L. T. Hobhouse,
Sociologist

the Making of Sociology series

EDITOR: RONALD FLETCHER

The Making of Sociology
vol. 1 *Beginnings and Foundations*
vol. 2 *Developments*
vol. 3 *Reassessments: Consolidation and Advance?*
RONALD FLETCHER
AUGUSTA COMTE
KENNETH THOMPSON
L. T. HOBHOUSE
JOHN E. OWEN

Karl Marx
Z. A. JORDAN

John Stuart Mill
RONALD FLETCHER

Herbert Spencer
STANISLAV ANDRESKI

Max Weber
J. E. T. ELDRIDGE

Sociology and Industrial Life
J. E. T. ELDRIDGE

Deviance and Society
LAURIE TAYLOR

L. T. Hobhouse, Sociologist

Professor John E. Owen

Ohio State University Press: Columbus

First published in Great Britain by Thomas Nelson and Sons Ltd

Printed by A. Wheaton & Co., Exeter

Library of Congress Cataloguing in Publication Data

Owen, John E
  L. T. Hobhouse, sociologist
  Bibliography: p.
  1. Hobhouse, Leonard Trelawney, 1864–1929.
2. Sociology—History. I. Title.
HM22.G8H68 1975 301′.092′4 74-18457
ISBN 0-8142-0235-7

To John Eric Nordskog

Contents

vii

Introduction by Ronald Fletcher

Professor Owen's study is the first major critique* of the work of Hobhouse to have been undertaken since Hobhouse's death in 1929, and is all the more to be welcomed because it comes from America.

When the 'current battle of paradigms'—the toy war of the professional post-war 'school-men'—is ended, and the theatrical uniforms are decently buried in the desert of unnecessary dust, a new view will come to be formed of the relations between British and American scholarship. That is to say, the more settled view, of what was already substantially seen and understood by men like Barnes, Becker, Sorokin, MacIver (before the post-Parsonian show distracted attention from it), will re-emerge with more secure knowledge. Then the place of Hobhouse will properly be seen. Indeed, Professor Owen's book is itself a significant contribution to the return and deepening of this sounder view.

The theoretical thought of continental Europe, Britain and the United States has always been more of a piece than apparent national differences have suggested. Just as, towards the end of the nineteenth century, there was the closest relation between the work of Comte and Spencer and that of the early Americans (Sumner, Ward, Giddings, etc.), so there was the same close interconnection of thought during the first few decades of the twentieth century. In this Hobhouse was quite central. Constructing his own system on a critique of the nineteenth century 'founders', he also acknowledged his debt to such American contemporaries as Small, Giddings, Ward and Ross. In the same way, he, in his turn, exerted considerable influence on some thinkers then active in the making of sociology in America—C. A. Ellwood and E. C. Hayes, for example. If such figures now seem of slight importance, this in itself is entirely due to the obscuring swirls of the post-war academic dustbowl. In fact, both were centrally representative of the most basic characteristics of sociology in America. Following Albion Small's influence in the 'Chicago School', they developed closer relations between psychology and sociology, dwelt on the understanding of interpersonal relations in social processes, and emphasized the application of sociology to ethical issues and the guidance of social change; all features of what the Hinkles have called the 'basic homogeneity of viewpoint' of the American tradition in sociology. Both men were central in American sociology, and were also cosmopolitan

*Earlier studies are mentioned on pp. 6–7.

ix

scholars of high reputation; Ellwood, in action as well as in sympathy, becoming a staunch European and President of the International Institute of Sociology in 1935–36. Hobhouse was a powerful influence at the roots of both.

It is of interest, too, that this study of Hobhouse should have come not from some viewpoint of partiality, touched with some commitment to one 'side' or another in ongoing arguments within Britain (as it might well have done if coming from a British-based protagonist) but rather as a matter of necessity, from Professor Owen's desire to understand the origins of academic sociology in Britain.

Certainly, though now a 'prophet without honour' in his own country, Hobhouse remains unquestionably the most considerable British sociologist of the twentieth century. He is, indeed, the only figure who can be counted 'great' in the sense that his work possesses a stature fully comparable with that of the other major 'founders' of the early decades of the century: Tönnies, Durkheim, Weber, and Pareto. In the system of sociological analysis that he accomplished, and the many dimensions that he clarified and developed, no other British figure approaches him. This can be clearly seen in his philosophical clarification of conceptual, theoretical, methodological, and ethical issues; his study of the psychological aspects of society (which led him into the experimental study of animal behaviour); the sheer range of his comparative studies of social institutions; and his systematic awareness of the relevance of sociological knowledge to the distinctive problems of modern societies Rooted in the nineteenth century founders (Comte, Spencer, Mill, etc); well aware of contemporary work (of Ward, Tönnies, Durkheim, and others); he critically developed the systematic analyses they had advanced, and carried out his own sociological investigations along the lines of enquiry they had laid down.

Comte, Mill and Durkheim had all stressed the importance of comparative studies of social institutions, couched within a classification of societies and guided by some hypothesis. Hobhouse undertook such studies. Durkheim especially had stated the need for the clarification of an ethic relevant to the collective conditions of modern industrial societies, informed, now, not by philosophical inference alone, but also by the new analysis and knowledge of sociology. Hobhouse clearly articulated such an ethic; both in philosophical terms, and with direct reference to such concrete social issues as property, the distribution of wealth and incomes, and the problems of control in industrial organization. From Comte onwards, through Marx, thinkers had wanted a science of society for the practical task of *social reconstruction*. Hobhouse acted on this; spending his time on wages boards; involving himself in journalism; devoting his mind to the problems of industrial relations, social administration, and the massive threats of twentieth century warfare. In all this, he made contributions of the most basic kind. In his studies of ethics, social philosophy, and social reform he is frequently shrugged off as a naive 'rationalist'; a 'Manchester Guardian "Liberal" ' some scornfully call him; but then it is never commonly realized by such arrogant half-scholars that it is a central part of the theories of Durkheim and Weber, too, to emphasize the growth of *rationality* in the making of modern social institutions, and, correlated with this, the pressures within social change towards the shaping of institutions that are *socially just*. Here is Durkheim, for example, who linked the division of labour in society with 'our whole moral life'.

> If we remember that the collective conscience is becoming more and more a cult of the individual, we shall see that what characterizes the morality of organized societies, compared to that of segmental societies, is that there is *something more human,* therefore *more rational,* about them. . . . It is not enough that there by rules; they must be *just* . . . In short, our first duty is to make a moral code for ourselves.

To this end, in keeping with the theories of others and the stringent requirements of science and philosophy alike, Hobhouse made perhaps the most substantial contribution of his time. Similarly, in his thorough discussion of 'evolution' and 'social evolution', he demonstrated quite definitively that the Darwinian interpretation could never be a sufficient explanation, whether in biology or in sociology, and his position on this has rarely been understood, so that latter-day pronouncements, such as those of Parsons, for example, are made in complete ignorance of it. The extent, too, to which Hobhouse sustained scientific accuracy in his methods, pursued empirical studies, and deliberately trained himself for them, even to the extent of seeking and submitting his data to laboratory experience, is generally quite unknown.

There is a further point of importance to which Professor Owen draws our attention. Though the parallel is not exact, Hobhouse can correctly be regarded as the 'Albion Small' of British sociology. One of the first Professors of Sociology in Britain (he and Westermarck held the first two chairs at the London School of Economics), it was he who was chiefly responsible for administratively establishing the subject, formulating the first basic courses of undergraduate teaching, and editing the first professional journal. It was from these foundations that the 'London Degree' became the pattern for University Colleges throughout the country and overseas.

All of which makes it plain that an account of Hobhouse's work has long been overdue, and that in this richly documented study, Professor Owen has filled, at last, a very important gap in the story of the making of sociology. Here is a sound and many-sided appraisal which will be as fresh and original for students in Britain as for those in any other part of the world, and will not be surpassed for a long time to come.

Suffolk,
June 1974.

Preface

Sociology has had a remarkably rapid rise on the British academic scene in the last fifteen years. L. T. Hobhouse was one of its founders who made solid contributions in defining the field and helping sociology to take root in Britain at a time when it was an academic outsider.

The present work is offered in the hope that current students of sociology may still learn something from the writings of an early pioneer. Even though contemporary research methods and theoretical frameworks have moved far from Hobhouse's sociological frame of reference, it is contended that a careful study of such an encyclopedic mind and founder of the discipline may yield stimulation and benefit to its current exponents.

I am indebted to numerous persons in British and American universities who, in manifold ways, offered help and encouragement in the preparation of this work. If the volume can serve to arouse new interest in what may be learned from British sociology's first academic representative, the author will feel amply repaid for his efforts.

J.E.O.   TEMPE, ARIZONA, USA.

I   Introduction

The significance of Hobhouse

What are the origins of academic sociology in Great Britain? It was through the attempt to answer this question that the writer first became interested in the contributions of Leonard Trelawney Hobhouse. The present work is an endeavour to indicate some of the specific contributions made by Hobhouse, and to relate them, by critical analysis and comparison, to the work of his contemporaries as well as to that of later exponents of sociology in Europe and America. The specific problem was to ascertain the particular contributions of Hobhouse, and to assess these endeavours in relation to those of other sociologists.

Although academic sociology had a relatively late start in Britain—being predominantly a post-1945 development, compared with the US academic scene, where sociology enjoyed an earlier beginning—the fact remains that sociology today as an academic discipline and field of research is essentially European in its roots. And together with Durkheim in France, Weber in Germany, and Spencer in England, Hobhouse may be rightly looked upon as one of the early pioneers who did valuable preliminary ground-work. Compared with the other three, his name is not as known in the field, and in the present author's view he has not received the recognition in America, or even in his native England, that his contributions merit. The reasons for this will be considered, together with a presentation of the points he stressed that are still pertinent and deserving of attention, and an analysis of areas where he opened up new paths for others to follow. Since his day, sociological research interests and methods have changed and some of the early directions followed by Hobhouse (e.g., a sociology of morality) have been left relatively unexplored. But the

1

work he did in his time had a solid foundation and was broad in scope.

Varied testimony has been offered on Hobhouse's importance. Emory S. Bogardus, at the time of Hobhouse's death in 1929, said:

> Leonard T. Hobhouse stood out for a quarter of a century
> and more as a leading social philosopher of England . . .
> His name remains, and will stand, as a tower of strength
> in the field of philosophic sociology.[1]

Floyd N. House refers to Hobhouse as 'the most outstanding and influential social philosopher of Great Britain', and notes that he was one of the first two men to bear the title, 'Professor of Sociology', in a British university.[2] John E. Nordskog, a former pupil of Hobhouse, speaks of him as follows:

> Americans have shared in the world's admiration,
> appreciation, and respect for the wonderful work
> representative of Professor Hobhouse as scholarly gentleman,
> philosopher, and sociologist . . . I confess to having
> regarded him as no less than the dean of sociologists in
> Europe. He was indeed outstanding as social philosopher
> not only in Europe, but was an international figure. His
> influence has for a generation spread out to the far places of
> the civilized earth through his connections with the
> *Manchester Guardian*, through his years of teaching at the
> University of London, where he was Martin White Professor
> of Sociology at the London School of Economics and Political
> Science, and by way of his many books and essays in
> periodicals. In public service he has been noteworthy. In his
> valuable books his work lives on.[3]

An earlier statement by Steeves and Ristine may be quoted, in affirmation of the importance of the work done by this sociologist:

> His place in the world of contemporary thought is secured by
> unusual breadth of intellectual vision and remarkable
> command of branches of study collateral with those in which
> he is specially interested . . . It may be inferred from the
> titles of Professor Hobhouse's work that their strength lies

in an exceptionally keen analysis of the bearing of evolutionary science upon the entire history of man and his institutions; this is illustrated impressively by his use of an enormous mass of scientific evidence from fields whose connection with his own is not always apparent to the casual student, and whose whole domain can be covered only by a scholar of exceptional erudition.[4]

This expression of praise for the erudition of Hobhouse is shared by Barnes and Becker, who refer to him as 'a social philosopher unsurpassed in any country for breadth and profundity of learning'.[5] But although these two writers state that, at the time of Hobhouse's death in 1929, many American sociologists had considered him in the first rank of the world's contemporary sociologists,[6] they nevertheless noted that he was not as well-known as he might have been.

In fact, despite the foregoing expressions of acclaim, Hobhouse is still comparatively unknown in his native England. Even in America, where sociology has enjoyed a much greater popularity, his writings have not received the wide attention given to many other sociologists. It is, indeed, doubtful whether the influence of his books has been felt by the majority of American sociologists, and outside the academic realm his name is still relatively unknown.

The wide erudition of Hobhouse, extending as it did into many fields, was, paradoxically, one cause of his comparative obscurity. Morris Ginsberg noted[7] that after Hobhouse had left his Alma Mater, Oxford, following a period of teaching there, he was never called back to lecture at that university. The academic authorities appeared to resent his having branched out into areas of study that transcended the orthodox academic boundaries and subdivisions.

Similarly, in America the trend toward academic specialization had, and has, gone so far, in sociology and other fields, that Barnes and Becker could declare[8] that it was considered quite permissible to be ignorant of the really great minds of the past, provided there was an acquaintance with such minutiae as the number of fire-plugs in Ashtabula on 16 January 1934.

Further testimony regarding Hobhouse's wide erudition and its implied influence on his comparative obscurity is offered by an English writer, Arnold S. Nash.

It is an ironic commentary on liberal rationalism that it has
so largely ignored the work of the one thinker, L. T.
Hobhouse, who might have saved it from its intellectual
bankruptcy. However, Hobhouse's scholarship in sociology,
anthropology, history, and comparative psychology was too
massive for the word-spinning philosophers; his sense of the
importance of epistemology and ethics separated him from
the fact-loving natural and social scientists, while his keen
appreciation of the reality of evil and the penetration of his
thinking was too much for the rest of the professional
intelligentsia, who preferred the more easily derived and
more comforting generalizations of H. G. Wells *et al.*[9]

The breadth of viewpoint that characterized Hobhouse's works
and his general method and approach have been labelled by the
rubber-stamp term, 'philosophical'. Herein lies one undoubted
reason for his comparative lack of recognition in the United States,
where the prevailing temper in sociology has been away from
philosophical treatment and broad generalizations in favour of
scientific analysis and empirical research. Barnes and Becker
speak of 'the Hobhousian tradition of viewing social life in its
total setting and in its relation to a scale of values',[10] and it would
be a truism to point out the lasting distaste for values and value-
judgements among sociologists and social scientists, despite
recent changes in attitude. The point is mentioned here, however,
only because it throws more light on the lack of attention that
Hobhouse has received. It would seem that he himself constitutes
a good example of a situation in science that he described as
follows:

There is a queer element of arbitrary fashion in the scientific
world which every now and then decrees that certain people
shall be ignored, no matter how sound their work, or that
certain hypotheses shall be treated as matters of faith, no
matter how flimsy their structure.[11]

Nevertheless, it is the aim of this study to show that Hobhouse did
make definite contributions, not merely to social philosophy and
ethics, but to scientific sociology. Partly on account of the prestige
of empirical research, the more theoretical aspects of sociology
have only recently received comparable attention. An attempt is

made in the pages that follow to show how, by his emphasis upon theory, Hobhouse rendered a service to the cause of social science. The general theme of the book is the sociological thought of Hobhouse, but the writer has not tried to set forth his theories in their entirety. The aim is more that of a critical exposition and analysis of his specific contributions. These contributions are illuminated by a study of the socio-cultural background from which his thought arose, and by an attempt to assess the relevant aspects of his sociology in relation to American sociological studies.

The method used has involved research in the original literary sources, aided by personal interviews with sociologists and others who knew Hobhouse as a writer and teacher. A delimiting of the field of research has been necessary, in as much as Hobhouse's thought covered a vast area. Indeed, one sociologist has said[12] that to attempt a review of his many works would be comparable to giving a summary of the *Encyclopaedia Britannica*. The present book does not touch on his study of political phenomena, or with the epistemological or ontological side of his work, or with his research into comparative psychology, to all of which fields he made contributions. Hobhouse's ethical theory is mainly considered as it bears upon his concept of social progress. Yet it may legitimately be claimed that Hobhouse's thought represents a systematic unity in which all the parts play an integrated role. The implication follows that no part can be taken out of its setting within the whole of his theory if it is to be thoroughly understood. The validity of this implication is granted, but it must be emphasized once more that the present work does not claim to be a complete and synthetic exposition of Hobhousian theory. The formative influences upon Hobhouse will be mentioned in relation to each area of his work considered, and a brief indication of the relation between the different aspects of his work will be given; but for a synthetic exposition of Hobhousian thought in its totality, the reader is referred to other works about him, as well as to the original sources themselves.

Many texts in sociology and the history of social thought in the past forty years refer to Hobhouse. Barnes and Becker, authors of *Social Thought from Lore to Science* and *Contemporary Social Theory*,[13] may be cited, as can Pitirim A. Sorokin, author of *Contemporary Sociological Theories*,[14] and Charles A. Ellwood, author of *A History of Social Philosophy*.[15]

The most authoritative work that specifically concerns Hobhouse is that by Hobson and Ginsberg,[16] published in 1931. This volume devotes space to the biographical details of Hobhouse's life, followed by an excellent summary presentation of his general theory in the areas of comparative psychology, sociology, ethics and social philosophy, theory of knowledge and theory of reality. The volume ends with a selected group of his essays and articles. The work constitutes a fine review of Hobhouse's theory, but does not lay detailed emphasis on the specifically sociological aspects. Nor does it make any comparison between Hobhouse and other sociologists.

A small work by Hugh Carter[17] attempts to give, albeit briefly, a general picture of Hobhouse's entire sociology. It furnishes a useful summary but pays scant attention to systematic theory and contains no evaluation of Hobhouse in terms of the contributions of other sociologists. The majority of the specific contributions dealt with in the present study are not considered by Carter.

John Eric Nordskog[18] has dealt with the political theory of Hobhouse in an article, 'Leonard T. Hobhouse: Internationalist'. International relations and democratic principles are considered in this article.

The philosophical thought of Hobhouse has been dealt with in a work by Nicholson, concerned with logic and social theory.[19] Dealing, as it does, with epistemological theory and metaphysical questions, this article does not have specific sociological relevance. It is, however, a good statement of this aspect of Hobhouse's work in relation to the philosophical outlook current in England during his formative period.

At the time of his death in 1929, obituary notices appeared from the pens of sociologists, for example, from Bogardus[20] and Ginsberg.[21] The article by Bogardus has been mentioned previously. The notice by Ginsberg set forth the contributions of his predecessor in the philosophical realm, and was later revised and incorporated into an article on Hobhouse's work on philosophy and sociology generally.[22]

The organization of the present study centres around certain aspects of Hobhouse's sociological thought, as follows: (a) his criticism of the mechanistic outlook in science and philosophy, with his emphasis upon assumptions and theory; (b) certain prolegomena to sociology and its methods; (c) the sociological study of morality; (d) the concept of social harmony as related to progress, and the opposing biological view of progress; and (e) purposive social development as an aspect of progress.

In each of these areas, an attempt will be made to indicate how Hobhouse's work constitutes a contribution to sociology. A further chapter will be devoted to comparing his work with that of other sociologists on each of these specific points, and the last chapter will summarize his contributions with the conclusions that have accrued. As a preliminary, certain biographical data may be set forth, with a study of the forces that moulded his life and thought.

Formative influences in the life of Hobhouse

Leonard Trelawney Hobhouse was born in 1864 at St Ive, a village near Liskeard in Cornwall, England, where his father was Rector of the parish church for fifty-one years, before serving as Archdeacon of Bodmin from 1877 to 1892. During the eighteenth century the Hobhouse family had been prosperous merchants in Somerset. Leonard Hobhouse's grandfather had been a barrister and a public servant of great distinction. Occupying several prominent positions in the government, he had been Keeper of the State Papers, and Permanent Under-secretary to the Home Office. The son who became Rector of St Ive, married the daughter of Sir Thomas Trelawney, from an old, well-known Cornish aristocratic family. An uncle of Leonard Hobhouse was Sir Arthur, afterwards Lord, Hobhouse. These facts regarding his élite antecedents are cited in view of Hobhouse's later espousal of the cause of democracy.

After a happy home life, Leonard Hobhouse entered Marlborough College, a traditional English 'public school'. His training was in the classics, though he also had access to library books in the social and political sciences, including the essays of Mill, Spencer and Mazzini. In 1883 he entered Corpus Christi College, Oxford, with a classical scholarship, and after a brilliant undergraduate career became a tutor at Oxford in 1887. While there he married Nora Hadwen in 1891, and the marriage lasted until her death in 1925. In 1897, he left Oxford to become a staff leader writer for the *Manchester Guardian*, and remained with the newspaper until 1902. A short period of journalistic activity in London followed. In 1904 Hobhouse became political editor of *Tribune*, but retired after a year and a half on account of a divergence of viewpoint between himself and the management. In 1907 he was appointed as first holder of the Martin White Chair of Sociology at the University of London, and also became the first editor of the newly founded *Sociological Review*. Since 1893 he had been writing books upon sociological and philosophical topics, and he continued to write leaders for the *Manchester Guardian*. His later years, though, were largely devoted to academic work in London, and the writing of scholarly works in sociology, ethics and philosophy. He found time to engage in a great amount of public work, as chairman of various committees and trade boards. His death occurred, at the age of sixty-four, in 1929.

Against the background of these biographical facts, what were the formative influences that shaped Hobhouse's sociological thought? It should be noted that he came from a family with a tradition of public service. His grandfather, besides his public appointments, had been a socially-minded landowner in Somerset, taking an active part in local affairs. He saw rural life from a public-spirited viewpoint and was concerned for the welfare of the tenants and persons under him.[23] The conception of public service played a large role in the life of his family. Henry Hobhouse's sons served in Parliament, and in the Church overseas and in England.

Another influence in the life of Leonard Hobhouse was that of his sister, Emily, who worked on behalf of prisoners of war in South Africa at the time of the Boer War. Her concern with post-war reconstruction in South Africa influenced her brother, and the denunciations of British imperialism that run through the pages of *Democracy and Reaction*[24] are better understood in the light of this humanitarian influence.

Against the religious outlook of his father, who was a High Church Anglican, Leonard Hobhouse reacted strongly in favour of a broader viewpoint. It appears that at an early age he also differed from the conservative political views of his father. A reconstruction of his own religious outlook took place, under philosophical influences to be discussed later. Apart from an article written just before his death in 1929,[25] Hobhouse's religious position is set forth in the pages of his philosophical and ethical works.[26] It may be noted in passing that a great gulf is represented between his rational humanitarianism and the conventional social attitudes of the class into which he was born in the 1860s. A further moulding influence may be found in his own family life. His keen feeling for the family, based on his early days in Cornwall and his long and happy marriage, greatly affected his outlook and valuations. Sir Ernest Barker has said that 'the experience of the family was the foundation of his belief'.[27]

The great external influences upon him were to be found, however, in the philosophical and social ethos of the last third of the nineteenth century. During Hobhouse's Oxford years an intellectual storm had arisen, at the centre of which was the evolutionary theory of Darwin. Long-held positions in science, philosophy and religion were being challenged. Hobhouse came to devote a vast amount of his attention to the implications of the evolutionary theory for social thought, in its psychological, sociological and philosophical aspects.

The biological theory was being used by people, who little understood it, as a justification for economic exploitation, competitive individualism and ruthless nationalistic expansion. A type of economic liberalism was current in the mid-Victorian era: a liberalism which was essentially one of laissez-faire. Its great defender was Herbert Spencer, and it was partly in reaction to the ideas of Spencer that Hobhouse formulated his own view of social evolution. He developed his theory as part of a general philosophy of evolution, as did Spencer, but whereas Spencer saw evolution as an automatic, mechanical and inevitable process, Hobhouse regarded it as a development of the power of mind, leading to a growth in harmony and correlation. Spencer's theory had minimized the power and importance of the human mind in the evolutionary process. The human mind, for the biological evolutionist, came to be regarded merely as a physical organ that had been evolved in the struggle for existence. It was 'a sort of glorified reflex action'.[28]

Harry Elmer Barnes has said[29] that Hobhouse is the one British scholar whose writings are of such quality as to place him as Spencer's worthy successor. This statement, be it noted, refers strictly to sociologists, and does not include the fields of ethnology, psychology, political science or metaphysics in Britain.

However, apart from the evolutionary emphasis, Hobhouse differed from Spencer in nearly all respects. The Hobhousian interpretation of evolution is one in which mind plays the dominant role, as opposed to the automatic and mechanical view of the Spencerians. Although they both saw society as an organic unity, yet Hobhouse rejected the 'organic analogy' that characterized Spencer's thinking. Spencer's definition of evolution, in terms of the integration of matter and dissipation of motion, constituted a purely physical science formula, namely, the redistribution of matter and energy.

This materialistic outlook was repugnant to Hobhouse, for if it were true that the human mind had played no part in man's development, but constituted merely one means among others of adjusting behaviour to the environment, then the possibility of 'progress' in the future rested on pure chance. Further, if, as Spencer averred, biological factors were the basic determinants in social development, and the struggle for existence were the law of life, then conceptions of justice and humanity were meaningless, and the unregulated competition of the later nineteenth century, with its social consequences, was perfectly in accordance with the natural scheme of things. Man did not have any right, on this view, to interfere with 'the laws of nature', but had to recognize that the survival of the fittest was the means of bringing about progress, since it would ensure the survival of the best types and the elimination of poor human stocks. This being the case, any artificial interference—whether through governmental legislation or other means—with competitive economic processes was socially harmful. Evolution is then made synonymous with progress, and a strictly individualistic and laissez-faire society will be the one most likely to survive and prosper.[30]

A great deal of Hobhouse's work and writing was motivated by the aim of refuting this outlook. He set about the task of showing that evolution was a process built around mind and its growth; he tried to indicate that society had grown through the developing power of mind in man, and its application to problems; he traced the developing awareness of man in relation to ethical principles, showing how moral evolution had consisted, through the centuries, in the extension of the principle of humanity; he worked out an ethical theory around the concept of a developing harmony, rather than an unmitigated struggle for existence; and he brought these various efforts together in a philosophical synthesis in which the concept of development, as a movement towards harmony and mental growth, was the central theme.

One positive influence exerted upon Hobhouse by Spencer was the concept of philosophy as a synthesis of the sciences. Hobhouse found, though, that this synthesis does not exhaust the work of philosophy, and he realized that an evolutionary philosophy would require a more careful examination of the results of the evolutionary sciences than Spencer had made.[31]

This leads, however, to another formative influence, namely, the method and outlook of science. At Oxford, Hobhouse's college, Corpus Christi, had had a philosophical tradition of its own: that of British empiricism. Hobhouse came to have the spirit of Locke and Bacon, in their respect for science and scientific method. As a study of philosophy, a rational empiricism appealed to him. He was driven to the study of facts. This led, first, to an empirical investigation in comparative psychology in which he tried to ascertain the growth of mental factors in animals,[32] and later to a study of the actual development of human customs and institutions.[33]

It was to science, then, that Hobhouse turned as a student to find a basis for philosophical theories. He was not content at Oxford to accept the then current philosophy, but engaged in actual scientific experiments in the University Museum with J. S. Haldane. These early studies were in the realm of physiology, and became the basis for his later work on the intelligence of animals. He was typically English in his empiricism. Barnes says of him:

> . . . Hobhouse lays down the premise that any valid body of thought must rest upon the methods and discoveries of the most recent scientific endeavour. Its truth must be ascertained by testing it out through a study of experience carried on according to scientific principles.[34]

The background out of which this empirical bias developed is to be seen in the Oxford philosophy current during the last two decades of the nineteenth century. It was an outlook in which first principles were uncritically accepted and the facts of experience made to conform to *a priori* axioms rather than being the basis for philosophical reflection.

This ethos will be described in subsequent paragraphs. At this point it may be stated that Hobhouse was convinced that philosophy had to take science into account. To build upon the foundations of experience and proceed piecemeal was preferable to setting up a complete *a priori* metaphysical system. Any valid philosophy, as distinct from empty speculation, would, he thought, have to come to terms with science and be based upon a synthesis of experience as interpreted by science.[35]

A further influence upon Hobhouse, related to the foregoing, was the work of Comte. He did not look upon Comte uncritically, but he regarded with favour Comte's view of a self-directing humanity and he shared Comte's emphasis upon the empirical method and approach. He also shared Comte's view of the interdependence of social life in all its aspects, and he recognized the consequent need for a synoptic social science. Comte's religious humanitarianism may be regarded as another formative influence upon Hobhouse. Finally, they both considered the idea of development as central in sociology, though it would appear that Hobhouse was influenced more by Darwin and Spencer than by Comte in this regard. And Hobhouse agreed with Branford's statement that '. . . the grand manner of the Positive synthesis, the wide philosophical survey of civilization as the field of man's effort, persistent through repeated checks and failures, to the rational ordering of his life' constituted the 'cream of Comtism'.[36]

Along with the positivism of Comte, Hobhouse was also affected by the social philosophy of John Stuart Mill and T. H. Green. He referred to Mill as 'one of those rare minds capable of life-long growth',[37] and 'a moral force', one capable of influencing character as well as intellect.[38] On account of his willingness to change his views, Mill was apt to be accused of inconsistency, but, in one of his earlier books, Hobhouse stated his obligations to Mill, despite the disfavour into which Mill's work had supposedly fallen.[39] Mill had shared Comte's general conception of history. He was, moreover, an ardent sympathizer with the working classes —a viewpoint that Hobhouse came to espouse. Mill also combined a vital enthusiasm for social progress with a critical and scientific temper, an outlook that was also shared by Hobhouse. They had similar views on the subjection of women, and Mill's emphasis on the value of individuality in human welfare was later to be reflected in Hobhouse's own social theory. Finally, the Utilitarian principle that Mill developed bears a close relationship to the theory of harmony that Hobhouse set forth.[40]

Hobhouse did not, however, concur in the Utilitarian view of pleasure as the greatest good, nor did he hold with the Utilitarians that happiness (pleasure) was the end of all desire. The identification of pleasure with happiness was criticized by T. H. Green, and Hobhouse sympathized with this criticism. He saw that a revaluation of the original Benthamite notion of value was needed. In place of pleasure, he substituted the concept of harmony.

But the impact of Green on Hobhouse was both positive and negative, for while Hobhouse found himself in favour with Green's social and ethical outlook, there were many points on which he differed from Green. It was out of this disagreement that his own distinctive theories came to be formulated. The rational human-itarianism of Green was shared by Hobhouse, but the meta-physical basis of Green's views was unacceptable to him. To understand this, it is necessary to consider the climate of philo-sophical opinion at the English universities during the time Hobhouse was at Oxford.

In the 1880s and 1890s the influence of Hegel at Oxford was dominant. This idealistic philosophy had laid its mark on British philosophy. According to Hegelianism, of which Green was a foremost British example, reality is spiritual, and the stress upon the spiritual element was so marked as to involve the complete ignoring of science. At the same time, an over-confident science, under the influence of Darwin and Spencer, was apparently working towards the 'despiritualization' of the universe. Hob-house, influenced by these two currents of thought, tried to formulate a valid philosophy that would do justice both to science and to moral and spiritual values. He could not accept the view that all reality is spiritual. This would render the spiritual element of no distinctive significance.[41] The basis of Green's views lay in the notion of a single eternal consciousness, and Hobhouse could not subscribe to this. Green had himself reached this position in an attempt to escape from the implications of the biological view of the world. In opposition to materialism, he evolved a 'spiritual conception' of life, based upon Hegelian notions.

While to Hobhouse this appeared fallacious, he nevertheless saw that an empirical rather than a spiritual view of mind might be derived from Green's 'spiritual principle', and that this empirical view could be identified with Comte's idea of a self-directing humanity.[42] If the notion of a permanent self-conscious-ness were philosophically invalid, the idea of mind and its development could nevertheless be shown to be empirical fact.

There are important similarities between Green's ethical theory, with its view of self-realization as the good, and Hobhouse's concept of harmony.[43] For Green, the good consisted in the realization of personal character, and the social good could only be realized in a society of persons, in which individuality, though retained, was integrated in a social whole.

The Hegelianism that Hobhouse encountered at Oxford was a dominant force in British thought at that time, and it was partly on account of his divergence from this prevailing intellectual tendency that he left the university in 1897. German thought in the English and Scottish universities had the effect of diminishing the impact of English empiricism, and it is significant that Hobhouse did not go along with the idealist tide, but maintained his empirical outlook. Unlike the German thinkers, he believed in checking large and vague conceptions by logical and scientific tests.[44]

The Hegelian theory of the state served as another influence that moulded Hobhouse's thought. It will be considered in connection with the First World War and his writing at the time.

Both at Marlborough and Oxford, Hobhouse had absorbed the classics. The Oxford honours course of *Literae Humaniores*, or 'Greats', is a combination of classical literature and philosophy. It was thus through a study of the ancient thinkers that Hobhouse approached the problems of his own day. Here is to be seen one cause of his concern with the problem of human values; it was the same problem faced by Plato in the *Republic*, the problem of 'justice', and it was dealt with by Hobhouse in *The Rational Good* and *The Elements of Social Justice*.

At the memorial service held for Hobhouse in June 1929, his colleague Graham Wallas said: '. . . to Hobhouse at Oxford the Athenian philosophers were real persons, and their penetrating inquiries as to the significance of human life still all-important and still unsolved'.[45] Similarly, Sir Ernest Barker has described him as an Oxford man nourished on Plato's *Republic*, and maintains that the Hobhouse conception of sociology has, in the last analysis, Plato for its father rather than Comte. He notes that Hobhouse, like Plato, was seeking for 'justice', and was torn between philosophy and politics. On this view, any interest in human problems is sociological. Such an interest may embrace in its scope political theory, biology, positivism, comparative psychology and anthropology, but it is essentially the range of interest of an individual seeking 'justice'.[46]

It may reasonably be inferred that Hobhouse's broad conception of the scope of sociology was at least partly due to his study of the classics. His combination of philosophy and science, of facts and values, represents a blending of the Platonic and the Aristotelian methods. If *The Rational Good* and *The Elements of Social Justice* are Platonic in their concern for ethical and spiritual values, *Morals in Evolution* and *Mind in Evolution* are Aristotelian in their emphasis upon factual data.

It is worthy of note, as Hobhouse himself points out, that the concept of harmony is Platonic in origin.[47] Finally, Hobhouse was, above all, a rationalist in his philosophy, and here he shows the influence of Greek thought. In this connection, the words of his successor, Morris Ginsberg, are pertinent:

> The driving force of Hobhouse's thought was an ardent humanitarianism, an intense desire to serve mankind, by bringing to bear upon the problems of human life the methods and principles of rational thought. Quite early in his career as an undergraduate at Oxford (1883–7), he became convinced that an adequate understanding of social problems could be reached only on the basis of an underlying philosophy, and throughout his work the philosophic spirit, the urgent demand for an all-round or synoptic view characterized both his treatment of scientific data and his handling of practical affairs . . . He illustrates in his life work his own view of reason as a continuous and comprehensive effort toward harmony in experience, whether in the field of practice or speculation . . .[48]

This rational humanitarianism was expressed in Hobhouse's attitude towards the Boer War, which itself constituted another moulding force in his life. The war in South Africa represented a challenge to his international and humane outlook, and he spoke and wrote against it with great vigour. It was during this period that he was working on the *Manchester Guardian* under C. P. Scott, a leading liberal editor of the day, and the paper was taking a pro-Boer stand that became very unpopular in the war atmosphere of Britain at the time. But throughout his life Hobhouse was an outspoken foe of imperialism whether in Africa, Ireland or elsewhere. He was regarded with favour by his uncle, Lord Hobhouse, at the time of his writing *Democracy and Reaction*. When Lord Hobhouse read the proofs of this anti-imperialistic volume he wrote to his nephew, 'You are . . . right in trying to bring about a saner mood by appeals to reason.'[49] However, conceptions of Empire were rife at the turn of the century and there was much talk of 'the white man's burden'. This outlook had been due in part to the biological doctrines of the evolutionists. The notion of the survival of the fittest had been used to justify racial domination and territorial expansion, and against this prevailing mood the humanitarianism of Hobhouse protested. He helped to transform the earlier, mid-Victorian liberalism, with its laissez-faire and individualistic concepts, into the newer liberalism typified by Gladstone, in which concern for humane values was brought into the political sphere. This newer political view, far from representing the 'survival of the fittest', espoused a modified collectivism and a programme of social reform. The Liberal Party, with which Hobhouse was affiliated through his *Manchester Guardian* connections, was returned to power with a great majority in 1906. In 1911 Hobhouse wrote his essay on *Liberalism* in which he tried to give a more positive content to Liberal thought and a firmer philosophical base than it had had in earlier days. He voiced a new liberalism in which conceptions of laissez-faire gave way to a deeper sympathy for the working classes and a more genuine interest in human beings as human beings. Gladstone in the world of politics, and Mill in the world of thought, were the representatives of this newer liberalism that followed the era of Cobden and Bright. A concern for social justice, at home and abroad, marked Gladstone's rule.[50]

Hobhouse was surrounded in his Manchester days with this newer ethos of the liberalism of which he was so definitely a part. He described the Gladstonian principle as the antithesis of the Machiavellian; it was a principle that proceeded on reasons of conscience rather than mere reasons of state. Despite Gladstone's difficulties in applying this principle in the world of European politics, Hobhouse nevertheless considered him, like Mill, to be a moral force.[51]

There was a strong affinity between Hobhouse's view of bringing ethical considerations into politics and the liberal tradition of

Gladstone. They were both in direct contrast to the imperialistic notions of the Unionist Party, led by Joseph Chamberlain—the party which Hobhouse regarded as attempting to nullify England's social gains. It is in the light of the then current imperialist ethos at the time of the Boer War that his humanitarian writings should be read and understood. This applies particularly to *Democracy and Reaction.*

A further basic influence upon Hobhouse's sociology was his own keen interest in the affairs of the world and his passion for social reform. Even as an undergraduate at Oxford, he had tried to organize the agricultural workers nearby, though Tory Oxford frowned upon such efforts. When he later became comfortably placed as a Tutor and Fellow in one of the most important colleges, he found even so that the academic life of this small world did not satisfy him. It would seem that one side of Hobhouse was always turned towards the outer world, while another side leaned towards the academic. In this balance between theoretical and practical affairs, he drew insight from actual human experience. Far from being an ivory-tower thinker, he was a sociologist living in the world of action. As J. S. Burgess says of him: '. . . his whole mental life is really a picture of his attempt to synthesize his interest in practical reality with his deep interest in philosophical speculation'.[52]

Apart from his journalistic activity, his participation in practical affairs was evidenced by years of work on trade boards, in which he is reported to have mastered the details of several trades in relation to labour conditions. Serving as the chairman on several boards, it was necessary to arbitrate between the demands of employers and workers, as well as to weigh the suggestions of government appointees. He served as chairman of nine boards and helped to found seven.[53]

This was only one aspect of the larger world of action that he found in London. A pertinent comment is made by Graham Wallas, who had himself combined the academic and the political life. Speaking of Hobhouse, he says that his 'main work was done, not in a delightful Oxford study, but in the midst of a great industrial city . . .'.[54]

In the world of events, the Great War of 1914–18 should be mentioned as a catastrophe that rendered his last years less happy than some of those preceding it. The war represented for

Hobhouse a reversion to barbarism. Concerning the outbreak of hostilities that took place in 1914, he said:

> To so many the world not only seemed different but became different on August 4th . . . It turned out to be in sober truth a different world from that which we knew, a world in which force had a greater part to play than we had allowed, a world in which the ultimate social securities were gone, in which we seemed to see of a sudden through a thin crust of civilization the seething forces of barbaric lust for power and indifference to life.[55]

This theme of the war is noted because it caused Hobhouse to re-examine his theory of progress. The war years were the setting out of which he wrote his *Metaphysical Theory of the State*, a vigorous denunciation of the Hegelian view of the God-State.[56] The strain of the war years left Hobhouse a tired man, and his wife's death in 1925 was a further blow. Although he lived until 1929, the effect of the war upon him may be compared with its effect on Simmel, though with Simmel the end came much sooner.

Hobhouse acknowledged the influence upon him of his contemporaries in the social sciences. He admitted that 'many new suggestions' had accrued from the work of Professor Stout, Graham Wallas, and William McDougall in general psychology.[57] A later expression of recognition was made for stimulus derived from the writings of E. A. Westermarck, R. M. MacIver, Morris Ginsberg and A. M. Carr-Saunders, in addition to Wallas and McDougall.[58]

In the chapter dealing with societal self-development, it will be seen that Hobhouse's outlook on the power of the mind to control life-conditions bears a resemblance to the 'social telesis' of Lester F. Ward. Hobhouse himself recognized this, and in the Preface to *Mind in Evolution* (1901), he wrote:

> The general conception of mental evolution presented in this volume was formed some fourteen or fifteen years ago when I had come into close contact with the criticisms then current on Comte, Mill, and Spencer . . . The general view of evolution which most closely corresponds to it, is to be found, I think, in Dr Lester Ward's *Outlines of Sociology*,

published in 1898. I mention these points as indicating the
general character of my obligations to other writers.[59]

Another point regarding formative influences upon Hobhouse's
life relates to a revealing incident described by Victor Branford in
1929. Branford claims that Hobhouse's mental powers had been
relatively dormant between 1906, when *Morals in Evolution* first
appeared, and 1916. As to the truth of this contention, opinion will
vary, but Branford notes that, in the early war years, Hobhouse
had considered resigning his Chair of Sociology; however, the task
of having to set forth the meaning and scope of sociology had the
effect of vitalizing his powers. The task in question was the writing
of a 12,000-word article entitled 'Sociology', which was printed a
few years later in the *Hasting's Dictionary of Religion and Ethics*.[60]
According to Branford, the mental effort involved in producing
this article had a transforming effect upon Hobhouse, clarifying
his concept of the field of sociology. Says Branford: 'A veritable
regeneration of his mental powers followed.'[61]

Branford then notes that the years following 1916 saw the
publication of *The Metaphysical Theory of the State* (1918), *The
Rational Good* (1921), *The Elements of Social Justice* (1922) and
Social Development, Its Nature and Conditions (1924). It is proble-
matical whether there was any causal relation between the article,
'Sociology', and the works that followed it, or whether this was a
case of *post hoc, ergo propter hoc*. It is not known to the writer
whether this theory originated with Branford, or whether it was
based upon conversations with Hobhouse.

There would appear to be more obvious truth in Morris
Ginsberg's contention that Hobhouse's whole life and work
furnish a good example of his own view of reason as an organic
growth in harmony. His life represented a harmonious balance
between different interests and embraced both the academic and
the practical realms. His thought seems to have followed a harmonious line of development, beginning as it did in epistemological inquiries that proceeded to empirical investigations into the
growth of mind in the sub-human and later the human level, and
from there to ethical theory and sociology, ending in a final effort
at philosophical synthesis.[62]

Having reviewed the background and formative influences upon
Hobhouse, consideration will now be given to significant portions

of his works, and his sociological contributions. The first subject developed will be his criticism of the mechanistic outlook in social science.

Notes and References

1. Emory S. Bogardus, 'Leonard T. Hobhouse, 1864–1929', *Sociology and Social Research*, XIV: 103, November–December 1929.

2. Floyd N. House, *The Development of Sociology* (New York: McGraw-Hill, 1936), pp. 148, 149.

3. John E. Nordskog, 'Leonard T. Hobhouse: Internationalist', *Sociology and Social Research*, XIV: 373, note, March–April 1930.

4. H. R. Steeves and F. H. Ristine (eds.), *Representative Essays in Modern Thought* (New York: American Book Company, 1913), p. 341.

5. Harry Elmer Barnes and Howard Becker, *Social Thought from Lore to Science* (Boston: D. C. Heath, 1938), Vol. II, p. 807.

6. ibid., p. 796.

7. In conversation with the writer.

8. *Social Thought from Lore to Science*, p. 809.

9. Arnold S. Nash, *The University and the Modern World, an Essay in the Philosophy of University Education* (New York: Macmillan Company, 1944), pp. 297, 298. Although Hobhouse may be considered the foremost political philosopher of the British Liberal Party, yet this party has been in eclipse since its days of strength before the First World War. Here perhaps may be found another reason for Hobhouse's comparative obscurity.

10. Barnes and Becker, *Social Thought from Lore to Science*, pp. 978, 979. In the present study, the term 'sociologist' is broadly used to include, according to Hobhouse's own definition, 'all who treat problems of social life in the scientific spirit . . .' (L. T. Hobhouse, 'Editorial', *Sociological Review*, I: 3–4, January 1908).

11. L. T. Hobhouse, 'Science and Philosophy as Unifying Forces', in F. S. Marvin (ed.), *The Unity of Western Civilization* (London: Oxford University Press, 1922), p. 171.

12. J. S. Burgess, 'Certain Concepts, Methods and Contributions in the Social Science and Social Philosophy of L. T. Hobhouse', *The Chinese Social and Political Science Review*, XIII: 126, April 1929.

13. Harry Elmer Barnes and Howard Becker, *Contemporary Social Theory* (New York: D. Appleton-Century Company, 1940).

14. Pitirim A. Sorokin, *Contemporary Sociological Theories* (New York: Harper & Brothers, 1928).

15. Charles A. Ellwood, *A History of Social Philosophy* (New York: Prentice-Hall, 1939).

16. J. A. Hobson and Morris Ginsberg, *L. T. Hobhouse, His Life and Work* (London: Allen & Unwin, 1931).

17. Hugh Carter, *L. T. Hobhouse and his Social Theories* (Chapel Hill: University of North Carolina Press, 1927).

18. John E. Nordskog, 'Leonard T. Hobhouse, Internationalist', loc. cit.

19. J. A. Nicholson, *Some Aspects of the Philosophy of L. T. Hobhouse: logic and social theory* (Urbana: University of Illinois Studies in the Social Sciences, 1928), Vol. XIV, no. 4.

20. Emory S. Bogardus, 'Leonard T. Hobhouse, 1864–1929', loc. cit.

21. Morris Ginsberg, 'Leonard Trelawney Hobhouse', *Journal of Philosophical Studies*, IX: 442–53, October 1929.

22. Morris Ginsberg, 'The Contributions of L. T. Hobhouse to Philosophy and Sociology', in *Reason and Unreason in Society, Essays in Sociology and Social Philosophy* (London: Longmans, Green, 1947), pp. 44–60.

23. See Leonard T. Hobhouse and J. L. Hammond, *Lord Hobhouse, a Memoir* (London: Edward Arnold, 1905), pp. 2–3.

24. L. T. Hobhouse, *Democracy and Reaction* (London: T. Fisher Unwin, 1904).

25. L. T. Hobhouse, 'Christianity', *Encyclopaedia of the Social Sciences*, III: 452–61, 1930.

26. See L. T. Hobhouse, *Development and Purpose, an Essay towards a Philosophy of Evolution* (London: Macmillan, 1927), and the final pages of 'The Philosophy of Development', in *Contemporary British Philosophy* (London: Allen & Unwin, 1924), Vol. 1, pp. 149–88. See also the final chapter of L. T. Hobhouse, *Morals in Evolution, A Study in Comparative Ethics* (New York: Henry Holt, 1925).

27. Sir Ernest Barker, 'Leonard Trelawney Hobhouse, 1864–1929', in *Proceedings of the British Academy* (Oxford: Humphrey Milford, 1931), Vol. XV, p. 4. See also Hobson and Ginsberg, *L. T. Hobhouse*, p. 30.

28. L. T. Hobhouse, *Development and Purpose*, p. xviii.

29. Harry Elmer Barnes, 'Some Typical Contributions of English Sociology to Political Theory, (II) Leonard T. Hobhouse and the Neo-Liberal Theory of the State', *American Journal of Sociology*, 27: 442, January 1922.

30. See Herbert Spencer, *Principles of Sociology* (New York: D. Appleton-Century, 1914).

31. Morris Ginsberg, *Reason and Unreason in Society*, p. 44.

32. L. T. Hobhouse, *Mind in Evolution* (London: Macmillan, 1901).

33. L. T. Hobhouse, *Morals in Evolution, a Study in Comparative Ethics* (London: Chapman & Hall, 1906).

34. Harry Elmer Barnes, 'Some Typical Contributions of English Sociology to Political Theory, (II) Leonard T. Hobhouse and the Neo-Liberal Theory of the State', p. 444.

35. See Hobhouse, *Development and Purpose*, pp. xix–xxi.

36. See Susan Liveing, *A Nineteenth-Century Teacher, John Henry Bridges* (London: Kegan Paul, Trench, Trubner, 1926), with Preface by L. T. Hobhouse, p. xiv. It is noteworthy that Bridges's interpretation of Comte's positivism was the main influence here. Hobhouse spoke of Bridges as one of the 'saints of Rationalism', a term that Gladstone used in connection with J. S. Mill. See ibid., p. xiii.

37. L. T. Hobhouse, *Democracy and Reaction*, p. 225.

38. L. T. Hobhouse, *Liberalism* (London: Williams & Norgate, Home University Library, 1911), pp. 106, 107.

39. L. T. Hobhouse, *The Theory of Knowledge, a Contribution to Some Problems of Logic and Metaphysics* (London: Methuen, 1896), p. ix.

40. See L. T. Hobhouse, *The Rational Good* (New York: Henry Holt, 1921), pp. 193–9. See also J. S. Mill, *On Liberty; Representative Government; The Subjection of Women* (London: Oxford University Press, 1933).

41. *Development and Purpose*, p. xix.

42. L. T. Hobhouse, 'The Philosophy of Development', loc. cit., pp. 149–50.

43. See T. H. Green, *Prolegomena to Ethics* (Oxford: Clarendon Press, 1890), and L. T. Hobhouse, *The Rational Good*, pp. 199–201.

44. L. T. Hobhouse, 'Science and Philosophy as Unifying Forces', loc. cit., pp. 173–6.

45. Graham Wallas, address delivered at the Hobhouse Memorial Service, St Clement Dane's Church, London, 27 June 1929, reprinted in *Economica*, IX: 247, November 1929.

46. Sir Ernest Barker, 'Leonard Trelawny Hobhouse, 1864–1929', loc. cit., pp. 20–21. It is interesting to note that the sociology curriculum at the London School of Economics and Political Science included a course for the sociological study of Plato's *Republic*.

47. See *The Rational Good*, p. 139, note; and *Morals in Evolution* (1919), p. 601.

48. Morris Ginsberg, *Reason and Unreason in Society*, p. 44.

49. See L. T. Hobhouse and J. L. Hammond, *Lord Hobhouse*, p. 242.

50. See L. T. Hobhouse, *Liberalism*, esp. Chapters 4 and 5.

51. ibid., pp. 102–6.

52. J. S. Burgess, 'Certain Concepts, Methods and Contributions in the Social Science and Social Philosophy of L. T. Hobhouse', loc. cit., p. 124.

53. See Walter A. Willis, *Trade Boards at Work, a Practical Guide to the Operation of the Trade Boards Acts* (London: Nisbet, 1920), with Introduction by L. T. Hobhouse.

54. Graham Wallas, Hobhouse Memorial address, loc. cit., p. 250.

55. L. T. Hobhouse, *The World in Conflict* (London: T. Fisher Unwin, 1915), p. 6.

56. L. T. Hobhouse, *The Metaphysical Theory of the State, a criticism* (New York: Macmillan Co., 1918).

57. L. T. Hobhouse, *Mind in Evolution* (1915), p. x.

58. L. T. Hobhouse, *Social Development, Its Nature and Conditions* (New York: Henry Holt, 1924), p. 15.

59. *Mind in Evolution*, p. vi.

60. L. T. Hobhouse, 'Sociology', *Hasting's Dictionary of Religion and Ethics,* XI: 654–65, 1921.

61. Victor Branford, 'The Sociological Work of Leonard Hobhouse', *Sociological Review*, XXI: 276, October 1929.

62. See Morris Ginsberg, 'Leonard Trelawney Hobhouse', *Journal of Philosophical Studies*, IV: 442, October 1929; and *Reason and Unreason in Society*, p. 44. See also Hobhouse, *Development and Purpose*, pp. xvii–xxxii.

2 Science and Mechanism

Hobhouse was repulsed by the mechanistic world-view of Spencer. How had this outlook arisen as a scientific philosophy, and why had it acquired such authority in the world of thought? These questions will be considered briefly as an introduction to Hobhouse's criticism of the assumptions underlying mechanism.

Attitudes towards science as a cultural product

The prestige of the mechanistic outlook has been connected with the general prestige accorded to science as a cultural achievement. The prestige of science has caused its methods to be spread over many areas and has given its outlook a dominance in twentieth-century thought. It receives much uncritical veneration and has almost become a religion for many of its exponents. Scientists are sometimes regarded with the same superstitious awe that the medieval masses showed towards their priests. Certain it is that the dominant modes of thinking today have been modelled on those of the natural sciences, in an effort to extend their methods to all areas of human experience. This is one result of the great prestige that has accrued to these methods of natural science. In this connection, Hobhouse says:

> When a great impulse is given to one science by some epoch-making experiment or some new and fruitful generalization, that science is apt to acquire a certain prestige in the minds of contemporaries, which gives it an influence over thought in every department, particularly in those departments where inquiry is still a novelty and

24

where there is no fixed tradition to regulate the methods
of approach.[1]

The reasons for such a phenomenon are sociological and historical,
since modern science is a cultural product, growing up in a socio-
cultural milieu. Between science and its milieu exists a reciprocal
interaction. The emergence of scientific method cannot be fully
understood without noting the stages through which it has passed
in history. With regard to the sociological study of science,
Hobhouse says:

> The history of science in the last century and a half has been
> of vast importance in the general evolution of society. But
> the student of society does not need to know, say, the history
> of the successive analyses and syntheses by which organic
> chemistry has been built up. What he does want to know is,
> for example, the way in which the progress of science has
> affected our view of the world, how it has recast the forms of
> industry, how it has reacted on literature and art, how it has
> affected religion and social theory. Again he is interested in
> the causes affecting the growth of science itself, the effects of
> political and social liberty, the influence of theological
> prepossessions, or of the prevailing system of education. In a
> word, he concerns himself with the place of science in social
> life, whether as affected by other agencies or affecting them.
> So regarded, of course, some of the actual achievements of
> science will interest him. Not only must he recognize the
> important bearing of theories like those of the preliminary
> scientific work which makes them possible, but he must also
> note as of transcendent interest the light which scientific
> progress throws, both by its success and by its limitations,
> on the power of man over nature. He must, as it were, assess
> the work of science as one form of human achievement, and
> one product of the human mind.[2]

Here, then, is one task of the sociologist as a student of human
culture—to look with objectivity upon science as one of the products
of that culture. Science has emerged out of a cultural background,
and a developing trend of thought has interacted upon the methods,

concepts and general pattern of scientific thinking. The recognition of this interaction may help to bring about an objectivity that is very different from the uncritical devotion to 'scientific' method, which, lacking any awareness of the intellectual forces in history which have moulded the scientific movement, is actually unscientific in its lack of perspective. Similarly, the slavish dependence upon one set of scientific tools involves the forfeiture of that experimental attitude which is basic to science. The scientist whose blind dogmatism and closed-mindedness regarding scientific orthodoxies spring from ignorance of both the historical growth and philosophical assumptions of science is as much to be pitied as the narrow-minded defender of a particular religious dogma or political creed. It is very easy to overlook institutions and thought-patterns which are part of the current ethos or climate of opinion; similarly, it is possible to be a scientist by profession without holding a scientific attitude towards science itself.

A more balanced attitude is held by those who, while respecting science and its achievements, nevertheless regard it judiciously and objectively. Hobhouse points out that after reason has been turned against supernaturalism, there arises a scepticism turned against itself, and there are found those who question reason much as reason questioned authority. He expresses their viewpoint in the following terms:

> Who, they ask, made science a ruler and judge over us?
> Science has her methods, to which she is welcome, but why
> should they be held superior to any others? Science, like
> theology, is human, the product of human thought . . .
> Her conclusions are not infallible, and her scope is not
> exhaustive. As to her first principles and fundamental
> assumptions, men have never yet come to an agreement
> about their nature, origin, and validity. The uniformity of
> nature which is assumed in all generalization is difficult to
> formulate in terms upon which all would agree, and has
> been admitted by distinguished men of science to be itself
> a matter of faith.[3]

Nevertheless, there is reason to believe that the above viewpoint towards science is not as prevalent as that which regards science as an idol of the intellectual world. Indeed, science has itself become a faith, or rather a philosophy, in the course of its recent history. The background to this situation, and its contemporary manifestations, will be now be considered.

Mechanism as a scientific philosophy

In the seventeenth century, scientific method became deified largely through the influence of Francis Bacon, Sir Isaac Newton and John Locke. Newton's investigations into natural phenomena led to a view of the physical world that came to constitute a metaphysics or theory of reality. Modern science in its beginnings did not draw itself loose from philosophy. On the contrary, it took over an entire metaphysical system based upon Newtonian physics— largely mathematical physics. Basic to this was the concept of material particles which move through space and endure through time. To this world of material particles acting in terms of mathematical laws, ultimate reality was attributed. Science thus became a metaphysics: a disguised metaphysics perhaps but a metaphysics nevertheless. And so Newton, who had said 'Physics, beware of metaphysics', became one of the fathers of the latter offspring. Hobhouse describes the consequences of this situation as follows:

> The physical conceptions of the seventeenth century
> had by the close of the nineteenth century reached the
> culmination of success. In the fundamentals they had stood
> the test of time and their applications had widened to
> embrace the whole field of physical phenomena. They seemed
> to hold the world in an iron frame of mechanism. The
> fundamental laws were so simple and axiomatic, the
> calculations so rigid, the verifications so pat, that only the
> metaphysician or the mystic could dream of an escape.[4]

Nature was reduced to a machine, or mechanism, as this passage states. Science came to be based upon assumptions that were mechanistic and materialistic.

Similarly, owing to the influence of John Locke, science in its outlook became involved with epistemology, for Locke was one of the intellectual progenitors of nineteenth-century naturalism. Underlying this philosophical viewpoint are two epistemological assumptions. The first is that only the sciences can give man valid knowledge. The second holds that the only real things that can be known are those that submit to the conditions laid down in the first assumption. Science, then, came to be looked upon as the only road to valid knowledge, the only key to truth. It has been pointed out by Hobhouse that much good knowledge is not scientific,[5] and more recently a prominent American scientist has said:

> Science is modern, popular and dominant. It needs no special pleaders . . . It cannot help being tempted to a certain arrogance and a conviction that the keys of truth are in its hands alone . . . [But] logic and reason are no monopoly of science . . .[6]

This view would be corroborated by Hobhouse. He held that the methods of physical science might be justified in terms of the purposes of science, but not as the basis of a theory of knowledge, because '. . . as an interpretation of reality it [science] still suffers from the abstractness which is the very condition of its success'.[7] He further noted that, as science advances, its more philosophically sophisticated exponents come to realize that physical science is only one way of attaining truth, that in the last analysis their concepts are derived from and have reference to the world of experience, that other forms of experience exist, and that concepts derived from the same source are equally worthy of respect, if mutually consistent. The aesthetic, the moral and the religious experience, and the whole experience of life and mind, have a right to demand autonomy of investigation. They have discarded the authority of physics as physics discarded the authority of religion. They rest on the same basis: namely, experience. And since all these autonomies must live together, self-determination cannot be absolute in the world of the mind any more than in the world of politics.[8]

Nevertheless, in the last quarter of the nineteenth century the natural sciences exerted a dominating influence upon modes of thought. There was manifested an attempt to compress all human experience into the preconceived moulds of mathematical physics, or, in effect, to superimpose a method upon all varieties of subject-matter. If the subject-matter in question did not, for example, lend itself to mathematical treatment, it was reinterpreted and adapted to make it fit such treatment. Similarly, the mechanistic philosophy gave rise to behaviouristic theories of man and his nature. Although modern science claims its independence of philosophy, it has actually been instrumental in spreading a philosophical theory of knowledge and of reality: namely, mechanistic materialism, which pervades much social as well as physical science. The view is frequently held that science is identical with the mechanistic approach to phenomena, and that the mental categories which underlie mechanism are still valid.

Hobhouse would contend, however, that it is not the object of science to reduce everything to matter:

> . . . it is often supposed that the distinctive object of science as opposed to humanistic or philosophical treatment is to resolve the mental into the material, the purposive into the mechanical, life and mind into physio-chemical forces. This is a mistake in definition: it is not in the distinctive character of science to assume any general explanation at the outset. It is the object of science to ascertain the facts with accuracy and completeness.[9]

He further states that to assume that all data must be of a mechanical character and lend itself to mathematical computation, if it is to be the subject of scientific investigation, is to identify science with mathematics, and for this there is no warrant.[10] But here, again, is seen the influence of Newton's mathematical physics, traces of which linger today in the emphasis on mathematical measurement as the only 'scientific' analysis of phenomena, physical or social.

The tendency of mechanism to reduce everything to matter is related to the abstraction that takes the part for the whole; if the mechanist cannot within the bounds of his own methods analyse every aspect of phenomena under investigation, he is apt to declare that the unanalysable segment does not exist, or is insignificant. Hence the tendency for the intangible and imponderable factors in human association to be ignored or compressed within the confines of mathematical analysis. To quote Hobhouse's pupil, colleague and successor, Dr Morris Ginsberg:

In its revolt against vagueness the mechanical mind seizes eagerly on those concepts which appear most easily verifiable, and then mistakes these luminous bits for the whole.[11]

The effect of this tendency of the mechanist to reduce everything to matter, and to interpret all phenomena in materialistic terms, is portrayed by Hobhouse in the following passage:

. . . when the biologist comes to deal with the actual behaviour of organic matter in the living organism, he is by no means disposed to let the physicist or chemist dogmatize as to what he must find. On the contrary he knows what he himself finds by his own methods, and this is often enough the very opposite of what pure physics would lead him to expect. The higher science, in fact, though dependent on the lower, ought by no means to merge its identity therein. This loss of identity Comte called materialism, because it hands over the higher, more complex, more subtle things of the world to be dealt with by methods appropriate to things of a coarser texture. It puts the living on a level with the inanimate, and the higher life with the lower. This lapse into materialism is precisely what has befallen the science of society in our own time. Volumes are written on sociology which take no account of history, no account of law, nor of ethics, nor of religion, nor of art, nor of social relations in their actual development, and, above all, have no consistent standard of value to measure the progress of which they speak. And their utterances are held to be the verdict of 'science' to which the mere student of society must yield.[12]

In view of the foregoing, what are the assumptions that underlie mechanistic materialism? What is the view of man and human relations to which they lead? Are these assumptions valid? Hobhouse's answers to these questions will now be considered. It will be seen that, just as biological categories and terms do not in themselves exhaust the field of sociology, so mechanism is inadequate to explain human relations.

Hobhouse's criticism of mechanism

As the term 'mechanism' implies, its viewpoint is that the living human being is simply a machine devised to meet a larger number of contingencies than any other machine, so devised that each contingency supplies the necessary stimulus to the necessary parts to act in such a way as is compatible with the maintenance of the organism.

Hobhouse points out that the term 'mechanism' appears to have arisen as antithetic to the term 'teleology', but he notes that a machine is as clearly something contrived with a purpose as anything can be. It is possible that the contrast between the purpose which lay behind the building of the machine and the blindness with which the latter acts has made the term current. But, however the term became current, the characteristics of a man-made machine are visibly those of mechanism if the details of the action are observed. In a machine, although the parts are so arranged as normally to operate in relation to one another so as to produce a certain result, yet each part acts uniformly without relation to the rest in response to the forces upon it. Each part acts uniformly in response to a given force independently of the condition of the other parts, and is independent of the results of its action. The action of any one part does not depend on the action of other parts as such.[13]

From this physical or mechanical point of view, the claim would be put forward by the mechanist that the human mind is simply the result of mechanical interactions between external phenomena and the physical structure of human sense organs. The mechanist would explain the nature of the human being by regarding him as a physical machine; any residue not reduced to materialistic terms would require only further investigation to be placed upon the same basis. Finally, a more complete knowledge would enable purposive action, artistic creation and philosophical thought to be reduced to a series of mechanical changes in nervous tissue.

Against this viewpoint, Hobhouse argues that there are two other categories which offer a more adequate interpretation of human action and relations. These are the categories of 'organism' and 'purpose'. Concerning them, he says:

A whole is mechanical when and in so far as its parts act
uniformly in response to the forces operating on each of
them, not varying in relation to the results of their action
or to the state of other parts. A whole acts organically when
and in so far as the operation of any part is varied in
accordance with the requirements of the whole as a self-
maintaining structure. A whole acts purposively in so far as
it acts are determined by their own tendency to produce
results affecting the whole.[14]

Hobhouse throws further light on the concept of 'organism' when
he says that 'a thing is called organic when it is made up of parts
which are quite distinct from one another, but which are destroyed or vitally altered when they are removed from the whole'.[15]

The human body is organic, since its life is dependent on the
functions of many organs, each of which depends in turn on the
life of the entire body, perishing or decomposing if removed from
the body. There is an interdependence of the parts, since the
requirements of the whole body influence each part.

The organic, for Hobhouse, is in general the character of a
whole whose parts are modified in their origin, development and
continued activity by the demands of the whole to which they
belong. Similarly, the requirements of each part have an effect on
the remainder. This definition implies elements that have a certain
character and tendencies of their own, but elements that cannot
fully maintain themselves or fulfil their tendencies without the
assistance of the others.[16]

It is apparent, then, that the behaviour of living beings differs
from the mechanical type in a constant adaptation to the requirements of the whole. The peculiar character of an organism lies in
its wholeness, and not in any particular part. This is in direct
antithesis to the mechanical system which sees distinguishable
elements as operating separately. In reality, they determine and
modify each other:

The true corrective . . . to the mechanical view is the
conception of the organism as a totality wherein all elements
and all life processes modify one another and lose that
independence which, as genuinely mechanical processes,
would be attributed to them.[17]

The mechanist, however, is apt to take the sum of the parts for the whole, and to regard the organic character merely as an extra part added to the others, upon which it acts in an ill-defined manner. The wholeness of the phenomena in question is reduced to one part among others. It is invented and added as a controlling force to the other parts. In this way, the mechanist tries to overcome the difficulties inherent in the conception of an organism.

Hobhouse maintained, on the contrary, that it is a simple matter of fact that there are differences between forms of behaviour, and that some forms of behaviour bear no resemblance to the processes of the machine; these latter are those usually attributed to the mind.

Involved in this assertion is a third category: namely, that of purpose, a form of explanation which mechanism expressly excludes. The definition of purpose which Hobhouse gives is as follows: 'A whole acts purposively in so far as its acts are determined by their own tendency to produce results affecting the whole.'[18]

There are, then, two distinct types of behaviour: the mechanical and the purposive; and the organic type will usually resolve itself into one or the other. Basic to the purposive type is the fact that behaviour is conditioned by its relation to the end or result of such behaviour. In the mechanical type, there is no such relation between action and its end, although the result is in fact produced. It is worthy of note that even a reflex action, which appears to be the response of a structure to a specific stimulus, manifests a divergence from the purely mechanical model. The reflex may be inhibited or varied, and these variations are all in one direction: they serve the requirements of the entire body as a structure maintaining itself through changes.

The distinction between the two modes of action, the mechanical and the purposive or teleological, is basic to Hobhouse's theory. In the teleological sphere a thing is done because it tends to produce something: namely, a change in a whole to which the thing is done belongs, or in which it happens. In the mechanical realm, no such elements enter into causation. A distinction is to be drawn, then, between teleology and mechanism as two modes of action, rather than between mind and matter as two substances.

Actions which are purposive may be termed teleological, that is, they are performed with an end in sight. In the view of Hobhouse, there is no theoretical limit to the plasticity of human purpose;

in contrast with this is the machine, which has no power of adaptation to an unexpected contingency, and cannot vary its course in a manner more appropriately suited to the end or result.[19] When purposive action takes place, this condition, and those of mechanical action generally, are reversed. And purposive action is a prime characteristic of mental life, as Hobhouse points out:

> Mind, as studied from outside, in its functions, is most clearly recognizable in the purposive act. Now the purposive act, again studied not from within but from without, is an act apparently directed by relation to its result. It chooses means to ends, rejects those that are unsuitable, varies its behaviour in accordance with circumstances, surmounts, destroys, or circumvents obstacles, adapts itself to an indefinite number of varying circumstances in accordance with their relation to the matter in hand.[20]

The human mind, on this view, is characterized by purpose, and that purpose has a vast range. Hobhouse describes teleology as 'a specific mode of causation, and in our experience it is the characteristic method of conscious intelligence and so of mind'.[21] Although he would grant that mental elements may act mechanically when not co-ordinated, he would nevertheless maintain that the mental always acts teleologically in greater or lesser degree, and that even in its 'mechanical' actions there is often found some trace of conative adjustment. Even the 'mechanical' actions involved in a man's lighting his pipe have reference to an end in view. This end in view, like the original desire, constitutes a determining factor. The importance of the end in view, even in the case of a supposedly 'mechanical' series of actions such as those involved in the lighting of a pipe, is expressed in the following passage:

> Ideas, perceptions, efforts, are taken up, pressed, discarded, varied, brought into relation in such a way as to serve the result, so that the purpose is an organization of elements determined by relation to the effect which it produces, and if we look to the centre of this organization, in the case instanced a desire, we find its very nature unstateable except

by an inclusion of reference to the result. It is nothing if not an impulse towards an end. The tendency to bring something about does not merely determine but rather constitute it.

Now, purposive activities, as we know them, rest on a central impulse of this type, and . . . involve awareness of what we are doing and anticipation of what is coming.[22]

This latter assertion is illustrated by another so-called 'mechanical' action that nevertheless involves an end and a recognition of an end. If a man requires a book which he remembers to have left in a particular place, and goes to get it, his memory has to contain some deposit of his previous dealings with the book and has to be combined with his need and his physical surroundings so as to discharge the actions necessary for finding the book. This deposit is only one of millions that his experience has formed. But provision must be made for selecting it out from them, combining it with other memory deposits, and bringing the whole to bear upon the problem of finding the book, which constituted the original end in view. The concept of relevancy of means to ends is basic to the entire procedure, even in such a simple 'mechanical' action as the one cited. The combination of activity that is represented here is relevant to an end. To admit this principle is to recognize a structure determined by purpose. To deny it is to lack a general plan to explain the activity-combinations, and 'either horn of the dilemma excludes mechanism'.[23]

The end in question, be it noted, may be immediate and individual, as in the above case; it may be a long-range individual end involving a lifetime's career, and in the complex structure of modern society an end may concern not merely the individual involved, but may reach out to his country, his church, or to humanity.

In conclusion, it may be repeated that mental activity is purposive, and purpose for Hobhouse is 'a state which determines acts in accordance with the results which they tend to produce'.[24] Since man has the power to act purposively, and since this type of action is the antithesis of the mechanical, man is not simply a reacting mechanism, as the behaviourists would claim.

The implications for social science that stem from mechanism include the view that mind is non-existent, and that human beings are simply machines that react to stimuli, without any thought or purpose involved, since these latter categories are meaningless except in terms of physico-chemical interactions. Also implicit in this viewpoint is the idea that value is a meaningless concept, while social evolution is considered to be predetermined: man is not a purposive or thinking being who can in any way direct his own future.

Hobhouse inclined to the view that the influence of mechanism was not as strong in the years preceding his death as it had been a few decades earlier, for, in this connection, he said:

> It was not till physical science had achieved the final triumph of the later nineteenth century that it began to doubt its own assumptions and a reconstruction set in, of which the end is not in sight, but which has gone far enough to shake the apparent simplicity and seemingly axiomatic character of mechanistic principles and to justify those who study the world of mind, of ethics, politics, religion and art in pursuing their course without the uneasy belief that their ultimate results can be nothing but superficial appearance, the underlying causes of which must be ultimately traceable to the mechanical interaction of physical particles.[25]

It would be an interesting task to try to estimate how far Hobhouse was responsible, through his research, writing and teaching, for the decline of mechanism in England. His criticism of the mechanistic position is sound testimony to the fact that it is more 'scientific' to inquire into the assumptions underlying a scientific theory than to accept the theory uncritically. For when scepticism is turned on science as science has applied it to theology, 'the way is opened to wider applications of scientific method and a more liberal interpretation of scientific principles . . .'.[26] And this had actually taken place in the world of thought as the principles of mechanism were critically examined. There had been a challenging of old ideas, and a change in the conceptions of physical science, from which a broader outlook had arisen. The foundations of physics had shifted and the way had been opened for a deeper and wider philosophy of science.

Mechanism furnishes an excellent example of how philosophical assumptions underlie the thinking of those who would be quick to disclaim any connection with philosophy. The behaviourist, for example, who is solely concerned with 'the facts' of physical stimuli and response, is apt to forget that he is assuming the metaphysical theory of materialism, though he has no right as a scientist to assume such a metaphysical theory at the outset of his research. The fact that such assumptions and underlying viewpoints exist, and colour supposedly 'objective' investigation, is, however, ground for the view that scientific endeavour might be advanced if more attention were paid to the original assumptions or postulates which the scientist brings to his work. It is contended that one of Hobhouse's indirect contributions, related to his criticism of mechanism as an underlying scientific viewpoint, lay in his study of assumptions and hypotheses. This will now be considered.

The importance of assumptions, hypotheses and theory

It is a commonly held view that the scientist proceeds in his investigations without any assumptions or presuppositions, since he is 'objective' and impartial. The scientist is supposedly simply concerned with ascertaining the facts of his particular field, but without preconceived notions or biases. He does not take anything for granted, but has the attitude of open-minded investigation, allowing his discoveries to take him where they will and following the facts wheresoever they may lead. His mind is free from dogmas, he has no unquestioned first principles at the outset of his research. He brings, on the contrary, an 'open mind' to the study of the phenomena under review.

This is the way in which many persons, scientists included, think of science, as opposed to theology, for instance, which starts out with certain dogmas or beliefs which are not open to question but must be accepted uncritically. But, Hobhouse implies, this view of science is erroneous, for science does make assumptions, and rests upon them from the start. Just as common action is based upon assumptions of which it may be unaware, so there are scientific workers who fail to realize that their minds are not 'open' in the sense of being empty of presuppositions. Indeed, scientists make assumptions all the time and at all stages of their research, albeit unconsciously.

As Hobhouse points out,[27] it is the work of logic to criticize and analyse these basic assumptions, for every assertion of fact or system of facts rests on assumptions, avowed or implied. Logic seeks to analyse the first type, expose the second, and test both. It leaves no assumption unexpressed, nor, if at all possible, untested.

If it is claimed that the scientist is without assumptions, it may be replied that it is in the light of assumptions that 'facts' are selected and their meaning interpreted. This is so, no matter how 'scientific' an individual may be. Among the assumptions of science that readily come to mind are: (a) the worth of the scientific quest, (b) the adequacy and relevance of the methods employed, (c) a belief in refined observation, (d) a belief in the existence of phenomena external to the observer, the trustworthiness of memory, an ordered regularity in natural phenomena and the judgements of the senses. Some less apparent presuppositions relate to the ethos or intellectual climate of the world of science at a particular time, as was seen in connection with mechanism. Whatever these assumptions may be, and whatever their source, they are basic to science in that the validity of science is bound up inextricably with *their* validity. Speaking of assumptions, Hobhouse says:

> If they are true, the results of science are trustworthy, and if not, not. That being so, it is clear that whatever validity attaches to the results of science, whatever confidence we can legitimately place in its generalizations, must attach equally to these assumptions.[28]

Assumptions are the first principles, the axioms which are unexpressed and taken for granted, and are therefore seldom held up to criticism as the scientist demands theories in other fields of study and belief be examined and criticized. They have special reference to scientific laws and generalizations, for they underlie them. If the assumptions are at fault, the laws will not apply. The law of supply and demand furnishes a case in point, for it assumes that men will always buy as cheaply and will sell as dearly as they can. This is an *assumption* about human motives, and, on some occasions, it has proved false, thereby rendering invalid the 'law' of supply and demand.

It is not merely in connection with generalizations, but throughout the entire realm of science and logic, that assumptions are crucial. Hobhouse has indicated[29] that they are basic to logic and that logic underlies all science, though this is sometimes forgotten. No overt reference may be made to the prior assertions that support a judgement, while perhaps the commonest assumption regarding science, as distinct from philosophy and theology, is that it is lacking in assumptions and postulates. Throughout the writings of Hobhouse that deal with science and logic is the implication that this is an untenable position, while he would be in agreement with Barnes and Becker in the judgement that '. . . it is quite impossible to engage in systematic rational discourse of any kind without making assumptions that cannot be proved by any amount of Pure Induction . . .'.[30]

This being the case, it should be apparent that theory and logic can aid the development of science by exposing and criticizing its basic assumptions. These assumptions are not necessarily valid unless they have been recognized, analysed and tested.

Besides pointing out the existence of assumptions, a further contribution of Hobhouse lay in his study of the role of hypotheses in science, and his indication of the difference between hypotheses and assumptions. He also pointed out some of the dangers inherent in the use of hypotheses. With regard to the way in which assumptions become hypotheses, he said:

. . . while there may be some first principles which are true axioms, needing no proof, there are others which at the outset are mere assumptions, taken up for the purpose of seeing what flows from them. These conclusions can be tested by experience, and if there is agreement, the assumption on which they depend stands uncontradicted. It may be true. If further results are elicited and the agreement with experience continues, it becomes difficult to believe that an assumption which works so well can be false. When it has stood very wide and complicated tests, we need not trouble ourselves to question it further. We may take it as true. This is the only way by which experience can establish a generalization. Any such generalization is at first a hypothesis, and in proportion as its consequences are found to conform to fact it becomes a recognized theory.[31]

The conclusion may be drawn that a hypothesis is a *conscious* assumption, taken up with the express purpose of seeing where it will lead. In this way, the scientist attempts to understand facts by means of conceptions drawn from experience. By beginning with certain facts, he formulates a theory that may lead to further understanding, while comparison of his results with observed and measured data may disprove the assumption.

Hobhouse insisted, though, that while an encounter with fact is a test of the invalidity of a hypothesis, it is not so easy to say when a hypothesis is proved. For hypotheses are long-lived, until they feel the impact of some fact which is indisputable. In the meantime, much energy may be lost in defending unproved positions. But, Hobhouse recognized, modern science often obtained worthwhile results by assuming positions it could not directly prove. This was so, however, because scientists had worked out methods of reasoning from these assumptions, and had compared the results with those of observation. An assumption so treated became a hypothesis; one which could not be so treated remained a conjecture.[32]

Hobhouse thus pointed out that assumptions that were tested by observation and reason have a scientific value in several fields. Abstract principles, when tested by concrete experience, provided good hypotheses, but they had to be tested, otherwise they remained in the realm of conjecture. But, when tested and found valid, hypotheses become part of the theoretical framework of science, and a basis for further advance. Hobhouse noted that scientists use established conclusions as well as unproved hypotheses. Every experiment, on this view, involves not merely probabilities but tested results which are part of the basis for further experimentation. What *has* been found then becomes a premise from which, with careful treatment, the scientist derives a knowledge of what *will* be found.

Hobhouse was aware that organized sciences tend to conform to a body of interconnected generalizations, not merely tested hypotheses but 'a mass of results each standing on its own basis of observation and calculation, positive evidence which we can have no specific ground for doubting . . .'.[33] Scientific verification, then, is a process involving further observations or further inferences from observed facts; in Hobhouse's view, a scientific hypothesis is an assertion of fact to be decided by comparison with other assertions of facts. He recognized that, when such a comparison was made, the situation might arise in which two hypotheses might be consistent with a great body of ascertained fact, but be irreconcilable with one another. Such a situation might develop at an incomplete stage of knowledge, but could not represent the objective truth, since truth is a unity and consistent throughout. Either or both of the hypotheses, on this view, would have to be revised before the truth could be known.

Hypotheses, then, consist of assumptions tested by observation and reasoning from known facts; they are part of the foundation of the scientific quest and a means of its continued development. But if the results of a hypothesis do not compare well with those of observation, the hypothesis must be rejected or revised. For it has to have a basis in facts. If it does not have such a foundation, but simply rests on vague possibilities, its scientific value is nil. In this connection Hobhouse praised the work of Darwin, noting that Darwin started from known facts and made inferences from those facts. His method was founded on empirical generalizations, and it resulted in a new epoch in science.[34]

Although it is necessary in science to make such tentative hypotheses, and to confirm them by calculation and refined observation, yet there are dangers in reasoning from hypotheses. Hobhouse showed wherein some of these dangers lay. For example, the way in which a hypothesis develops through being tested by facts and empirical data does not constitute a theory of proof. It involves the fallacy of the 'inverse' method, which Hobhouse explains as follows:

If the hypothesis is true, certain observable facts will follow. They do follow, therefore the hypothesis is true. This is inherently bad logic, and the theory that there is no proof obtainable from experience but this is the parent also of much bad science.[35]

It follows from the above that careful logic is obviously required in the framing of hypotheses and in their subsequent use; for a hypothesis may assume more than is warranted, and it thus commits itself to that which its inverse method cannot prove. It is an error, then, to conclude that all that is involved is true merely because the results follow and are in accordance with the facts. A hypothesis which is merely assumed can never be substantiated by going to the facts, nor does it explain the facts. In this connection, a good example of fallacious logic, cited by Hobhouse, consists of 'if the principles are true, the results must follow. But here are the results, therefore the principles are true.'[36] A hypothesis cannot be 'proved' in terms of its results, and to attempt to establish it thus is logically unsatisfactory.

Since this point is of some importance, the following passage is cited in full, as a statement of the characteristic stand taken by Hobhouse on hypotheses:

> ... bare consistency with the facts is not, by careful thinkers, held sufficient as a final demonstration of a hypothesis. More than one hypothesis may be consistent with the facts, and it is clear that more than one hypothesis cannot be true ... A hypothesis may well accord with the facts without being itself true, when it contains within it descriptions and generalizations which are true. Thus, I suppose the Ptolemaic system of the universe summed up a mass of recorded observations and generalizations as to the movements of the planets, which were in the main perfectly sound, and eking these out with certain further suggestions which were not based upon experience, or were based on a faulty interpretation of experience, it formed a certain concrete picture of the material universe. On the basis of this hypothesis, the motions of the planets and the occurrence of astronomical events became, in great measure, capable of being predicted, and so for a long while the hypothesis accorded with known facts, and not only accorded with them, but assisted ... in the practical requirements, if we may so call them, of reducing these facts to order and anticipating the future. The hypothesis served this purpose in virtue of the element in which it was sound, as being derived by legitimate generalization from well-attested experience. But so far as there is no test to discriminate what is sound from what is unsound, and so long as we look to bare consistency with fact as constrasted with necessitation by fact, we cannot make this distinction.[37]

Mere 'consistency with the facts' does not constitute a sound proof of the validity of a hypothesis. It is an error to use a hypothesis as the basis for a deduction from which conclusions can be drawn with which the 'facts' agree.

While the use of hypotheses is necessary for the advancement of science, great care must be used in formulation, with due regard for the facts already established. Similarly, the dangers of attempting to argue backwards from their results must be kept in mind. The sound elements in a hypothesis have to be separated from the unsound, if fruitful results are to be forthcoming, while nothing can atone for failure to begin with the facts of experience. All of which serves to illustrate a point previously noted: that sound logic is essential in any science, not just in the use of hypotheses, but elsewhere also. This leads to another related contribution of Hobhouse: his emphasis upon the use of sound logic and theory in sociology.

It was seen in connection with mechanism that theoretical viewpoints underlie even the most rigidly 'scientific' thinking. For this and other reasons, Hobhouse would contend that sociology as a science, or indeed any field of study, cannot be content to limit itself to 'scientific method' and leave all questions of logic to the philosophers. On the contrary, any study that seeks valid knowledge must depend upon sound logic at every step of the way. It is understood that logic refers not merely to correct methods of reasoning and the examination of the criteria of validity in thought, but comprises reflection upon the entire topic at hand. Logic or philosophy is concerned with the conditions under which valid knowledge may be obtained, and is used here in the sense of sustained and comprehensive analysis.

In the formulation of a sociological system or frame of reference, reasoning plays a major role, and in the criticism and refinement of a sociological system, more reflective reasoning is called into play. The presuppositions and postulates underlying the original system are criticized and analysed. In dealing with the relation between parts of a system, theory is utilized. In studying the relevance and adequacy of any particular method in sociology, logical reflection and comparison lead to a more balanced point of view than that expressed in uncritical devotion to one methodological tool or the current fashion. In short, it can be said that most of the important issues in contemporary sociology are questions that scientific research alone is inadequate to cope with, because they are issues that involve theory at every turn.

The need for logic and sound theoretical foundations in sociology is implied throughout all Hobhouse's writings. This is natural, in view of his early Oxford training in philosophy. It has been seen how he brought to light some of the theory underlying mechanism, and showed how theoretical assumptions lie behind and beneath scientific endeavours.

Nevertheless, theory is apt to be currently cast aside by some sociologists in the attempt to 'get the facts', while abstract arguments will be distrusted, as Hobhouse noted three quarters of a century ago. Writing in 1898, he contended that the prevalent intellectual tendency of the time was to distrust abstract arguments, a tendency that he thought had been growing for nearly one hundred years.[38]

The ignoring of theoretical issues and the tendency to regard abstract questions as taken for granted are not new. This chapter may appropriately close with a discussion of a criticism that Hobhouse made concerning Comte. Comte is often regarded as the father in sociology of empirical method, as distinct from 'metaphysical' thinking. Yet, as Hobhouse shows, Comte himself furnishes a good example of the importance of metaphysical assumptions and the way in which they unconsciously become a part of the scientist's system of research.

Hobhouse pointed out that Comte founded his whole system on a negative answer to the question of whether knowledge leads to the heart of reality. This, says Hobhouse, is 'the fundamental question of metaphysics'.[39] The positive method of Comte is said to deal with 'phenomena' and the 'laws' of phenomena, abandoning the search for origins, causes and purposes. Knowledge, according to Comte, should be restricted to facts, to 'phenomena'. The implication is that the facts with which investigation deals are 'phenomena'. Behind them lies the real world, a Forbidden City containing the causes of all that happens and its ultimate origin and purpose. Positivism sees these fundamental problems as insoluble. It simply seeks to know that which is of concern to humanity. This conception of the limitation of all knowledge strongly coloured Comte's philosophy.

But, argues Hobhouse, the definition of positive method itself rests on *metaphysical* conclusions. The distinction between phenomena and reality is a *metaphysical* distinction. The denial that ultimate causes and purposes can be known is a *metaphysical* denial. The abandonment of speculation as to the ultimate origins or purposes of things is the result of a *metaphysical* scepticism. To drop all this metaphysical theory and begin with the positive method would be to look for data in experience. But it does not appear from the positive method whether this experience is an experience of phenomena only; whether there is a valid and general distinction to be drawn between phenomena and a reality beyond this phenomena does not appear. Distinction between phenomena and the real order of things, together with restriction to the former, is not a first principle on which method depends. If it is true, it is a result to which sound method should lead, and if false, one which it should disprove. It is an error to attribute to the positive stage a certain theory of the limitation of human knowledge. For until the method has been carried through, it is not possible to tell whether or not the ultimate problems are insoluble.[40]

Such, in brief, is the Hobhouse criticism of the theory underlying Comte's positivism. Although he was sympathetic to Comte on many points, this particular criticism is one more case of how 'the facts' cannot be divorced from the theory that undergirds them. Hobhouse noted that, when any special science probes far enough, it reaches fundamental questions of validity and meaning. It is because it has been found possible, and up to a point profitable, to investigate without regard to these deeper questions, that they have been reserved for philosophy. But, Hobhouse maintained, knowledge and truth represent a unity, and cannot be broken up into separate compartments without the appearance of artificiality and abstraction; therefore the separation of philosophy and science has been in many ways unfortunate. For, in its investigation of truth, careful formulation of statements and systematic ordering of data, philosophy itself aims at being scientific. It analyses, clarifies and compares. Its analyses may sometimes be imperfect, but it seeks the remedy in further and better analysis. Social theory, on this view, is clear and consistent analysis regarding society and its ramifications. Its ends are comprehensive, consistent and connected.[41] It is not to be confused with empty speculation.

In summarizing this chapter, it may be repeated that Hobhouse made a contribution in his criticism of the mechanistic view of life and mind; he refuted the idea that scientists have to assume materialism at the beginning of their investigations in order to be scientific; and he insisted upon the need for recognizing and examining the assumptions of science as one of the tasks of logic. In addition, Hobhouse pointed out how assumptions, when tested, become hypotheses, and he showed some of the dangers inherent in reasoning from hypotheses. He stressed the importance of sound logic in dealing with hypotheses, as in all aspects of science, and he noted that the historical separation of science and philosophy had been unfortunate for both.

In Chapter 3 we will consider other contributions of Hobhouse relevant to sociology.

Notes and References

1. L. T. Hobhouse, *Social Evolution and Political Theory* (New York: Columbia University Press, 1911), p. 21.

2. ibid., pp. 109, 110. The need for a sociology of science is also expressed by Morris Ginsberg in *Studies in Sociology* (1932), pp. 11–12, and by F. J. Wright, *The Elements of Sociology* (1942), Chapter 11.

3. L. T. Hobhouse, 'Faith and the Will to Believe', © *Proceedings of the Aristotelian Society* (London: Williams & Norgate, 1904), Vol. IV, pp. 87, 88. (Reprinted by courtesy of the Editor of the Aristotelian Society).

4. L. T. Hobhouse, *Development and Purpose*, p. xxxvi.

5. L. T. Hobhouse, *The Theory of Knowledge, a Contribution to some Problems of Logic and Metaphysics*, p. 2.

6. Edmund W. Sinnott, *Time*, L: 95; no. 17, 27 October 1947.

7. *Development and Purpose*, p. xxxvii.

8. ibid., pp. xxxvii, xxxviii.

9. *Social Development, Its Nature and Conditions*, pp. 240, 241

10. op. cit., p. 279. In connection with the mechanistic approach, it is interesting to note that the approach to a problem, and the method used in formulating the problem, in any field, will determine the nature of the solution. If mathematical methods are used exclusively in the formulation of a scientific problem, the outcome will be expressed in mathematical terms and will have little meaning outside mathematics. The question may be raised whether the methods of mathematical treatment are suitable and adequate for dealing with the problems of human relations, or even for all problems within the natural sciences themselves. To superimpose upon social reality the abstract methods that have been derived from Newtonian physics is comparable to remodelling a lock to fit a certain key, rather than finding a key that will more closely resemble the

characteristics of the lock. This is the situation that has arisen through the view that only science, in the sense of mathematical physics, represents the key to truth.

11. J. A. Hobson and Morris Ginsberg, *L. T. Hobhouse, His Life and Work*, p. 105.

12. *Democracy and Reaction*, pp. 97–9.

13. L. T. Hobhouse, 'Are Physical, Biological and Psychological Categories Irreducible?', in *Life and Finite Individuality*, edited by H. Wildon Carr (London: Williams & Norgate, 1918), pp. 62, 63. (Reprinted by courtesy of the Editor of the Aristotelian Society, © 1918 The Aristotelian Society).

14. ibid., p. 67.

15. L. T. Hobhouse, *Liberalism*, p. 125.

16. L. T. Hobhouse, "The Philosophy of Development', loc. cit., p. 168.

17. L. T. Hobhouse, 'The Law of the Three Stages', *Sociological Review*, I: 275, 276, July 1908.

18. 'Are Physical, Biological and Psychological Categories Irreducible?', loc. cit., p. 67.

19. ibid., p. 69. See also L. T. Hobhouse, 'The Place of Mind in Nature', in *Methods of Analysis*, Aristotelian Society, Supplementary Vol. VI (London: Williams & Norgate, 1926), p. 120.

20. *Mind in Evolution* (1915 edition), pp. 14, 15.

21. 'The Philosophy of Development', loc. cit., p. 177.

22. 'Are Physical, Biological and Psychological Categories Irreducible?', loc. cit., p. 66. (Reprinted by courtesy of the Editor of the Aristotelian Society, © 1918 The Aristotelian Society).

23. *Development and Purpose*, pp. 405–6.

24. *Mind in Evolution*, p. 163.

25. L. T. Hobhouse, 'Comparative Ethics', © *Encyclopaedia Britannica*, 6: 163, 14th edition, 1937.

26. ibid., p. 164.

27. *The Theory of Knowledge*, p. 3.

28. *Development and Purpose*, p. 414.

29. op. cit., p. 480.

30. Harry Elmer Barnes and Howard Becker, *Social Thought from Lore to Science* (1938), Vol. II, p. 997. Related to this position is the view that there are no 'bare facts', since all facts are interconnected. Every fact is clothed in premises, assumptions and other theoretical habiliments, and in viewing the facts a 'point of view' is always involved. This point of view colours the inter-

pretation of facts, regardless of the origins of the viewpoint. The theory of knowledge which involves the concept of a 'camera-mind' looking at entity-facts or objects is false. The mind, whether of the scientist or layman, is not blank at the outset of its investigations or observations, but on the contrary is full of presuppositions derived from past experience, previous training, the intellectual climate of opinion or personal bias.

31. *Development and Purpose*, pp. 291, 292. The task of criticizing assumptions belongs to logic, and when and if a scientist attempts by logical, rational methods to criticize his assumptions, he is filling the role of logician or philosopher. His presuppositions are philosophical, not just scientific. They transcend science and scientific method, as some of the more philosophically sophisticated scientists have shown. (E.g., see A. N. Whitehead, *Science and the Modern World* (New York: Macmillan Company, 1926); and A. S. Eddington, *The Nature of the Physical World* (New York: Macmillan Company, 1929); also F. S. C. Northrop, *Science and First Principles* (New York: Macmillan Company, 1931).) For this reason, they demand philosophical treatment, namely, rigorous, comprehensive, critical analysis. This will aid the development of science, since its advance consists not merely in extending its range of valid data, but in the revision and reconstruction of its theoretical foundations, which are made up of assumptions and first principles. If these are false or inadequate, they can wreck an experiment. More important, they can hinder the entire development of science, until revised and corrected. Thus, Einstein aided the advance of science by his criticism of Newtonian physics, a criticism which was based upon a *philosophical* analysis of space and time. But philosophy was disdained by many contemporary physicists as being little more than empty speculation and vague theorizing, and thus the foundations of physics remained Newtonian until fairly recently. More awareness among physicists of the Newtonian assumptions lying behind their science, with analytical criticism of these assumptions, would have greatly accelerated the development of modern physics.

32. *Development and Purpose*, p. 130.

33. ibid., p. 336. See also L. T. Hobhouse, *The Rational Good*, p. 183.

34. *Social Evolution and Political Theory* (1911), p. 113. See also *Development and Purpose*, p. 295.

35. ibid., p. 292.

36. ibid., p. 135.

37. 'Faith and the Will to Believe', loc. cit., pp. 97, 98.

38. 'The Ethical Basis of Collectivism', *International Journal of Ethics*, 8: 138, January 1898.

39. *Social Development, Its Nature and Conditions*, p. 36, note.

40. 'The Law of the Three Stages', loc. cit., pp. 268, 269.

41. *Social Development, Its Nature and Conditions*, p. 204. See also *Development and Purpose*, p. 136. In connection with the implied importance of social theory that runs through Hobhouse's writings, the following passage by Barnes and

Becker is illuminating: 'It has been customary to be enthusiastic over the trend toward minute specialization and "fact-gathering" that is characteristic of present-day American sociology, but there are grounds for mixed feelings. True, there is probably less unfounded speculation at present than there has been in the past, and for this we may be thankful. But speculation is not the same as rigorous, comprehensive, theoretical analysis, and of the latter there is far too little. The naïveté of most American sociologists when confronted with basic epistemological and methodological problems is deplorable . . . seeing that certain methods are applicable to physical, chemical and biological problems, we have jumped at the conclusion that they can be carried over *en bloc* to sociological problems. Our Comtean heritage has much to do with this, but the general drift of thought during the nineteenth century is at least equally to blame'—*Social Thought from Lore to Science*, Vol. II: pp. 990, 991.

3   Some Prolegomena to Sociology

Hobhouse emphasized certain topics which, in their entirety, constitute a series of thought-provoking themes in sociology. As a first-generation pioneer in the days when sociology was in its infancy, he was naturally concerned with the framework, scope and methods of this new science. This chapter will present some of the areas where he rendered a service to sociology as a new discipline.

It is a prime characteristic of science that it is empirical in its outlook and methods. What were the ramifications of the empirical approach and outlook, as interpreted by Hobhouse?

Empiricism

The basis of empirical or 'positive' method in social science is usually associated with the name of Auguste Comte, though the approach can be traced back to the work of Bacon, Galileo and Descartes. In their particular realms of interest, they concentrated on observed facts rather than traditional outlooks. Comte, however, is usually regarded as the father of sociology, since he laid the foundations of empirical sociological method and stressed observation and classification of phenomena and the elimination of theological views and metaphysical premises.[1]

But metaphysical premises are inherent in Comte's sociological system, as has been noted. What Hobhouse did was to analyse some of the aspects of empiricism, and to show that a broad definition of 'experience' is required if sociology is to be a realistic description of human association. Although it certainly could not be claimed that Hobhouse was one of the first sociologists to espouse empirical method, yet he was one of the earliest to insist upon taking into account all the varied aspects of experience. He pointed out the dangers of limited views of the concept of experience, and insisted that it should not be restricted to the observable or the sensory. There are important implications for sociology here, and the first part of this chapter will try to set forth the significant aspects of this general approach.

Hobhouse favoured the empirical outlook, for despite the limitations of scientific method the principle of building from experience was for him sounder than metaphysical analysis and speculation. He maintained that experience and thought remained the sole basis of knowledge, and experience could be reconstructed by means of observation and experiment and could undergo a similar process of refinement by analytical and comparative methods. At the outset of his career he wrote that '. . . the basis of reasoning is always one or more observed particular facts'.[2] On this view, inference involved a process of generalizing from observed particular cases, and any law that claimed to be axiomatic and self-evident, but which could not be exhibited as such by reasoning, had no claim to validity.

As an example of the way in which first principles have been overthrown or revised with the growth of science, he cites the field of geometry in which consistent systems can be set up by denying certain axioms which from Euclid's time have been held to be necessary presuppositions of geometrical knowledge and to require no proof. Euclid was once regarded as the model of rigid reasoning and the pattern of precise thinking, but was later accused of redundant and defective proofs in some of the simplest of his propositions. His definitions are seen to presuppose the point at issue and his axioms are subject to question. It is shown to be possible, says Hobhouse, to build consistent geometries which negate his axioms and contradict the assumptions which were formerly regarded as primary principles based on the constitution of the human mind, revealed as self-evident to intuition.[3] Herein is seen a further instance of the way in which presuppositions and first principles are, in more ways than one, 'basic' to the development of science, and cannot be ignored by even the most empirical investigators, except at the risk of invalidating their conclusions.

Hobhouse gave attention to the ramifications of empiricism and pointed out that the majority of the results of science could be regarded as established by reasoning from experience, that is, established upon tested facts and careful inferences and hypotheses drawn from the facts. He maintained that the only valid principles were those that emerged out of human experience, and that thought which was not educed logically from experience was precarious.[4] And so because of the difficulty of finding any other method of detecting and establishing grounds that are not precarious, the scientist insists on empirical foundations.

A further point noted by Hobhouse, relevant to this topic, is that empirical method does not arise in history fully equipped at any particular date, as a casual glance at Comte's hierarchical system might erroneously suggest. On the contrary, Comte himself held that the empirical or 'positive' method has been in constant use from the days of primitive man until the present time. It is not a new invention, nor is it a complete and perfect instrumentality for the acquisition of knowledge. The test of experience is not recent, but has been variously applied from the days of the earliest thinkers. Intelligence has developed, and Hobhouse notes that Comte does not suggest the rise in human affairs of a new faculty to which improvement in method is due. The lowest known savages employed observation and made legitimate inferences from observation.[5]

It is in the modern period, though, that science has used empirical methods with such remarkably successful results, in terms of scientific purposes, as to have become associated with these methods. This began in the natural sciences and extended to the social sciences.

It may at this point be asked whether Hobhouse himself was empirical in his outlook and methods. He was both a sociologist and a philosopher, but he held that since the marks of science were detachment of attitude, tentative advance and systematic inquiry, there was no reason why philosophy and metaphysics should not become scientific in this sense, for 'it is at bottom a question of bringing to the study of fundamental questions the same qualities of detachment and intellectual self-restraint that are universally demanded in the historian or the laboratory worker'.[6]

He also pointed out that positivism, when applied to the foundations of science and the theory of knowledge, sought to remake on its own lines the categories which in the development of thought had half-unconsciously grown up, by investigating each and asking impartially what form of experience it expressed. In so far as metaphysicians follow this method, Hobhouse would maintain that they could be regarded as 'positive' thinkers.

It may be claimed that Hobhouse himself sought to do this in his analysis of the theory of knowledge and in his investigations of the categories of mechanism. The testimony of other writers can be appropriately quoted in this regard:

> The aversion for sustained thought manifest among many contemporary American sociologists has led them unduly to discount Hobhouse because of the marked philosophic cast of his researches; the emphasis upon 'work' as opposed to 'armchair speculation' has gone so far that it is considered quite proper to be wholly ignorant of the really great minds of the past if only one knows the number of fireplugs in Ashtabula on January 16, 1934. Let it be proclaimed from the housetops that for all the social philosophizing in which Hobhouse indulged, he never was guilty of mere speculation... Social philosopher he undoubtedly was . . . but the most rigidly scientific of social scientists can learn much from Hobhouse.[7]

The same writers cite Ernest B. Harper as follows: 'He fed on factual material which he digested with the aid of brilliant hypotheses.'[8] And J. A. Nicholson points out that Hobhouse insists on a reconstruction of method, favouring the one which is usually associated with British philosophy, namely, the method of science. He further notes, regarding Hobhouse's methodological approach:

> His whole treatment of this problem is strongly reminiscent of Bacon. He contrasts as did Bacon the two methods, the one tending to attain its generalizations with rather too much facility and then, regarding them as sacrosanct, proceeding deductively; the other placing all the stress upon the investigation of facts and insisting upon the tentative nature of the generalizations formed from these.[9]

Empirical method, applied to practical affairs, is implied in the following:

> We must start from the place in which we find ourselves. We must understand society, know how it works, before we

can improve it. Science must be added to philosophy before we can have a social art.[10]

And finally, '. . . the validity of abstract reasoning in social affairs is only to be tested by a close and yet comprehensive survey of the facts of social life'.[11] However, although Hobhouse was a devotee of empiricism and looked to the facts of experience for his generalizations and social policies, he nevertheless pointed out that it is a profound error to limit the concept of 'experience' at the outset. He maintained that to use arbitrary or *a priori* conceptions in deciding the range of experience is to limit the validity of inferences and experiments that follow therefrom. No data of experience must be ignored, and no inference or judgement that is founded upon experience can be rejected if rational procedures are to be adhered to. All experience of life and mind—the aesthetic, the moral and the religious—has its place and demands autonomy of investigation. An all-round treatment of experience is thus required. For example, he noted the frequent claim that science should be limited to the range of observation, and he maintained that it would destroy science.[12]

Hobhouse insisted that 'experience' should not be restricted to the observable. On the contrary, reasoning must be combined with the observation of empirical phenomena, as Comte himself stated, and it is necessary to recognize connections or general relations between the parts of experience, so that the observed can be used as the basis for dealing with what is not yet observed. For when Comte defined the object of positivism as 'co-ordination of observed facts', he was introducing into his method something beyond actual observation of data, whereby the co-ordination was to be carried on. A further consideration is that empiricism or positivism implies and assumes that knowledge is and should be limited to the factual, to 'phenomena' and its 'laws', so that the search for origins, causes and purposes may be disregarded. This, however, involves a theory of knowledge and reality. A scientific method has thus become a metaphysic, despite the efforts of its founder to differentiate and separate science from metaphysics. But the metaphysical assumption that only 'phenomena', the factual, can be known, is an unproved assumption without any basis in science. It is a philosophical position taken up at the start of investigations that disclaim any connection with philosophy.

Comte was not the first to assume this type of philosophical stand, for John Locke, usually viewed as one of the fathers of empiricism (if not *the* father), defined experience in terms of sense-experience. Hobhouse did not follow this limited view of 'experience', for he stressed the importance of intangible and imponderable factors in human association and the significance of non-sensory data. The following gives a good example of how the term 'experience' legitimately includes several varieties of data:

> 'Chair' or 'table' is as much a concept as constitutionalism or liberty; all four alike . . . are drawn ultimately from our experience, and, what is more important, have validity and meaning by reference to our experience . . . But, whereas a chair can be tested by sitting upon it, the meaning and value of such a concept as constitutionalism may require the histories of several nations for several generations to determine.
> In a sense then it will be seen that the 'higher' conceptions, to distinguish them provisionally by that convenient epithet, are relatively remote from direct, immediate and easy observation. They spring from experiences and relate to experiences, but the relation is so indirect as to be easily left out of sight.[13]

And thus it is that the non-sensory and imponderable factors in human experience are often 'left out of sight', in accordance with the notion that only the observable and the measurable have significance for science. Hobhouse showed that this is not a position that is warranted by scientific investigation *per se*, but is simply an assumption that grew up in the course of scientific development. He pointed out that it is purely arbitrary to believe, as do the mechanists and behaviourists, that if the existence of something cannot be demonstrated by the evidence of the physical sense organs, as they are involved for natural science data, it does not thereby exist.

It should be noted that not all scientists, whether in the realm of nature or human relations, make this false assumption. Nor do all of them hold to the view that science consists purely of factual phenomena and laws relating thereto. Like Hobhouse, Barnes and Becker differ from this viewpoint:

> The epistemology and methodology of sociology are not overwhelmingly popular subjects . . . The most common epistemological notion seems to be that there are 'lots of facts' lying about which when sorted into piles and counted will enable us to discover 'laws' that exist independently of the observer . . . Pure Induction is a god to whom the appropriate genuflections must always be made. Linked with this is the belief that sense-data—things that one can see, touch, taste, smell and hear—are and should be the sole object-matter of sociology—in our opinion it is sheer nonsense.[14]

From which several conclusions may be drawn. First, empirical method, especially in the social sciences, cannot legitimately restrict itself to sense-data, but has to include the adaptation of methods of gathering evidence to the subject-matter at hand. For it is an error to regard the materials of the senses as the whole of knowledge. The senses are one means of deriving knowledge, but not the sole means, and it is purely arbitrary to look upon them as the only key to knowledge. Nor is knowledge limited to factual phenomena and their laws. For there are no 'bare facts' standing independently on their own; on the contrary, since truth is a unity, every fact is related to every other fact.

A related conclusion is that more attention might profitably be paid to the theory of knowledge, and analysis made of the range and validity of sociological knowledge. Some of the basic issues in the social sciences would appear to be connected with this question, the answers to which are often uncritically assumed. The problem of ascertaining the range and meaning of valid knowledge, together with that of what constitutes appropriate tools for acquiring such knowledge in sociology, still remains, and to limit knowledge to sense-data is no solution. Here is another indication of the need for carefully examining the presuppositions lying behind method and knowledge processes. A final conclusion is that concepts must not be limited to the data of the senses, because certain concepts, such as 'liberty' and 'constitutionalism', to use Hobhouse's examples, transcend the immediately tangible and observable. The main points suggested by Hobhouse regarding concepts will be briefly reviewed, as a further contribution in the nature of a 'prolegomenon' to sociology.

Concepts

The importance of concepts in sociology is well-known, since some of the significant general advances in this science have directly accrued from the introduction and diffusion of new terms. Hobhouse was aware of the importance of concepts and the disadvantage of sociology in having to draw its conceptual tools from the vocabulary of everyday speech. He observed that social investigators should avoid introducing into the defining term the associations which appertain to it in another capacity. To keep this rule in mind would aid the development of sociology, since the terms used would be less confusing. The organic analogy furnishes a prime example of how confusion can be caused through vague terminology and unfortunate metaphor. The main point raised by Hobhouse in this connection was his suggesting three criteria for the clarity and comparison of concepts: (a) precision, (b) lack of ambiguity and (c) ease in identification.[15]

A further consideration is that concepts should be related to human experience rather than being derived from the mere analysis of conceptions, since concepts can become highly abstract and fail to express the essence of the data with which they are concerned. The dangers of speculation must be guarded against, and some connection with the objective order of things maintained. Concepts, according to Hobhouse, tend to form a world of their own, and instead of being based on the empirical order which they are supposed to reflect, this empirical order is made to conform to a conceptual system. This was a characteristic of the 'metaphysical stage' that Comte described. It set up its own system of conceptions and regarded the world of experience as data that had to conform to the conceptual order. If it did not so conform, it was considered unreal.[16] The 'metaphysical stage' involves the application of a recognized concept to an experience in an attempt to explain the latter. But, says Hobhouse, 'the concept may contain nothing to show what are the observable conditions under which the given experience is found'.[17] To the extent that concepts are not derived from experience, but derived by deductive reasoning from other concepts, the metaphysical or dialectical stage still obtains.

A further point regarding concepts is that they can give rise to many difficulties if the categories of thought that they involve are seen as the vehicles of ultimate truth, absolute and unchangeable.

Hobhouse points out that there is a profound contrast between the fixity and narrowness of abstract concepts and the plasticity, boundlessness and variability of experience. Conceptual thought is apt to draw lines of distinction and definition which become stumbling-blocks when gradations of meaning and the continuity of nature are to be dealt with. He notes that there have been epochs in the history of ideas when categories of thought solidified into hard moulds into which all experience had to fit.[18] For this reason, no set of concepts can exhaust the individuality of a single thing. The concrete, the individual, the changing and the variable are elusive and indefinable.[19]

Finally, Hobhouse pointed out that concepts must undergo change and revision. It is unscientific, he said, to look upon concepts as fixed and rigid. When concepts become set into hard inflexible moulds, the advance of thought is hindered. The growth of science and knowledge consists, at least in part, in revising both conceptions and the thought-systems out of which they emerge. It is true that conceptual fashions are apt to persist after the needs for which they arose no longer exist. But this is simply an example of cultural lag, as is the continued use of concepts in one field after they have been rendered obsolete by the progress made in another. The building up of concepts, as an aspect of mental culture, has taken a long time and represents a gradual process of co-operative mental interaction. Hobhouse claimed that conceptions were not made of cast iron, but had to grow with a developing human experience and be adaptable to wider knowledge. Comte had recognized this, for the revision of concepts and categories was an inherent part of his positivism. In this connection, Hobhouse said:

> . . . it is readily intelligible that what has appeared first as a
> myth and afterwards as a metaphysical theory should yet
> later be expressible as a positive truth. What is at one time
> a command of God may at another be recognized as a
> condition of a healthy and happy life.[20]

According to Hobhouse, positivism sought to reconstruct the familiar categories that had grown up almost unconsciously in the development of thought, and relate them to the form of experience they allegedly expressed. Thus, myth developed into metaphysical theory which later could be expressed in a more empirical way.

But to constrict a concept to myth, or, indeed, to constrict and 'mould' it at all, is fatal to intellectual development. As long as the conceptions formed at a certain level of experience were regarded as the ultimate measure of all things, the attempt to interpret experience systematically was doomed to failure. The limited value of conceptions must be recognized.

In conclusion, concepts have prime importance for science and sociology, but they must be precise, unambiguous, easily identifiable and connected with rather than abstracted from the facts of experience. The need for analysing the elements that go to make up a concept has to be seen, for a concept may refer to a class of objects containing individual differences, but concentrate on one or two qualities or characteristics shared in common, ignoring the differences. The concept does not give an exhaustive description of its content, but rather a distinguishing outline. It is a framework of definition, not a comprehensive and all-inclusive analysis. In the development of thought, concepts have tended to become fixed in hard moulds which have retarded the growth of knowledge. But as they have nevertheless developed in the past, they may be expected to grow in the future, since knowledge is a process that is dynamic and should not be regarded merely as a fund of information. The dynamic nature of knowledge, with the implications for sociological method that flow from it, will form the topic of the next section, as another theme of Hobhouse in a 'prolegomena to sociology'.

The experimental attitude

It was the contention of Hobhouse, expressed in nearly all his writings, that knowledge at any stage is incomplete and partial, that no finality is to be found, that fresh experience might lead to new data and new conclusions, and that therefore a tentative, experimental attitude should be taken with respect to contemporary knowledge, methods and perspectives. With the growth of knowledge, there is a modifying of old views, and few indeed are the truths of which it can be said that they are unmodifiable. Indeed, 'the advance of knowledge is a process of modifying conceptions'.[21] The implication is that there is no finality in knowledge and truth, and it is an error to suppose that complete and final truth has been obtained in any field. Similarly, human thought at any particular stage only represents a stage, not the termination of the journey. At every point, new facts gained are mere elements in a wider whole. Nor is knowledge to be limited to the extension of factual material. Hobhouse claimed that growth in understanding of the facts was as equally important as their continued acquisition.

The system of knowledge that has been established is not, on this view, to be looked upon as a closed and final system, since further truth may always bring the need for amending past findings. Reason is therefore to be seen as 'the method of growth in understanding'. Herein lies its strength, rather than that it has achieved finality in truth. New data have to be related to the old content, and the latter modified, with an attendant change in the meaning and value of long-held conceptions.[22]

No interpretations, then, in sociology or elsewhere, may be regarded as final; on the contrary, the value of the latest conclusions and theories must be regarded as tentative and subject to constant revision. For since thought has been a growing phenomenon, Hobhouse would insist that the present stage has no more right to be seen as ultimate than had those previous stages which were regarded as equally sacrosanct by their exponents. This emphasis is well expressed in the following passage:

> . . . the conception of development must affect the content of all our thought, scientific or other. Truth as such is not relative in the sense that it only professes to hold good for the thinker, but the truth that is accessible to us at a given stage is as much and no more than our mental structure can compass, conditioned as it is by our psycho-physical limitations, the conceptual methods which we absorb from our predecessors and contemporaries, and the little strength of our own efforts to adapt and improve them. Thus our most fundamental conceptions become ways of apprehending reality or of co-ordinating experiences that have lost all sacrosanct immutability and may require revision and supplementation like everything else that belongs to growth. The structural principles of thought are conceived not as rigid moulds into which all truth must fit, but rather as plastic elements of a growing structure which may be modified without loss of identity to take a wider and fuller experience within their grasp.[23]

In this viewpoint of Hobhouse, methods inherited from the past and absorbed from the contemporary mental climate should be seen with some perspective. In this light, the categories of science and sociology can be viewed not as unchangeable frames into which new data and fresh insights must fit, but rather as 'plastic elements of a growing structure'. What are now regarded as first principles should be seen as subject to revision, with a developing knowledge. In this process, error can be eliminated, understanding deepened, and the area of knowledge expanded.

There is here an implied need for objectivity in looking at the contemporary thought-system and its ethos, rather than the uncritical acceptance of all its premises and implications. Just as Comte made a contribution by pointing out how thought runs through stages, so Hobhouse notes that Comte's conceptions need revising. He claimed that it would be hardly reasonable to suppose that a hypothesis advanced in the infancy of anthropology, and prior to the modern development of science, should warrant the same respect that was accorded to it a century ago. Such a phenomenon would be more characteristic of the theological than the positive stage.[24]

Hobhouse called attention to one aspect of the scientific attitude that is often overlooked, by stressing the need for an experimental and tentative approach to methods used and results hitherto gained in science. There is need, not merely to extend the territory of science, but to modify those results which have been regarded as best established. The truly scientific attitude involves the willingness to change, or at least to question, basic concepts and assumptions.

An implication that has reference for sociological research relates to the holding of an experimental attitude towards the methods employed. Since knowledge is in process of growth, the methods of social science might profitably be held liable to criticism and revision, with the understanding that they do not represent the ultimate techniques for acquiring relevant data. Constant correction of methods and principles might lead to significant advances, as might adaptation of research techniques to the subject-matter in hand.

The scientific attitude, according to Hobhouse, will not claim to have attained complete knowledge; on the contrary, it will constantly correct its premises, principles and conclusions. Its certainty is that of being on the right road, rather than having arrived at the end of the journey. The scientific attitude involves the awareness that there is always an undiscovered area of knowledge, and that knowledge should not be looked upon as departmentalized into tight segments in which the whole of one section can be known independently of the others. No area of knowledge, scientific or other, can be taken in complete isolation from the remainder, and no partial view should be regarded as final without any consideration of the bearings of other viewpoints and investigations from other sources. This last-mentioned point regarding the experimental approach leads to another contribution made by Hobhouse: the early warnings he expressed concerning the tendency towards overspecialization in sociology and social science.

The dangers of overspecialization

At the outset of his career as a teacher of sociology, Hobhouse declared that sociology was 'a science which has the whole social life of man as its sphere'.[25] The task of sociology was to regard social life as a unity, and to interpret it as such. It would in this way serve as a synthesis of the more specialized social sciences, though this was not its only function. Hobhouse is also said to have used the term, 'General Sociology', to denote 'the synthesis of the various social sciences: . . . the general study of the origin, development, structure and function of human society in all its various forms'.[26]

The unity of social life cannot be broken up into departmentalized divisions without the dangers of abstraction and specialization entering into the investigation. Indeed, the problem before sociologists, he thought, was to bring together in vital connection the inquiries which had hitherto been made separately. Such a synthesis was demanded by the nature of the subject itself, and it was futile to take any part of the life of society and think of it as being entirely separated from other parts; no one set of conditions could be isolated with complete disregard for the rest of the life-history of society.

Sociology was for Hobhouse a synthesis of the special social sciences that had arisen from the various forms of interaction. Sociology was concerned with the relation of parts in a whole, based upon accurate description. As an example, economics dealt with the conditions of production and distribution of wealth, but sociology was more directly concerned with the life that people led under those conditions; it attempted to analyse the effects of economic forces on social interaction, together with the effects of political institutions, religious and moral ideals, and literary forces. Its task was to interpret societal life as a unity, in its entirety. A complete account of a society, on this view, would include its religion, ethics, laws, industrial organization, the characteristics of the people (racial and acquired), class structure, geography and physical surroundings.[27]

The specializations that had arisen in an effort to understand better these various aspects of the socio-cultural reality were for Hobhouse a necessary evil, and he insisted that an attempt must be made to relate the particular aspect singled out for study to the larger whole that constituted society. A significant expression of this point of view is seen in the following passage:

> . . . if we are to achieve permanent and assured good we must as far as possible keep in view the life of society as a whole and seek not jealously to magnify our own little sectional interest at the expense of the others, but rather to correlate it with the work that others are doing and endeavour to induce in them the same spirit. In sociology as in all sciences specialism is a necessity and it is also a danger. It is a necessity for the simple reason that human capacity is limited and it is not given to man to acquire sound knowledge and adequate skill in many departments at once. It is a danger because social life is no more divisible into independent sections than the human body is divisible into independent organisms.[28]

Hobhouse claimed that specialities were a danger, partly because they did not yield a sociology; they gave no theory of the nature and development of society, nor did they give any account of the general trend of culture. And they answered no questions regarding progress and retrogression, questions which for Hobhouse were basic to sociology. He therefore made a plea for co-operation between the specialists, and for the larger view that could see beyond its own particular area and relate it to other fields of knowledge and research. No particularistic view of society could be regarded as the whole of sociology; some forces in human society transcend the divisions made for academic and research purposes.

In 1908, Hobhouse observed that the advance of social study in the years previous to that date had consisted more in the growth of special sciences than in the development of basic ideas. The division of sociology into special branches was in accordance with the usual conditions of the growth of science; it was only natural that divisions should be made, but this nevertheless constituted a danger to the future development of the science, especially if there were no cohesive bonds between these separate specialities.

The function of *general sociology* assumed importance in this respect, for it was not merely a synthesis of the other special sciences, but a vitalizing principle running through all social inquiry, acting as a stimulus to research, correlating results, setting forth the life of the whole in the parts and bringing from the study of the parts a deeper comprehension of the whole. In making specific investigations in the social science field, the possibilities for specialization were unbounded in their variety, but the investigator could not help being aware of the forces that transcended all his boundaries. For example, what could be known of the family and its history without some study of ethics, religion, law and even governmental organization? Again, asked Hobhouse, how far could a study of law or government be carried without any account of religion and ethics? Errors were bound to be made when one side of societal interaction were treated as though it stood alone.[29]

Hobhouse recognized that it would be necessary to point out these facts, were it not for the pride of specialization that sometimes renders investigators unmindful of the work being done in other fields and apt to regard their own specialties as all-important. His warnings would appear to have been vindicated, in view of the subsequent trend towards specialization that has taken place since he wrote. It should be noted, though, that Hobhouse was more concerned with the rise of special social sciences, and in America it is also sociology itself that shows the trend towards departmentalization. Specialized interpretations have naturally arisen and been looked upon as the latest 'scientific' approach to human relations. The view of sociology as a synthesis of the various social sciences is not widely held. The view is more prevalent that sociology has its own subject-matter, centring around social interaction and human culture. But the criticism made by Hobhouse against excessive specialization would still appear to be valid and relevant, in view of the conflict of 'schools of thought' that is currently in evidence. Hobhouse's pupil, Charles A. Ellwood, has said that 'as to the sociologists of the present, it is notorious that they are not agreed as to social philosophy or even as to concrete methods of studying social problems'.[30] In this situation, the plea made by Hobhouse in 1908 possesses relevance; in a conflict of sociological and methodological viewpoints, a synthesis of the best elements of all schools of thought would have value, as would any 'general sociology' that finds the links joining more specialized branches. And since 1940 a rapprochement and synthesis of different methods and approaches has taken place.

This section will conclude with a review of the analysis made by Hobhouse of the functions of a sociological journal, written when he became editor of the newly-founded (1908) *Sociological Review*. In its first editorial, he pointed out that its function is not to produce a ready-made scheme of sociology but rather to assist in the work of 'General Sociology', bringing specialized work together and affording a common ground for the discussion of such investigations. It should, for example, help the economist to become more familiar with work being carried on in the comparative study of law, or social philosophy, and give the student of the history of ideas some acquaintance with political and industrial development. In fact, it should put all students of society in touch with the best knowledge and thought regarding the implications of biology and psychology for their own specialities, and give them all the chance to protect the study of society from being lost in one of its subdivisions. It should serve as a counteracting force against any attempt by a few specialists to usurp the whole field of sociology for their own purposes. Finally, it should maintain a balance between research and applied sociology, approaching all questions of contemporary interest without bias, except that of showing that issues of the present time, like those of history, can be viewed in the spirit of science with a detachment of outlook that springs from desire to find the truth.[31] The foregoing still constitutes an illuminating set of criteria by which contemporary sociology journals might be studied and evaluated.

The next section of this chapter will give Hobhouse's analysis of one specialized methodological approach that enjoys popularity in current American sociology.

Measurement

It is sometimes claimed that society cannot be an object of scientific treatment comparable to physical or biological phenomena, and that the term 'social philosophy' would be more appropriate for the study of social life. Hobhouse regarded this view as unfounded, since it rested on a narrow and restricted use of the term 'science'. He maintained that sociology should be broadly scientific, prompted by the dispassionate desire for truth, rendered in accurate statement, and setting forth systematically the relations between facts. It is worth noting that, on this view of the term 'scientific', philosophy itself aims at being so characterized.

With regard to scientific methods in sociology, Hobhouse pointed out that the sociologist had to resist the tyranny of intellectual fashions in method and approach. It was necessary to guard against the too easy acceptance of one dominant factor in social life, whether it be racial, environmental, economic or any other. Similarly, the sociologist should realize that there was a tendency for an idea or a method to be popularized and extended to all areas of thought.[32] A prestige-making discovery in one field tends to such an extension of method into areas where it may be unsuitable. The mere fact that a method or technique has led to good results in one field of research is no guarantee that it will do so in all fields of endeavour. For example, culture may be studied in many ways and from many angles, but it will require methods of analysis that are different from the study of animals in a laboratory.

During the period (1907–29) that Hobhouse held the Martin White Chair of Sociology at the University of London, much emphasis was placed upon techniques of measurement in sociology, and this trend has continued since 1929, particularly in the United States. Hobhouse maintained that there was a place in social science for measurement, but that there was nothing to warrant the identification of science with mathematical measurement. It is this mistaken presupposition that leads the mechanist to demand that all data be made to lend themselves to mathematical treatment. For Hobhouse, the equating of science with measurement was a very one-sided view, notwithstanding the fact that in science, as opposed to ordinary common-sense thinking, both terms and relationships had to be accurately defined.

A similar error that Hobhouse noted is that of regarding analysis as a function destined to resolve everything into mathematical terms. The function of analysis is, on the contrary, that of clearing up what is obscure and confused. The operation of clarifying conceptions is one that involves analysis, as does any reasoned discipline, but this operation is by no means to be restricted to mathematical analysis.

The type of thinking that would so limit analysis involves the fallacy of regarding the precisely identifiable and measurable as the whole of phenomena, a viewpoint that arose from the influence of Newton's mathematical-physics. The correlation of experience by mathematical formulas required that data should be exhibited in a form in which measurement would be common to all. Any changes had to be analysed into their component factors and each of these had to be measured, the unit of measurement being adhered to consistently. The scope of science, conceived in this way, depended on the concepts through which data became measurable. Thus, says Hobhouse, Newton required the conception of 'space' in three dimensions, 'time' in one dimension, 'mass', and 'force'. Such were the foundations of Newtonian physics. But, asks Hobhouse, how far could this interpretation of experience, which was essentially mathematical, be carried? Could it cope with all the data of sense, with the secondary qualities of sound, colour, temperature, taste and smell? Could it deal with social relations, with mental phenomena? How could it be made to cover ethical relations, or solve the problems of religion and belief? Could it give an account of reality in the philosophical sense? How could the intangible and imponderable factors of human association be expected to yield to such mathematical treatment?

As a student of ethics, Hobhouse further pointed out that the English Utilitarians had tried to base an ethic upon this mathematical basis, regarding happiness as the sum of pleasures minus pains. But they forgot the important fact that happiness lies in qualitative, rather than quantitative, conditions of personal and social life, and that these qualitative conditions can be only very imperfectly rendered in any mathematical terms. Even the practical difficulties in a working democracy are related to the inadequacy of numerical majorities to measure the effective will in a community.[33]

Hobhouse's criticism of this mathematical viewpoint, and his revelation of its limitations in the social science field, would appear to be relevant to the contemporary situation in American sociology.[34] In the attempt to make psychology and sociology 'scientific', there has been much concentration upon quantitative measurement, with little concern for the qualities of what is measured and even less concern for those aspects of human experience that are not measurable with the tools at hand.

Hobhouse recognized that there is an important place for measurement in the social sciences, since it is partly through instruments and tools of calculation that experience can be interpreted and enlarged, and general laws deduced from data. By means of statistical description, exactitude and clear classification may be obtained. He pointed out, though, that it is a requirement of statistical treatment that the data under review be capable of being stated in terms of some unit that is constant.[35] Do the phenomena of social life always meet this condition? It would be difficult to give an affirmative answer, apart from the possibility or the desirability of reducing all data to statistical terms. Hobhouse gives an example from the realm of law:

> There is no social measuring rod by which we could compare degrees of obedience to law. Civilized societies, with their records of criminal statistics, might, indeed, repay investigation from this point of view, though there is no department in which statistics are more apt to mislead, and that is saying a good deal.[36]

And again:

> . . . in dealing with nationality we are confronted with one of those political forces which may be very real and very stubborn, but which yet are neither measurable in statistics nor easily compressed into the four corners of a rigid definition.[37]

It is very difficult to reduce the intangible and immeasurable factors in society to mathematical terms without encountering the dangers of artificiality and abstraction. Nor can mathematics be used to 'prove' anything of importance outside of the realm of mathematics. Hobhouse indicates the fatuity of attempting such 'proof' when he says that if the Western nations had exemplified the highest ideals of world peace in the days prior to 1914, 'they would certainly have convinced some German professor, who would have returned home and proved to his countrymen by statistics that their gods were false'.[38]

If human experience is to be interpreted with realism and validity, logic and sympathetic imagination will have to be combined with statistical analysis and instruments of measurement. In the illumination of social and psychological processes, relatively little aid is to be offered by statistics. It is not against statistical methods in themselves that Hobhouse's criticism is directed, but against the misuse of this research tool. He recognized that there is a role for statistics to play in sociology, as there is for experimentation that may help to verify hypotheses. He believed that this experimental research would become more pronounced in sociology,[39] and this has certainly happened since his writing in 1908. Yet it is a profound fallacy, as he noted, to regard one research tool as all-sufficient for the description, interpretation and explanation of the rich and many-faceted subject-matter of the social sciences.

The criticism made by Hobhouse of narrow and one-sided methods of social study developed out of his recognition that the roots of sociology were much broader, historically and philosophically, than the contemporary specialized viewpoints would lead one to suppose. This suggests a further contribution that he made to sociology.

The roots of sociology

Many present-day social scientists would claim that sociology has no connection with philosophy, but this overlooks the fact that, historically, they are related to each other. Hobhouse portrayed the historical and philosophical heritage of modern sociology. He made an attempt to distinguish the principal roots of sociology in their growth and interactions, as one means of achieving a clear conception of what the subject covered. The essential points of this contribution will be briefly surveyed.

Of four main roots that Hobhouse distinguished, the first is political philosophy. For a long time the fundamental questions of social life were dealt with chiefly under the aegis of political thought. Hobhouse noted that systematic political thought began in close relationship to the general trend of metaphysics and ethics, for two reasons. First, political philosophy, whether that of Hobbes, Locke, Rousseau, Bentham or Mill, bears a strong resemblance to general philosophy in its methods. It begins with common conceptions of law and government, liberty and obligation, individual and society, and examines these principles of human association which are usually taken for granted by the average man. It deals with the most general conditions of life in society and the social bond, and thus parallels contemporary investigations into broad sociological principles.

Secondly, political philosophy has been intimately associated with moral philosophy. Political thinkers have concerned themselves with the question of what society ought to be and not just what it actually is. Social problems are, for them at least, partly ethical problems.[40] This tradition goes back to the Greeks, though in its modern form it took shape in the seventeenth century, being related to the political and religious conflicts of that age. In fact, Hobhouse made the generalization that systems of political philosophy have always been formulated in connection with some historical situation. As an example, the younger Mill reconsidered the Utilitarianism of Jeremy Bentham in the light of the political needs of a generation which recognized that problems of government were not as simple as the Benthamist formula would imply.[41]

Historically, then, it was as a branch of general philosophy that systematic investigation of social affairs began. Plato's *Republic* dealt with metaphysics, ethics, aesthetics, psychology, education and political theory, while, for Aristotle, ethics and politics are parts of a wider political inquiry which is subordinate to his conception of man's place in nature. And the concern of the Utilitarians with the ultimate *ends* of human action has been noted. The relations of man in society, the question of the ideal for society, and the function of institutions in enhancing or detracting from that ideal, were the topics under philosophical review. This embraced three inquiries, the first dealing with facts, the second with values, and the third with the application of ideals and values.[42]

The second root of modern sociology is related to the first, namely, the philosophy of history. Hobbes, Locke and Rousseau represent thinkers who regarded history in a broader and deeper sense than the record of thrones and battles. They did not seek to interpret the past, or to find a key to the future, in terms of progress. Their concern was not so much with actual history as with conceptions that were independent of history, the conceptions that generally underlay the social bond. No history was actually necessary to them. They simply analysed conceptions, with little or no regard for the facts of experience. It was here that Comte represented a well-known advance. 'Sociology' was his term. Beginning in Latin and ending in Greek, it indicates the hybrid character of the discipline. Comte justified this, says Hobhouse, by the remark that the science itself is of hybrid origin, namely, as involving both the analysis of conceptions, and the recorded facts in which human history was to be read; the Comtean method was a union of a careful analysis of conceptions with a wide and comprehensive grasp of historical facts. Hobhouse also notes that it was inherent in Comte's personality to stamp his system with the rigidity of a dogma and give the young science a premature fixity of form.[43]

The third root of sociology is to be found in physical and biological science. The influence of physical science upon thought-patterns and intellectual traditions was mentioned in the previous chapter. It is only necessary to note at this point that philosophy and reflection on social matters have always been profoundly influenced by the status and achievements of the contemporary science. In the seventeenth century the great mathematical and physical discoveries affected not only philosophy but biology and medicine. Similarly, the eighteenth century was a period when the mathematical method ruled sociology. It appeared to be the fact, said Hobhouse, that whatever science was most flourishing and progressive acquired a dominant influence over the general trend of thought at the time.[44]

Science, and more especially biological science, has left its mark upon social investigation and theory. The influence of Darwin in bringing about a dominance of biological concepts in sociology is well-known. In popularizing sociological concepts in England,

Herbert Spencer also accelerated the tendency to superimpose biological principles upon sociological data. The prestige of this biological science, due to its success in its own realm, was brought to bear upon social questions. The latter were referred to biological principles for their interpretation and decision.

The effect of the prepondering influence of biological conceptions will be considered in a later chapter. As far as sociology is concerned, it may be stated that Hobhouse regarded this biological influence as reactionary, since attention came to be turned away from historical facts, from psychology, and from comparative studies. To understand the life of society, its past growth and possible future, Hobhouse would maintain that it is necessary to take into account all that the biologist had to say regarding the physical conditions of life, heredity and natural selection. But to learn the nature of social institutions, the sociologist must study *them*, rather than attempting to deduce their nature from conditions that apply to tigers and snakes as much as to human beings. The last word of biology is thus the first of sociology.[45]

The fourth root of sociology is the most recent, namely, the modern tendency towards specialization.[46] The half-century that preceded Hobhouse's appointment to the University of London in 1907 had witnessed the development of several subdivisions of social study—economics, anthropology, comparative ethics and religion, comparative jurisprudence, and psychology, to mention only a few. As a process, specialization is still in operation and specialization within the field of sociology itself has taken place rapidly.

The foregoing influences constitute for Hobhouse the main roots of sociology in history—political philosophy, philosophy of history, modern science and specialization. It may be added that, by calling attention to the historical background of this science, Hobhouse has suggested the possibility of looking with greater objectivity and perspective at its present condition, problems and methods. The final section of this chapter will relate to a question that arises from the first of these four roots: the place of values and value-judgements in a scientific approach to social phenomena.

The separation of facts and values

The place of values in sociological analysis is a topic of long-standing debate. On the one side are those who are concerned with ends, norms, meanings, values, purposes and questions of social philosophy. On the other are those who claim for sociology the rank of a science, thereby insisting that value-questions be excluded. The facts of social life, the objective and statistical description of social phenomena, and the attempt to delineate variables and causality in social interaction are, for this school, the marks of scientific sociology.

Hobhouse averred that both approaches, the scientific and the philosophical, had their value in sociology. He insisted that the two approaches should not be confused but should be kept separate and distinct. He held that in whatever way the actual and the real were related, they were also distinct, and in respect to any particular investigation there should be no doubt as to which of the two was being considered.

On this view, a complete sociology would include a social philosophy and a social science. It would not be a fusion but a synthesis of the two inquiries. Hobhouse made this distinction because it had too frequently been ignored. The metaphysical treatment of society had had the prime defect of not distinguishing between questions of fact and questions of value. In analysing the actual constitution of society, it had appeared to be simultaneously determining what that society ought to be. When issues of fact are coloured by judgements of value, they should not be fused but kept separate. To confuse the two, and to seek the facts of social life, at the same time colouring them with 'ethical varnish', represents a fruitless investigation. Only when science and philosophy have both completed their tasks, when the facts are known and the values fixed, is it legitimate to compare the two results, and to ask how far, if at all, the facts conform to the standard that has been established. Since the two methods converge upon this question, Hobhouse contended that they are both legitimate and necessary for a complete sociology.[47] And yet they represent two very distinct methods of approach. Many persons confuse them, or pass from one to the other without realizing the step they are taking, mixing the 'is' and the 'ought', mingling the facts of social life with some ideal to which society should conform.

To repeat, Hobhouse maintained that the distinction between the desirable and the actual, between facts and values, should be adhered to strictly. He regarded the distinction as 'the foundation of true social method'.[48]

Although Hobhouse insisted on the distinction between the factual and the normative, the scientific and the philosophical approaches, he pointed out that values and human purposes are integral aspects of social experience. He looked upon the interplay of human purposes as fundamental for sociology as mass and motion for physics or the metabolism of cellular tissues for biology. While he recognized that all types of conditions—physical, biological, enivronmental—interacted upon purpose, he maintained that the feature which made sociology a unique discipline is the web of human purpose in which individuals interact on one another and on their surrounding conditions.

Again, purpose and its relations to ends form the subject of moral judgement, and thus ethics and sociology tend to have the same subject-matter, though they regard it from different viewpoints. This topic will be concluded with the observation that Hobhouse was one of the few sociologists to stress the importance of human purpose as a social force. A typical expression of his emphasis on this element is seen in the statement that 'the heart of social life is human purpose'.[49] Similarly, Hobhouse made it clear that values are inextricably interwoven into the subject-matter of sociology, since human values and ideals are social facts.[50] Any topic of sociological investigation is charged with the ideals, emotions, interests and values of men and women. Ideals and the values they represent are among the social forces that the sociologist studies, though, until fairly recently, there was a tendency to overlook the valuative aspects of human association.

With this mention of values, the 'prolegomena' to sociology are brought to an end. The following chapter will be concerned with a related contribution of Hobhouse, that of his study of man's evolving awareness of values, as shown in socio-cultural development throughout the centuries.

Notes and References

1. Emory S. Bogardus, *The Development of Social Thought* (New York: Longmans, Green, 1940), p. 232.

2. 'Induction and Deduction', *Mind*, XVI: 519, October 1891. See also

Development and Purpose (1927), pp. xix, xx, 117, 118. It is interesting to note that according to the approach to knowledge outlined above, there is no purely *a priori* knowledge, though mental functions may be described as *a priori* in that they are independent of the objective order. Thus, a person does not remember because he experiences memory, nor does he infer because he hears and sees inferences at work. The functions of memory and inference, to take these two examples, are *a priori* activities which the mind does not learn from experience, but possesses independently of experience. But while function is thus *a priori*, formed knowledge is not. For it cannot be made to depend on certain universal first principles that are self-evident. See *The Theory of Knowledge*, p. 591, and *The Rational Good*, p. 72.

3. *The World in Conflict*, pp. 42, 43. See also *Development and Purpose*, pp. 353, 354.

4. *The Elements of Social Justice*, 1922, Preface, p. iii; and *Social Development, Its Nature and Conditions*, p. 239.

5. 'The Law of the Three Stages', loc. cit., pp. 277, 278, July 1908. In view of his criticism of Comte's assumptions, it is worth noting that Hobhouse nevertheless praised Comte as a sociologist who, despite the uncritical use he sometimes made of his data, did at least have the merit of looking for his sociological explanations in society itself. The same could be said for Buckle; similarly, Darwin was a prime example of another scientist who based his theories on the facts already at hand. See *Social Evolution and Political Theory*, pp. 17, 18.

6. 'The Law of the Three Stages', loc. cit., p. 274.

7. *Social Thought from Lore to Science*, Vol. II, p. 809. Similarly, a leading British sociologist makes the pertinent observation that Hobhouse's entire system was grounded on and substantiated by empirical and even experimental knowledge. See Ronald Fletcher, *The Making of Sociology, A Study of Sociological Theory* (New York: Charles Scribner's Sons, 1971), Vol. II, p. 123.

8. Ernest B. Harper, 'Sociology in England', *Social Forces*, xi: 337, March 1933, quoted in Barnes and Becker, *Social Thought from Lore to Science*, p. 809.

9. J. A. Nicholson, *Some Aspects of the Philosophy of L. T. Hobhouse: Logic and Social Theory*, p. 73.

10. *The Metaphysical Theory of the State*, 1921, pp. 87, 88. An interesting comparison suggests itself regarding this statement and Charles Horton Cooley's 'we hear it questioned whether sociology is a science or a philosophy. It is both, and an art also.' See Charles Horton Cooley, *Life and the Student, Roadside Notes on Human Nature, Society, and Letters* (New York: Alfred A. Knopf, 1927), p. 160.

11. L. T. Hobhouse, 'The Roots of Modern Sociology', in *Inauguration of the Martin White Professorships of Sociology*, 17 December 1907 (London: John Murray, 1908), p. 19. This article consists of an address delivered by Hobhouse on the above-mentioned occasion at the University of London. Other addresses included in the volume were given by the Vice-Chancellor and by E. A. Westermarck, this one dealing with 'Sociology as a University Study'.

12. 'The Law of the Three Stages', loc. cit., p. 267.

13. ibid., p. 270.

14. *Social Thought from Lore to Science*, Vol II, p. 997.

15. *Development and Purpose*. p. 264.

16. This is the case with the investigators who start out with restricted concepts of 'experience' that confine it to the data of the senses, the material phenomena that are readily observable and tangible. In this sense, the scientists who set out with a preconceived conceptual system, as do the mechanists, behaviourists and devotees of sensory data, and then try to compress the whole of the social reality into the moulds of this system, are 'metaphysical' rather than 'positive'; for they are not following the method of going to the data of experience first and constructing their concepts therefrom. Instead, they approach the world of experience—social, moral, aesthetic and religious—with a ready-made set of concepts that, for them, constitute the whole of empirical phenomena, and anything that does not fall within those prescribed limits is declared unimportant if not non-existent. Similarly, the data that do conform to the methods of investigation prescribed are regarded as the whole of experience. Hobhouse says (*Development and Purpose*, p. 265) that this is a crude fallacy that consists of taking the 'precisely identifiable and measurable' elements for the whole, discarding the residue as metaphysics or mysticism or sentimentality. One reason for this view probably lies in the difficulty of summarizing and expressing the intangible and the imponderable. It is a natural tendency, in reacting from conceptual vagueness, to find validity only in those concepts which are most easily verifiable in experience. (See 'The Law of the Three Stages', p. 275.) Scientists and philosophers of this type start their investigations with a strictly limited concept of 'experience', in terms of which they judge experience. The 'logical positivists' come to mind in this connection. However, despite the limited conception of experience to which empirical method gives rise, it still retains great value, in that concepts must be based upon empirical data rather than being made the thought-moulds into which the data must fit.

17. 'The Law of the Three Stages', p. 271.

18. See *Morals in Evolution*, 1925 edition, p. 620, note; and *Development and Purpose*, p. 260.

19. This danger in the rigidity of concepts is suggestive of the difficulty of making social surveys which transcend the limitations of 'snapshots of a community', i.e. glimpses of a community taken at one particular point in time, as contrasted with 'moving pictures of a region', portraying social change and processes.

20. 'The Law of the Three Stages', loc. cit., p. 276. See also *The Theory of Knowledge*, p. 606.

21. *Development and Purpose*, p. 427.

22. 'The Philosophy of Development', loc. cit., p. 156.

23. ibid., pp. 139, 140.

24. 'The Law of the Three Stages', loc. cit., p. 262.

25. 'The Roots of Modern Sociology', loc. cit., p. 7.

26. See Ernest Barker, 'Leonard Trelawney Hobhouse, 1864–1929', loc. cit., p. 18.

27. ibid., pp. 21, 22.

28. *Social Evolution and Political Theory*, p. 6. See also F. Muller-Lyer, *The History of Social Development* (London: G. Allen & Unwin, 1920), translated by E. C. Lake and H. A. Lake, Introductory Note by Hobhouse, p. 5.

29. L. T. Hobhouse, 'Editorial', *Sociological Review*, 1: 7–9, January 1908.

30. Charles A. Ellwood, *A History of Social Philosophy* (New York: Prentice-Hall, 1939), p. 555.

31. op. cit., pp. 9, 10.

32. *Social Development, Its Nature and Conditions*, pp. 11, 12.

33. L. T. Hobhouse, 'Comparative Ethics', *Encyclopaedia Britannica*, 6: 163, 14th edition, 1937. See also *Development and Purpose*, pp. 136, 137.

34. It is illuminating to note the large amount of space currently devoted to statistical research in American sociology journals.

35. L. T. Hobhouse, Morris Ginsberg and G. C. Wheeler, 'The Material Culture and Social Institutions of the Simpler Peoples, an Essay in Correlation', *Sociological Review*, VII: 210, July 1914.

36. *Morals in Evolution*, p. 23.

37. L. T. Hobhouse, 'Irish Nationalism and Liberal Principle', in *The New Irish Constitution, an Exposition and Some Arguments*, edited by J. H. Morgan (London: Hodder & Stoughton, 1912), p. 363.

38. L. T. Hobhouse, 'The Soul of Civilization, a Dialogue', *Contemporary Review*, 108: 164, August 1915.

39. 'Editorial', loc. cit., p. 7.

40. ibid., p. 4.

41. 'The Roots of Modern Sociology', loc. cit., pp. 8–11.

42. 'Sociology', *Hasting's Encyclopaedia of Religion and Ethics*, XI: 656, 1921.

43. 'The Roots of Modern Sociology', op. cit., pp. 11–14.

44. ibid., p. 15; see also *The World in Conflict*, p. 41.

45. 'The Roots of Modern Sociology', pp. 15–18.

46. ibid., pp. 18–22.

47. *Social Development, Its Nature and Conditions*, pp. 12, 13, 91, 92. See also 'Editorial', loc. cit., pp. 4, 5.

48. *The Metaphysical Theory of the State, a Criticism* (1921), p. 17.

49. *Social Development, Its Nature and Purpose*, p. 12.

50. op.cit., pp. 13–16.

4 The Sociological Study of Morality

Hobhouse gave a set of prolegomena to the study of morality. He expressed the concept of a morphology, or classification of social phenomena, as a sociological tool. He showed the significance and role of custom and tradition in the development of morality. He gave a theory of the development of moral codes, together with three principles of historical interpretation in the light of which the growth of institutions might be analysed. Finally, he traced the rise of ideas and practices in certain important areas of social organization.

The first part of this chapter will seek to clarify the scope, nature and methods of this general theme. Later sections will deal with custom and tradition, with the three principles of Hobhouse that illuminate the nature of the social bond, and with his tracing of the rise of moral ideas and practices.

Method and scope

Hobhouse regarded the sociological study of morality as being concerned with the rules, principles, regulations and ideals that guide or inspire human behaviour. He gave it the title of 'comparative ethics', and the question arises of whether it should be considered a branch of philosophy rather than of sociology.

However, while philosophy is interested in the ultimate validity of ethical conceptions, comparative ethics is concerned with the fact that they actually exist and exert a social influence, regardless of their philosophical validity. It studies concepts and rules as they play their role in individual and group life, and as they are related to other aspects of human interaction. It tries to interpret the differences between societies and classes as far as customs and codes are concerned, and it attempts to assess the place of the moral factor in social and cultural evolution.

Hobhouse regarded this study as a science since it was possible to compare customs, laws, religious demands and moral codes as historical facts, without reference to their relative value. The sociological analysis of morality, then, is empirical in its character and methods. It is concerned with the facts of morality, as expressed in customs, rules and concepts.

Hobhouse was insistent on the need for seeking all the relevant facts, as far as was possible. He had little respect for the method which began with a theory and then sought out those facts which would support the theory. On the contrary, he maintained that a theory should develop out of the facts. He noted that theories of social evolution could easily be formed with the aid of preconceived ideas and judiciously selected corroborative facts. The development of a theory which actually grew out of the facts themselves and expressed their significance presented many problems.

Like Comte before him, Hobhouse argued for the empirical data to be sought, extracted and arranged with the same impartiality that the natural scientist displays in describing and classifying his various forms of data. The present writer maintains that Hobhouse was one of the earliest investigators to apply this approach to the historical study of morality. Covering a vast range, the topic involves the life of the contemporary world on its various aspects, its science and philosophy, literature, religion, laws and customs, economic structure, political systems—all that is termed Western civilization. In addition, there are the old Eastern civilizations, and on an older cultural level the semicivilized, barbarous and primal communities whose independent life is receding into the past. The history of human ancestry is also required, together with the evidence of archaeology.[1]

Hobhouse showed the close relationship between ethical evolution—the rise of customs, rules and moral ideas and practices—and the broader flow of cultural evolution. He gave a new interpretation to the cultural approach by pointing out that it can throw new light on the problems of comparative morality. Throughout his *Morals in Evolution*[2] runs a constant emphasis upon the fact that moral rules and practices arise in a cultural setting and can only be interpreted in the light of their cultural environment. He attempted to take the various phases of culture, and upon an analysis of their ancestry and growth to ask what their development implied. In particular, he attempted to review the cultural past with reference to law and justice, marriage and the position of women, inter-group relations, role and status within groups, and property relations.

An important issue, raised and stressed by Hobhouse as part of the 'prolegomena' to the sociological study of morality, concerns the distinction between the objective analysis of moral and cultural evolution and the attempt to assess that evolution in terms of progress, retrogression, and normative judgements. Just as he insists on the necessity for distinguishing between questions of fact and questions of value, so he indicates as a preliminary necessity to this type of study the need for finding the facts of man's moral history, before attempting to impose value-judgements upon a part of the facts.

He noted with emphasis that the prime object of the study of moral evolution was to inquire into the lines of development, to discover what the ideas and practices of mankind had actually been at different times and places, and to ascertain whether any broad lines of development could be laid down. The discovery of what was ethically sound or unsound had no part, he claimed, in this type of investigation.[3]

He regarded questions of value and social progress as falling within the scope of sociology, unlike many social scientists, but he nevertheless recognized the difference between the impartial search for facts of the social past and the evaluation of those facts in terms of some standard or norm.

At the outset of his main study of ethical evolution, Hobhouse states that his object is 'to trace the evolution of the ethical consciousness as displayed in the habits and customs, rules and principles, which have arisen in the course of human history for the regulation of human conduct'.[4] In studying this evolution, one main purpose is the grasping of a certain development as a whole. In this study Hobhouse gave the concept of a 'social morphology', or 'systematic arrangement of the types that we find in accordance with their affinities'.[5] This concept does not refer to a mere collection of sociological data but to a systematic arrangement of types. It is clarified by the following explanation:

. . . by social types we mean examples of all the leading
forms of human achievement which result from the interaction
of individuals—types of social institutions, forms of

government, principles of law, types of the family, and, again, intellectual, moral, and artistic traditions, religions, ethical systems, sciences, arts. We need not merely to collect and enumerate the successive achievements of mankind in these various directions, but to arrange them in some way that will exhibit their affinities and interactions, that will help us to appreciate the lines of social development. We need a classification leading up to a social morphology.[6]

In the field of comparative sociology, Hobhouse saw a morphology as the first step towards the introduction of order and system. It represented the ascertaining and classifying of the actual forms of an institution. The classification, though, had to throw some light on the problem of origins and show how institutions have grown and developed. Its aim is to distinguish between the various phases or forms of social life and so to attain a comparative view of the stages through which they have passed. Later pages of this chapter will be concerned with one example of classification that Hobhouse set forth.

Related to this concept is another 'prolegomenon' to this type of investigation: the fact that all the strands that make up social evolution are interrelated. The history of law, for example, is linked up with economic systems, political development, family life and religious ideas. Even in reviewing the religious history of one nation, a full understanding will involve the history of other countries. This type of evolution is not merely national, but cultural. All strands are inseparably interwoven and related.

A further basic point is that the investigator must distinguish between actual codes and rules, as means of social control which have binding force, and those precepts which are mere ideals in a culture but which receive little practical assent. Similarly, it is not possible to measure or investigate the degree to which actual conduct has conformed to codes and rules. All that can be hoped for is a comparison of recognized customs and ideas as expressed in mythology, literature and art. The main concern is with practice, and with those practical moral codes that were real expressions of what groups actually felt, did and thought, for the normal conduct of individuals is based upon those rules that have social force behind them. Hobhouse stresses this point.[7]

The danger of taking facts and incidents out of their cultural setting has been alluded to in earlier pages. The entire life of a group, with its current system of values, must be considered.

A final point of importance relates to the non-linear character of social and moral development in history. This process does not emerge in a 'straight line' nor advance step by step with the growth of civilization. Indeed, one side of a culture may develop yet bring with it no corresponding change in moral practice or idea. Moral development represents a winding curve rather than a linear growth.[8] It involves culture growth and culture contact in all their ramifications. Similarly, the interaction of social forces being what it is, the growth of an institution cannot be regarded as a single continuous process from its origin to its contemporary form. There is, then, no attempt to trace a continuous cultural or ethical evolution, but rather the effort to compare cultures and institutions that have been subject to ubiquitous cross-currents of contact and interacting influence.

But the growth of certain types of institutions and concepts can be traced and described, and thereby the main lines of classification can be drawn. It was found by Hobhouse that certain types predominate at certain stages of culture while below and above that level the types grow rarer until they finally disappear. In other words, a predominance of given types of institutions at given levels of culture is seen.

Hobhouse grew up in the last quarter of the nineteenth century, a period in which ideas of 'evolution' were dominant in Western thinking. Much attention was being paid to the study of man's past history, and visions of a straight-line march towards 'progress' were widely entertained. Many keys had been offered for the explanation of man's social past, and many theories set forth which tried to show the 'meaning' of history and social evolution.[9]

Hobhouse did not attempt to give any explanatory theory of social evolution, but he did trace the rise of moral awareness in society and pointed out three principles of social organization. He called these the principles of *kinship*, *authority* and *citizenship*, and he showed how certain types of social structure developed in connection with them.

Kinship, authority, citizenship

What are the forms of social organization in which evolving moral practices and ideas are found ? To answer this question, Hobhouse turned to the nature of the social bond itself—the tie which holds the individuals in a society together while separating them from other societies. No single or simple bond can be discerned, since human beings live and act together from many motives and under the influence of diverse factors. But leading forces may be seen among the conditions which make for social unity and continuity, and Hobhouse noted three which were so prominent as to give their character to society as a whole. He tried to show that these three principles of kinship, authority, and citizenship constituted a fundamental principle of social classification. Certain forces make for union and are common to the life of all society; for example, a mutual interest or consciousness of kind tends to hold individuals together, fostering a type of co-operation. Similarly, religion acts as a social bond, but the religious element is common to all forms of society.

Kinship Primitive groups generally appear to be based on kinship. The relationship of mother and child may be described as natural and universal. Men have always lived in societies, and ties of kinship underlie every form of social organization. It appears probable that in the simplest societies these ties, extended and strengthened by religious beliefs, were the most important ones, for out of descent and intermarriage there arises a tissue from which small but close and compact communities are formed. As children grow up they will want partners and will seek them outside the circle of their own parents, brothers or sisters. The most simple social group, then, will be composed of two or more families living together united by cross-ties of intermarriage. A few families may occupy a tract of jungle or bush, though this type of isolation is unusual.

Hobhouse points out that the community will ordinarily have some contact with others. By increase of numbers, intermarriage, conquest and assimilation, it will become larger.[10] Through intermarriage a larger unity may be reached, and the status of the woman from the new group determined; her brother may take a sister of her suitor for his wife. Above the isolated family group there is a stage at which the kindred is the beginning of a wider but looser organization known as the tribe. Intermarriage is still the basis for this wider union.

The kindred may assume various forms whose genesis and

significance are matter for controversy. But it definitely constitutes a type of social structure which in some form persists through human history. Hobhouse is in accordance with fact when he notes the universality of kinship. The tie of blood is, in one sense, the foundation of the lower forms of society, and the family group runs through all forms of both primitive and advanced society. The local group represents a small unit based on near kinship and perpetuated by descent from parent to child, while a larger unit— the tribe—keeps its parts closely related by intermarriage, together with magical beliefs. Such are the typical elements of early society.

Hobhouse's contribution lay in his portrayal of how the principle of kinship is a dominant factor in early social organization. It constitutes a means by which the structure of primitive society may be analysed and interpreted.

For example, the kindred may grow numerically, intermarry with others, and form a tribal union while at the same time preserving an enlarged family structure. It is in the nature of a clan—a type of enlarged family. Kinship may be based on 'father-right', the child inheriting its father's name and status, with the government resting on the eldest male descendant. Hobhouse gives the patriarchate of Genesis as an example of how a man might dwell with his wife, their sons with their wives, their grandchildren and possibly great-grandchildren, with the common progenitor becoming the ruler.[11]

In this type of social organization, the father would hand over his authority to the eldest son or to the son most fitted for the honour by virtue of natural gifts. There is, however, another form of primeval society in which a husband might remain a member of his own clan or group, the mother and her children remaining associated with the group of her birth. Descent then continues in the female line; the daughters find husbands outside the group, and the sons, though attached to the group, find their wives in another family. In this system, descent goes by 'mother-right'.

Although the clan may be maternal or paternal, it has certain characteristics which will vary in detail from clan to clan. There are, for example, many ways in which the power of the head is granted and his appointment made; again, the clan may be ruled by a council with varying powers.

One of the main contributions of Hobhouse within this general theme of the kinship principle is his portrayal of the effects of exogamy and endogamy. Marriage outside the clan means that a man will belong, under mother-right, to a different clan from that of his wife and children. Exogamy thus brings in a cross-division or cleavage that cuts through family and clan life. This principle has contributed to the formation of organized society, for the practice of marrying outside the family would entail that every local group would consist of persons from two or more families. A strongly felt tradition helps to safeguard the practice and put the pressure of social condemnation on those who violate it. The effect of exogamy, then, is to give a form of social union that cuts across the clans, on the basis of which there is the local community of several intermarrying clans residing near each other. In the case of father-right, exogamy will still form a bond of connection, a link between separate stocks, but the wife passes out of her family and into her husband's and her children belong to him. The community, in either case, is joined by many interwoven strands of affinity and blood relationship.

The rule of endogamy, according to Hobhouse, has the tendency to strengthen the group to which it applies. It intensifies the life of the clan, separating the clan from the rest of the world. The union of different clans means a breaking-down of endogamous rules. An example that Hobhouse gives concerns Rome, where marriage appears to have been originally limited to the *gens*. The patrician *gentes* formed a circle of intermarrying clans, excluding the *plebs* until the *jus connubii* was obtained in 455 B.C.[12]

In the modern world, it is interesting to note that the principle of endogamy still obtains, as evidenced by the social disapproval typically expressed towards interracial marriages. It is a great separating tendency between those of different traditions, skin colours and cultures.

In conclusion, it may be noted that father-right and mother-right represent social forms that are in a sense natural and primitive, despite the many gradations to be found between them. But Hobhouse has emphasized a fundamental point in describing early society as constituted by ramifications of direct descent and intermarriage from the primeval group of mother and children. The kinship system, as he indicates, is predominant in the lower and earlier stages of culture.

Kinship alone does not 'explain' every aspect of primitive society. Hobhouse simply treats it as a principle which is basic to early social organization and structure. Other factors, such as primitive magic and religion, codes and organization for mutual defence, are important, as are the simple needs of human fellowship and co-operative tasks. In addition, the strength of the blood-tie maintains a common pride which is the source of warlike prowess. Hatred for the enemies of the clan is a reflection of love for the clan itself. But the existence of enemies is related to a new principle that arises with the growth of society. This new principle of authority was seen by Hobhouse as characteristic of the advance towards civilization.

Authority A significant change in social organization is related to the power-system of the early group. The primitive group has few social distinctions or gradations. There is the chief or leading member, but his powers are often only little developed. The entire social organization is an outgrowth of the ties of blood, inter-marriage and neighbourhood. But, says Hobhouse, when a group enters upon a career of conquest, it must have discipline in a greater degree than that accruing from the position of the elderly leader or chief. It requires a war-chief with unlimited powers, and with a following. In quarrels with neighbours, weaker peoples will be reduced to a dependent status. Stronger tribes may raid them for cattle, or greater rewards. The distinction between conqueror and conquered will become one of master and slave, or upper and lower caste. More power is given to the chief in the interests of internal discipline, while religio-magical conceptions invest him with new sanctities and potentialities.

Hobhouse has presented a significant portrayal of the existence of status—and structure based upon a status-principle in early society—for the principle of authority is essentially one involving status-gradations and power. He maintains that all the great civilizations appear to have experienced this stage of evolution, though the despotic system develops among people who are still in the barbaric stage, as, for example, among certain West African tribes. The monarch may become a man-god like the Pharaohs. Similarly, Hobhouse notes that, in England, the theory of divine right arose when feudalism passed into absolutism and the king proclaimed himself to be God's viceregent.[13]

Such is the second stage of social evolution. Hobhouse shows how it arises, usually from military demands and the changes they incur in social organization and relationships of a vertical type. It is a stage in which social and political unity rests upon a military basis. This makes possible more binding ties than those of kinship and neighbourhood. In fact, it demands such ties. Hobhouse points out the subordination–superordination relationship by noting that military organization holds one tribe together while holding others in subjection. The authority is not that of naked force, once it has been established. The element of social control enters in through the sacrosanct aura that surrounds the ruler and exerts influence over the minds and wills of the subjects. Such a government is essentially government from above. The relationship of ruler and ruled involves imposed duties—military service, tribute, new laws, ordinances. At this stage of society, says Hobhouse, law is in the nature of a command imposed by a superior upon an inferior.[14]

Hobhouse has portrayed the form of social control as it operates in primitive society. He has described the subtle change that takes place in societal structure, mores and expectations as a result of the principle of authority. He notes that the ideas prevalent in society are affected by this change. Custom, though sacred in the primitive kinship group simply because it was customary, and because supported by religious and magical conceptions, tends to be broken up. Law is no longer the direct expression of the common life, but a command from above. Hobhouse has shown how the principle of authority runs through the entire life of society. There may be a feudal hierarchy of lord and slave, from the monarch to the lowest subject, as in medieval England, or a hierarchy of castes, as in India.[15]

The principle of subordination extends to the present day and is expressed in modified ways such as class distinctions and conceptions of social, political or economic inferiority. It would appear to be almost inherent in advanced social structure.[16] What Hobhouse did was to note how it arose from military needs and the demands of an expanding social organization, and to point out how it affected every aspect of social interaction.

He showed the rise of a social hierarchy in which the majority of the people are at the bottom of the scale, as opposed to the conditions of equality that existed in primitive times. A despotic social system tends to lower the condition of the masses, as in slavery, caste systems or serfdom. The entire societal structure is permeated with the dominating influence of subordination. With the growth of social groups in their economic life, further differentiation ensues, and the sanctions of religion are used to widen and deepen the principle of authority.

It is to the credit of Hobhouse that he nowhere indicates or implies that the old forms of organization die out entirely. He did not fall into the error of presupposing any direct change, historically, between the two social systems. Hobhouse had too much historical sense to assume that the change was anything but gradual, or that it took place in a 'straight-line' fashion. He noted specifically that the old forms of organization would still keep some of their vitality despite the effects of conquest. Among the conquered, similar institutions would be found, and some compromise would have to be made with these.

Nevertheless the principle of authority is seen to give rise to three forms of social organization. First, there is the absolute monarchy in which the king is divine and rules without restraint. Secondly, there is the feudal monarchy, more adapted to larger areas where the power has to be delegated and a hierarchy formed out of the ruling classes. Thirdly, the empire is formed out of an aggregation of kingdoms. National boundaries are transcended, and differences exist between the degrees of unity and local freedom. Hobhouse sets forth a hypothesis that the idea of a moral duty to subordinates grows in proportion to the degree of unity achieved, despite the conception of law as based on authority and the societal system on relations of subordination of class to class.[17] And it would appear that the command of the ruler was not entirely divorced from considerations of duty to his subjects, as evidenced by the benevolence to the poor shown by the feudal rulers of Egypt. The administration of justice in the Persian Empire furnishes another example, as does the Roman concept of justice. The duties of the ruler are thus relative to an organization which, by its very defects, creates the necessity for them.

To summarize this topic of the principle of authority, Hobhouse has outlined and described the ramifications of a principle that belongs to periods of expansion in culture and improvement in the arts of life. He has portrayed how the principle furnishes a method for the forming of large communities, and for maintaining internal order and social control with greater ease than is displayed by the primitive clan. He has also shown how the principle of authority tends to carry forward distinctions of rank and class.

It is in so far as authority embodies or makes possible the third principle, that of citizenship, that the last-mentioned tendency is avoided. For it is from a sense of social solidarity that the principle of citizenship arises. The thought of Hobhouse in relation to this third principle of social organization will now be considered.

Citizenship There is no particular point in history at which the civic state comes into being. On the contrary, there is an evolving of the authoritarian type of government into the higher stage in which moral force and the willing co-operation of free citizens are fundamental to social order. Under the principle of citizenship, the relation between government and the governed is inverted. Order and harmony are no longer under the authority of a superior, for under this highest form the people who possess citizenship are the state. Government is not their master, but their servant, and its officials are bound by law, as are all subjects.

One main feature of this type of organization is that law ceases to be a command from above, but becomes an expression of the will of the citizens who obey it. A certain equality supersedes the former hierarchical system, resting upon a recognition of reciprocal obligations that transcend supremacy of power. Laws are made and remade with an awareness of social needs. The actions and agreements of the citizen become moulding factors in his life, rather than mere status. A sense of personal right develops, and the whole community exercises powers and performs functions formerly left to the clan leader, the family or authoritarian body. Other characteristics of the state include responsibility of citizenship and legislative government that expresses the majority will. Government is seen as a function in which individuals act as public servants; its laws and acts represent popular decisions. The citizens possess rights, valid both against the government and against other individuals. The individual assumes greater importance; he is a citizen, a part of the state, and as such has rights that he lacked under the authoritarian régime.

Hobhouse has set forth the concept of the state as the regular organ in a civilized community which maintains common rules. It is the fabric of the law, government and defence by which rule is maintained. It is not the community, but a system of institutions within the community, an association including legal and administrative machinery together with the constituent authority upon which government rests.[18]

It may be asked whether a primitive community does not have a state. But a single chief does not constitute a state. It is difficult, however, to fix the exact point at which a community is furnished with state organization. It presupposes responsible individuals with civic rights and obligations, and a responsible government expressing in its law and administration the will of the people. These are, for Hobhouse, the two essential features of the state.

He also pointed out the limitations on citizenship, with special reference to Greece and Rome. It is important to note that the number of citizens in a community may only be a fraction of the whole number of people living there. Again, the degree of civic rights may vary greatly among the citizens. Force may play a major part in the relations between citizens and non-citizens. Hobhouse has described the political relations of the Greek city-states. Here the distinction between the freemen and the slaves remained. Since citizenship was not universal, it should be noted that the despotic principle operated even within the stage of citizenship.[19] On the other hand, Greek and Roman history consists in large part of the breaking down of class barriers and the extension of political rights to ever-increasing numbers of the population.

Rome represented an authoritarian system, though a certain civic spirit was retained and has come down to posterity in the concept of a world-state based on law. The idea of citizenship was not lacking, but civic unity was deficient. Slavery was much in evidence. Hobhouse points out that the extension of the principle of citizenship was an important cause of Rome's downfall, for citizenship was granted until it took in the entirety of Italy and later the whole free population of the Mediterranean basin. This was fatal to the free self-government of a city-state. The Italian population could not meet in the forum to elect consuls or pass a law, and the extension of citizenship only reduced its political value.[20]

The above furnishes a good example of how social development does not advance in one straight line with all features of a civilization proceeding at a uniform pace. It is illustrative of the point made by Hobhouse to the effect that development on one side of societal life may work a disharmony or disorganization on another side.

Hobhouse has given another contribution in describing the

principle of citizenship in the modern state. With the abolition of slavery, the principle of citizenship has been carried nearer to its conclusion, though modern inequalities of wealth reduce political equality to less meaningful terms. As early as 1910, Hobhouse said that 'there can hardly be true political equality as long as the economic tendency sets strongly towards overwhelming inequalities of wealth'.[21] But he also noted that modern government does not mean a monarch or mercenary army or the exacting of tribute. On the contrary, it represents an organization of the common life. In national consciousness, each people feels itself to be one, drawing distinctions between itself and others.

He also pointed out a modern phenomenon: the movement towards self-government as a dominant feature of modern social organization. He insisted that it could not be studied in isolation, for it was part of a wider attempt to broaden the basis of civilization, to lessen artificial barriers of birth, nationality and sex, and to raise the masses of people from subservience to a share in the common heritage and common life. It is a movement that is sociological in the broadest sense, and not exclusively political; it deals with the mass of social and economic conditions on which political freedom and social harmony rest. Hobhouse notes that the struggle for the franchise is fundamental in this movement.[22]

The principle of citizenship, then, has not yet been carried to any complete stage. It is by no means universal, as problems of colour and absolutism still testify. Hobhouse makes the significant generalization that 'to base liberty on law, and the common life with efficient social co-operation on liberty, is the specific problem of contemporary statesmanship'.[23] It may be noted, in conclusion, that the authoritarian principle blends with the citizenship principle, especially where dependencies and subject races are concerned.

To summarize the three principles, in primitive society ties of kinship engender the close association of the small local group, and later the closely knit clan, within the larger unity of the tribe. These associations may possess vital force, compactness and durability; but they are narrow, self-contained and tend to be mutually hostile. They are adapted only to crude economic conditions and an elementary level in the arts of life. With growing civilization, they yield to the rule of force by which larger aggregations of human beings can be held together. Finally, the principle of citizenship makes possible a form that is as organic as the clan and as wide as the empire, but it adds a measure of freedom to the individual and a flexibility to the whole structure. It involves the concept of a 'common good', and in its later stages demonstrates the possibility of a world state.

From these three stages, seven forms of social organization arise. They are, in the kinship stage, the clan, maternal and paternal, and the tribe; in the authoritarian stage, military or bureaucratic despotism, feudal monarchy and the international empire; in the stage of citizenship, both the city-state and the national state.

These types of societal system are not mutually exclusive. It cannot be said that humanity started with a system of kinship, passed on into a system of authority and ended with that of citizenship. As the scale of culture ascended, there was no succession in serial order. What have been distinguished by Hobhouse are certain principles which form certain types of societal structure which may be regarded as means of reference whereby other social forms may be placed. The types may exist contemporaneously, or may be blended in various ways. What is claimed is that the three principles and the different forms of the social bond that develop from them are predominant at successive stages in the order given.

For example, the kinship system is supreme in the lower and earlier stages of culture, the system of authority characterizes the advance towards civilization, and the principle of citizenship is developed and expressed in the higher and more developed civilizations.

Hobhouse has thus set forth a significant hypothesis as to the rise of the state, and the development of societal structure. He has thrown light on the evolution of societies, by an analysis of the social bond that adheres in communities at various stages of culture. It should be noted that no value-judgement is involved in referring to the levels of culture. The stages distinguished are historical, and no normative significance is implied.

The next sections will be concerned with the study that Hobhouse made of the evolution of moral ideas and practices. The three previous sections of this chapter dealt with the broader aspects of social evolution. The remainder of the chapter will consider his study of some of the particular social forms that arise and develop within the wider trend of social evolution generally.

Morals in evolution

One of the most important works of Hobhouse lay in his depicting the trend of historical development in man's customs, mores and moral ideas. His *Morals in Evolution*, first published in 1906, and reprinted during his lifetime in 1915, 1919 and 1925, represented a pioneer attempt to portray human development with specific reference to five main areas of societal organization: (a) law and justice, (b) marriage and the position of women, (c) inter-community relations, (d) class relations and (e) property and poverty.

What Hobhouse attempted was to ascertain the principal characteristics of moral development and to depict the entire process in outline. For this study, as he noted at the outset,[24] no hypothesis concerning the causes of evolution was required. The aim was simply to distinguish and classify different forms of moral ideas and practices. Even if the theory of evolution were undermined, provided such a study were based on recorded facts, its results would still stand. Ascertainment of facts rather than the psychological forces underlying morality was the main concern of the investigation. But to arrive at the facts necessitated the use of many specialized conclusions taken from the works of other investigations in ethnology and cultural sociology.

Morals in Evolution is the volume by which Hobhouse is probably best known in America. It is also one of the most distinctively sociological of his works. It is a contribution to the literature of social control, as well as to comparative sociology and the sociology of morality.

The method used by Hobhouse was historical. He went to the facts of man's past development, as revealed in written records of customs, mores and ethical ideas. He gave an outline of the process on the basis of this research, utilizing the records of ethnographers and anthropologists.

Law and justice Hobhouse has shown that a long evolution has preceded modern law, with its distinction between civil and criminal justice, its consideration for motives and intentions, and its concepts of impartial authority and individual responsibility. Primitives made virtually no distinction between civil and criminal law, or between deliberate intention and accident. The notion of an impartial court was not familiar to them, nor was the use of evidence and testimony.

The historical analysis of law and justice is connected with the three stages of social organization described above (pages 83–93). In early societies, pure self-redress was found, but came to be organized under a code of custom. In small kinship groups, redress was obtained by retaliation. Family solidarity brought support to the individual wronged. Vengeance, as Hobhouse points out, develops in this way into the blood feud. The earliest law in the Old Testament is 'he that sheddeth man's blood, by man shall his blood be shed'.[25] Justice at this level is that of a united kin in sympathy with an injured relative, rather than of an impartial party viewing the facts of the case.

Hobhouse defines justice as 'the rendering to each man his due as judged by an impartial authority',[26] or 'the definition and maintenance of obligations, and obligations include what is due to people, their rights, and what is due from them, their duties'.[27]

As a concept of social duty, judged by an independent authority, justice is not distinctively conceived among primitives. It was not entirely unregulated, however, for primitive custom tended to control retaliation, as is seen in the famous *lex talionis*. The Code of Hammurabi, for example, although barbaric, contemplated organized courts of justice with rules of procedure and evidence. It was not, however, the most ancient code; the code of Ur Engur preceded it.

Another feature of primitive justice which Hobhouse distinguishes is the principle of payment for damages, or compensation. Involved in this, as in primitive relations generally, were differentiations of status between the persons injured. Hobhouse found that the system of composition extended over a large part of the barbaric world, including the Malay Archipelago, New Guinea, certain Indian hill tribes and the Somali of East Africa.

The blood feud was another means of social control. A tribe might refrain from aiding another tribe for fear of the blood feud that would ensue. The blood feud was a private war between families. The entire body to which the offending member belonged could be held responsible by the entire body to which the injured individual belonged. The clan or family was regarded as a unity, and redress was a group concern. Similarly there was a failure to distinguish between accident and design, a primitive failure in which theories of witchcraft and possession played their part.

Hobhouse traced the influence of the theory of collective

responsibility and found that it persisted until recent times. In France, for example, even up to the time of the Revolution it applied to the families of those guilty of political offences. On the other hand, Ezekiel stresses the concept of individual responsibility; children are not to be punished for the sins of their fathers.[28] One characteristic of evolving justice is the eliminating of the collective responsibility theory.

Under an evolving social order and a developing central authority, redress falls into the hands of an impartial administration of justice through a growing sense of the need for public safety. The development of public justice can be regarded as the process whereby reparation of private wrongs becomes a public responsibility, and the inflicting of private wrongs becomes a public crime. Occasional group intervention, based on common resentment and indignation, becomes defined in rules of custom. The fear of the blood feud may also be a cause of conciliation or arbitration on the part of the leading men of the group. Two means of settlement of disputes that Hobhouse distinguishes are the set fight and atonement for a crime. With the development of social groups, crimes become a breach of the peace.

Three main levels of justice which Hobhouse noted include, then, (a) self-redress, with or without composition or the regulated fight; (b) assistance or control of the avenger by public force; and (c) a fully established system of public justice to deal with serious crimes. Most civilized peoples can be said to show an evolution from the private to the public system of justice.[29] Hobhouse has noted Ancient Egypt as an exception, for here there was no evidence of private justice or any transitional stage.

Hobhouse reviewed Roman law, with its distinction between private and public crime. He also analysed the well-developed system of public justice in Greece. He noted a reversion to barbarism in that Greco-Roman justice was followed by that of the early medieval era, with its military-caste habits. He also gave a portrayal of medieval legal procedures, with its use of the 'oath', the 'ordeal' and tortures. He traced the rise of the court as a means of trying cases, obtaining facts and giving verdicts based on its own judgement while enforcing sentence through its own officers. He pointed out that this concept of the court required the formation of an effective governmental organ, with an executive force sufficiently powerful to raise its officers above the fear of revenge.

Hobhouse analysed medieval justice as an authoritarian system in which public authority was more concerned with the maintenance of order and the efficient repression of crime than with considerations of justice to individuals. He portrayed some of the barbarities of medieval law that extended into the modern period, and showed the rise of humane conceptions and practices that worked to alleviate the conditions in gaols, for example, during the nineteenth century. He sketched the development of penal reform, and at the end of his factual analysis of legal history, he insisted on newer methods in which the criminal will be seen as a 'case' to be understood and cured, rather than merely crushed and punished. The right to be punished involves the modern view of being helped in the path of reform. Finally, Hobhouse shows that, in self-governing societies, legislation expresses the will of the people, in accordance with the principle of citizenship. He makes the important point that there is no real antithesis between liberty and law. Provided the law is impartial, liberty may be obtained for a whole community, since law restrains individuals from their attempts to abuse or ill-treat their fellows.

Hobhouse showed the gradual rise of the concept of individual rights, and he noted that modern law frames its rules so as to regard certain basic rights and duties as belonging to all human beings, irrespective of rank, age, sex, race or even citizenship'.[30]

In addition to tracing the maintenance of legal rights and the development of public justice, Hobhouse showed the rise of the principal *human* rights, and his contributions here include marriage and the status of women throughout the centuries.

Marriage and the position of women One of the first points to be noted in this connection is that an institution such as the family cannot be studied apart from the culture that bred it. Marriage is interwoven with religious conceptions, economic conditions, class and caste distinctions, psychological forces, property, political obligations and societal organization generally. This dependence of the family upon the wider cultural context is fundamental to an understanding of its evolution.

Hobhouse analysed marriage historically under the following headings: (a) the number of parties to the union, (b) the restrictions imposed upon marriage, (c) the stability of the relationship,

(d) the methods of obtaining a mate and (e) the relations between husband and wife in the family.

He found no certain evidence that group marriage has ever existed, or that complete promiscuity has ever been a positive institution, socially sanctioned, as distinct from extreme looseness in the sex relation. The above distinction is basic, as is the difference between polygamy's being *permitted* and being prevalent. Hobhouse made the general conclusion that polygamy tends to be permitted in the uncivilized world, while polyandry is, by comparison, the rare exception as a practice, owing to poverty and the number of women.[31] He also found that, in higher civilizations, monogamy becomes so widespread as to be almost universal.

As for the impediments imposed on marriage, Hobhouse found that some type of restriction was practically universal, especially the prohibition of marriage between parent and child, or brother and sister. He made the generalization that failure to prohibit becomes rarer in direct proportion to the nearness of the relationship.

A further significant generalization was his statement that 'endogamy belongs to the backwaters of cultural history',[32] since intermarriage enlarges the boundaries of communities, strengthens the bonds of peace and brings about a great variety of human types. Hobhouse is the author of the generalization that father-right predominated among all Indo-Germanic peoples, Semites and Mongolians, groups that have developed the historic civilizations. Similarly, mother-right is broadly confined to the uncivilized world.

Hobhouse also found that, among preliterate peoples, the position of women is generally inferior to that of man in respect of personal rights. He came to the conclusion that some marriage institution is universal, as is some type of social control over sex relations. Primitive restrictions on marital choice dominate any individual claims. The maternal family separates the interests of the father from those of his household, while the patriarchal family is more close-knit but furnishes no independent status for the wife and mother. Patriarchy consolidates family life, but confirms the dependent position of woman.[33]

The investigations Hobhouse made into marriage under civilization involved analysis of available records of family life in ancient Babylon, Egypt, India, China, Arabia, Greece and Rome.

He studied the Code of Hammurabi, the Vedic and Brahmanic literature, Chinese codes and Hebrew laws, besides calling upon his own profound knowledge of the classical era, its history and literature.

He also analysed the roots of the modern European marriage law, which he saw as threefold in its origins, involving Roman law, primitive Teutonic custom and the Christian doctrine of marriage. This analysis was based upon a study of the history of the family since the days of Rome, up to the modern period, and covering the Middle Ages, the influence of Canon Law, the Protestant Reformation and modern divorce law.

He stated that the family began with a relatively loose organization which passed to a state in which close-knit relations were reached, though at the expense of the wife. In the higher civilizations, equal freedom for both parties tends to be reconciled with family solidarity. In woman's position, the idea of respect for human personality gains ground; in the early stages, there is little respect for women as such, and division of labour often acts to their disadvantage. Under the principle of authority, the wife was in a dependent position, but in the modern world she has gained greater independence in several areas of life. The modern ideal of the family is that of a cooperative unity, a little society whose common welfare is important for each member.

Relations between communities In primitive society generally the governing principle of ethics is the dependence of morals upon the group system. Moral obligations, Hobhouse pointed out, were intra-group obligations. Rights and duties did not attach to individuals as individuals, but as members of the group. Hobhouse noted that early morality was group-morality, and distinctions were made between the obligations binding members of the group and those that held with respect to out-group members.

He further pointed out that this relation still holds, for civilized man is organized in groups on the basis of nationality, race, religion and class. The sociology of morals, or the comparative study of ethics, largely consists of tracing the rise of wider concepts of obligation. In tracing such a development, Hobhouse contributed to the sociological study of morality. He pointed out the operation of the 'in-group' and 'out-group' distinction among primitives, and described the treatment accorded to members of the out-group at various historical epochs and in different cultures.

The hostile relations that existed between small groups of early society have been analysed by various writers. What Hobhouse specifically did was to describe the effects of this conflict from an in-group and out-group viewpoint, with particular reference to status, as arising from group membership. He showed how group-morality was a determining factor in deciding the allocation of human rights.

He indicated how, among primitives, the outsider had no rights at all, in principle, and he set forth the hypothesis that this principle is a main differentiating factor between primitive and civilized ethics. The following passage is significant in this respect:

> Moral rights and duties are founded on relations between man and man, and therefore applicable to all humanity. To deny this applicability is merely to throw back civilized ethics to the savage state. If there is one thing which differentiates the ethics of primitive man from the ethics of civilized man, it is precisely this. The primitive man recognizes duties to the members of his family and to the members of his tribe which are often exacting enough, but to the stranger he recognizes no duties excepting in so far as he has entered into certain special relations with him which are guaranteed by supernatural sanctions. Thus, if the stranger within the gates has no host to protect him, he is 'rightless'.[34]

Hobhouse has shown, in effect, that the development of civilized morality has consisted, on one side, of extending the areas of moral obligation until they include the whole of humanity. His study of inter-group mores involved the analysis of moral concepts and practices in ancient Assyria, among the Hebrews, in China and in Vedic India. He found that in the East generally the preference for peace rather than war made itself felt, despite the barbarism of early Chinese warfare and the references to war in the Vedas.

He also reviewed war mores among the ancient Greeks and Romans, with particular reference to human rights. Rome exemplified the principle of group-morality, since enemies or 'strangers' were rightless.

Regarding the influence of religion on inter-group mores, Hobhouse found that Mohemmedan teaching rested on the distinction between Moslem and non-Moslem, while the Christian Church accommodated its teachings to the mores and expectations of a military age. It was seen that the influence of medieval canon law was not considerable, as the barbarities of the Middle Ages testify.

The principle of 'humanity' was emphasized by Hobhouse, and he noted that, since the time of Grotius, rights and duties have been based, in theory, upon universal attributes of humanity. This was a principle which transcended national distinctions and destroyed the basis of group-morality. Hobhouse traced the rise of this principle, as expressed in international law, up to and including the First World War, and found a great divergence between ethical theory and actual practice. At the end of his historical study of the role of group-morality, he expressed a characteristic internationalism, emphasizing the view that a true patriotism was the corner-stone of a true internationalism. International law, on this view, rests on the concept of humanity as the ultimate group.[35] At the time of the First World War, he said:

> Political morality is not super-morality, setting ordinary
> obligations aside. It is morality extended and defined,
> stripped of the limitations of class or national prejudice,
> generalized for application in great impersonal organizations,
> the only thing that can save such organizations from
> becoming inhuman.[36]

He further states that the repudiation of the distinctions made by group-morality is common to all higher ethical and religious teaching, according to which law and protection are to be granted to all human beings simply as human beings. To deny the validity of international ethics in principle is impossible without denying the basis of civilized ethics as a whole.[37]

The contributions of Hobhouse in relation to his study of intergroup mores may be summarized by the statement that he reviewed the 'group-morality' of primitive society and showed the rigid demarcations to which it gave rise; he also traced the disappearance of the personal element from warfare and the change in the treatment of conquered individuals; finally, he portrayed the rise of the concept of humanity, the implications of which are diametrically opposed to those of group-morality. He emphasized this concept of humanity as the ultimate group, and showed how the rise of civilized morality has largely consisted in its gradual application to practical affairs.

His historical study indicated the gradual (though not unilinear) decline of group-morality, with the extension of the area of moral obligation. He recognized the distinction between the ideals of thinkers and statesmen, and the actual practice of nations. Group-morality at the present time coincides with the boundaries of the national group, but the mere existence of international ideals is significant. The civilized world, he noted, had passed through the age of the blood feud, custom had restricted the quarrel, and even if international tribunals possessed no powers of enforcement, the pressure of world opinion and religious ideas were forces on the side of such organizations. But, writing at the time of the First World War, he recognized that the future of such a world tribunal posed a question to which any answer would at that date be premature.

Class relations Hobhouse traced the rise of the principle of group-morality. The primitive group, he noted, was usually small and homogeneous. With the growth of society, new knowledge, advancing industrialism and a developing societal structure, classes tend to be formed, differing degrees of rights and duties are distributed and the growing society assumes a definite structure with differentiations of status. Here rights and duties are not inherent in the individual *per se*, but are determined by social, political or religious considerations.

For Hobhouse, the operation of this group-morality principle is one of the dominant facts of social evolution.[38] To trace its development is largely to follow the history of slavery and serfdom. He recognized that the conception of a 'rightless' class was widely diffused throughout the uncivilized world, though many variations presented themselves.

What Hobhouse did was to trace the variations in the relationship of subordination–superordination, as manifested in the history of slavery in Mohammedanism, in the early Babylonian Empire, in Egypt, among the Hebrews, in Vedic and Brahmanic India and in China. From his own extensive knowledge of classical antiquity, he described slavery in Greece and Rome in addition to portraying the degree of 'rightlessness' and status-manifestations in all these cultures.[39] He set forth a delineation of the history of class-relations, with particular reference to status and human rights.

His study was not confined to early epochs, but extended into the medieval period with its hierarchical feudal system. Hobhouse showed that the Church accepted the institution of slavery and made little effort to abolish it. Pagans were regarded as an 'out-group', a source of slaves for the Western European nations. But the Church did exert an indirect influence in ameliorating the position of the slave and curtailing the rights of the master. In Europe, slavery came to be virtually unknown by the twelfth century, with the great exception of Negro servitude.

Hobhouse gives a succinct historical treatment of English serfdom from the medieval period until recent times, and traces the development of legislation affecting serfs and labourers. He also traced the abolition of Negro slavery and noted that the principle of natural equality tended to undermine the structure of subordination.

He raises an important issue when he makes the conclusion that as long as class, racial and national antagonisms exist, group-morality has not been overcome. He also concludes that there has been an ethical evolution in the change from small primitive groups, in which captive enemies or peaceful strangers were rightless, to wider conceptions of obligation and humanity. An important conclusion is that group-morality is currently coincidental with the boundaries of national states.[40]

Within the communities of mankind, growth has brought divisions and distinctions between individuals, but Hobhouse concludes that humanizing influences have worked to mitigate these barriers, and that in the modern world they have largely been overcome, in comparison with the past. Humanity, though, was becoming one by a widened consciousness of obligation, a response to the claims of justice, a greater forbearance towards differences of types, and a more enlightened conception of human purposes. Personal freedom had been made possible for the classes which formerly lacked it, and the concept of humanity had made itself felt in the modern period.

Property and poverty Apart from his consideration of this subject in *Morals in Evolution*, Hobhouse has also set forth elsewhere[41] a brief account of the evolution of property, and various references to the topic are found in his other writings. The main conclusions that he reached may be summarized as follows:

In early society, the individual was not in any way separate from his group. The realm of private property was very small and individual power of contract and economic advancement was even more restricted. Land was communally owned and individual enterprise had little incentive. Small personal holdings and possessions pointed to individual ownership, but occupation and use were the basis for the recognition of such property. Songs and dances represent group property. An absence of wealth was combined with an absence of pauperism. Social growth and development of organization brought inequalities, dominated in the economic sphere by private ownership and free contract, modified in early civilization by feudal tenures and caste divisions. At this stage, individual status, rather than effort or initiative, determined much. These restrictions were gradually eliminated and individuals became free to enter into occupations, gain wealth in all forms and dispose of it at will. But economic liberties are secured by the social order supported by the state, which demands that rights must be related to the common good; private property and free contract are not exempt from this condition. Individual rights and social duties are basic to modern conceptions of property and contract. There is the concept of a reciprocal obligation between the state and its citizens, giving rise to state aid to the poor and the investigation of the underlying causes behind poverty and other societal maladjustments.

Unlike some researchers in this field, Hobhouse showed an awareness of the difficulties involved, and expressed some of them as follows:

> In no department of the study of comparative institutions
> are the data more elusive and unsatisfactory. The divergence
> between legal theory and economic fact, between written
> law and popular custom, between implied rights and actual
> enjoyment, enables one and the same institution to be
> painted and, within limits, quite honestly painted in very
> different colours.[42]

Hobhouse also mentions the need for careful logic and good inferences upon observation, and the keen scrutiny of supposed 'differences' between primitive peoples and conditions, differences which can often be more legitimately attributed to the personal viewpoint or bias of the particular investigator.

He stressed the importance of land as a factor around which the evolution of primitive property turns. He also showed three conditions under which the system of communism works well. Understood as the system which, excluding all personal belongings, makes the common wealth dominant, communism operates in a well-ordered family where the fundamentals of wealth are shared by all the members. Secondly, it works well in very primitive communities where nobody has risen above the rest and where all are concerned with daily needs. In this case, all are born and bred in one tradition in which they form a kind of enlarged family. Thirdly, communism functions among individuals united by a common purpose or a common need; in a shipwreck personal considerations are subordinate to the needs of the group. As long as the common dominates the purely personal, communism will function. In the first case, says Hobhouse, it dominates through strong natural affections. In the second, personal initiative is restricted by absence of opportunity for individual gain or advancement. In the third instance, a common need or purpose holds individuality in check.[43]

He also noted the changes that took place in the idea of property during and subsequent to the Industrial Revolution. The structure of manufacturing and exchange, the role of stock, property as power and capitalism generally, represent many contrasts between modern and primitive economic systems.[44]

In this evolution, Hobhouse distinguished three general stages, related to the principles of kinship, authority and citizenship. In the first stage, the fruits of the earth were open for all to gather. General poverty was combined with general opportunity. In the second, labour is more organized, status develops in the form of master and slave, lord and vassal, superior and dependant. Discipline is more dominant than freedom. In the third stage, the individual is free in his career, but competition and inheritance give a large share of the products of industry to the few and little to the many. Hobhouse makes a striking generalization when he says that 'the man of property and the man of none are the contrasted figures of modern civilization . . .'.[45]

He stressed the need for equality between the parties to a contract.

He clearly showed how the right to enter into an agreement may be used by a stronger party to inflict harsh terms on the weaker.[46]

He also expressed the significant insight that the fundamental fact of modern capitalism was not inequality in itself, but 'the entire dependence of the masses on land and capital which belong to others'.[47] The distinctive meaning of capitalism is not to be seen merely in the fact that existing wealth is utilized in the production of more wealth. What capitalism does is to introduce the employment of those who lack the means of production by those who do possess this means.

Accordingly, Hobhouse questioned the absoluteness of property rights and held that they should be seen in relation to the social organization as a whole, and defined according to its needs. To improve the social order, society has to have a right to a share of the wealth which it helps to create and produce.[48]

Hobhouse made a criticism of laissez-faire conceptions of governmental functions. He argued that a consistent individualism would involve the abolition of the police and state machinery in an effort to ensure complete individual liberty. The individualists had a very restricted view of the function of government.[49]

A related point that Hobhouse raised concerned the distinction between unsocial and social freedom. The former he regarded as the right of a person to use his powers without regard for the wishes or interests of other persons. Such freedom is antithetic to all public control, while social freedom rests on restraint, yet is a type of freedom that is conducive to harmony in society.

His study of historical attitudes towards the poor and helpless, from primitive to recent times, drew upon material relating to ancient China, India, Israel, Islam, Greece and Rome, the medieval period and modern legislation.

Two of his striking generalizations indicate his social consciousness. He wrote that '. . . civilized society throughout its history has in very large measure consisted in the imposition upon the many of an order of life wherein the essential benefits are reaped by the few . . .',[50] and 'the power of organized capital is the standing danger of democracy'.[51]

In summary, the quasi-communism of primitive groups tends to give way to a system of free contract and individual ownership, with a diminution of the restrictions due to caste and feudal status as the principle of citizenship manifests itself. The development of individual freedom in economic matters has affected social organization profoundly and has given rise to questions of social control. It may also be added that it has given rise to questions of social progress. The entire topic, dealing as it does with man's past evolution and his cultural and societal growth, naturally leads to issues of social advancement and the norms of progress.

Chapters 5 and 6 will be concerned with perspectives on progress in society.

Notes and References

1. *Development and Purpose*, 1927, pp. 188, 189.

2. A seventh edition of this classic of 1906 was published in 1951, with a new introduction by Morris Ginsberg (London: Chapman & Hall).

3. Review of Edward A. Westermarck, *The Origin and Development of the Moral Ideas*, in *Sociological Review*, II: 402, October 1909.

4. *Morals in Evolution*, p. 1.

5. *Social Evolution and Political Theory*, 1911, pp. 111, 112.

6. ibid., p. 118.

7. *Morals in Evolution*, pp. 22–4.

8. ibid., pp. 31, 32.

9. See Pitirim A. Sorokin, *Society, Culture, and Personality, their Structure and Dynamics, a System of General Sociology* (New York: Harper & Brothers, 1947), pp. 679, 680.

10. *Development and Purpose*, p. 209.

11. *Morals in Evolution*, pp. 46, 47.

12. *Social Evolution and Political Theory*, p. 132. Hobhouse makes frequent references to social conditions in Greece and Rome. This is natural, in view of his classical education in public school and Oxford.

13. *Morals in Evolution*, pp. 54–6; and see also *Social Evolution and Political Theory*, pp. 134, 135.

14. *Liberalism* (1911), pp. 7–10.

15. See *Social Evolution and Political Theory*, pp. 137, 138.

16. It is interesting to note, in comparison, that according to Simmel the most important relationship in social interaction is that of leader and followers, in

which the principle of subordination is fundamental. It is a 'form' of socialization that makes social relations possible. See Nicholas Spykman, *The Social Theory of George Simmel* (Chicago: University of Chicago Press, 1925), pp. 95, 112. Also, E. A. Ross saw domination as a basic principle of the primitive social group. See his *Principles of Sociology* (New York: The Century Company, 1920), Chapter XI.

17. *Morals in Evolution*, pp. 58–60.

18. *Social Development, Its Nature and Conditions*, pp. 50–52.

19. *Morals in Evolution*, pp. 63–6.

20. *Liberalism*, pp. 13, 14.

21. *Government by the People* (London: The People's Suffrage Federation, 1910) p. 12.

22. ibid., pp. 4, 18.

23. *Development and Purpose*, p. 228. See also 'Democracy and Civilization' *Sociological Review*, XIII: 130, July 1921.

24. *Morals in Evolution* (1919 edition), Preface, pp. v, vi.

25. *Genesis*, 9: 6.

26. *Morals in Evolution*, p. 74.

27. *Social Development, Its Nature and Conditions*, p. 259.

28. *Morals in Evolution*, pp. 74–87. It is also interesting to note that the Assyrian codes were probably the earliest to make demarcations between unintentional and intentional wrongs. See G. R. Driver and J. C. Miles (eds.), *The Assyrian Laws* (Oxford: Clarendon Press, 1935).

29. 'Comparative Ethics', *Encyclopaedia Britannica*, 6: 159–60, 14th edition, 1937.

30. It should be noted that this represents a marked difference from earlier legal phases, in which cases of homicide, for example, were distinguished according to the social status or caste of the slayer and the slain. Equality before the law as it is now understood involves an impartial enforcing of the penalties, and these will be the same whoever the slayer and the slain may be. There is, implied an equal protection of life and limb for everyone under the law, and equal penalties for everyone violating the law. Modern law holds certain fundamentals of right and duty equally applicable to all human beings (*The Elements of Social Justice*, 1922, pp. 115–17). Such equality before the law has not yet been completely attained in actual legal practice.

31. *Morals in Evolution*, pp. 132–42. See also *Social Development, Its Nature and Conditions*, p. 20.

32. ibid., p. 118.

33. *Morals in Evolution*, pp. 167–78.

34. *Democracy and Reaction*, pp. 199, 200.

35. *Morals in Evolution*, pp. 268, 269.

36. *The Metaphysical Theory of the State*, p. 137.

37. *Democracy and Reaction*, pp. 200, 201. In connection with internationalism, the following passage is significant: 'There are very few men who can be as ardent in their patriotism as Mazzini, and yet at the same time conceive of their country as the servant rather than the mistress of humanity. The ordinary patriotism is, if made the highest end of life, a narrow, exclusive, and in the long run a self-destructive idea'—*Mind in Evolution* (1926), p. 390.

38. *Morals in Evolution*, pp. 271, 272.

39. ibid., pp. 273–98.

40. It is interesting to note that there are distinctions to be drawn within the operation of this principle at the present time, e.g. between the United States and Canada, or between Spain and Portugal, and the two sides of the Iron Curtain.

41. 'The Historical Evolution of Property, in Fact and in Idea', in *Property, its Duties and Rights Historically, Philosophically and Religiously Regarded, Essays by Various Writers* (New York: Macmillan Company, 1922), pp. 1–33.

42. ibid., p. 3.

43. 'Christianity', *Encyclopaedia of the Social Sciences*, III: 453, 1930.

44. Property as an institution represents both a concept and a structure, though its conceptual aspects are less apt to be considered. Hobhouse was aware of *both* these aspects of property, as is suggested by the title of his article dealing with its evolution.

45. *Morals in Evolution*, pp. 331, 332.

46. For elaborations of this point, see *Development and Purpose*, p. 227; *Morals in Evolution*, pp. 335, 336; *The Elements of Social Justice*, pp. 79, 80; *Liberalism*, pp. 82–6; and the volume by Hobhouse entitled *The Labour Movement* (New York: Macmillan Company, 1912), pp. 94, 95.

47. 'The Historical Evolution of Property, in Fact and in Idea', loc. cit., p. 22.

48. This principle underlies much modern legislation in England. It involves a refashioning of the concept of property, just as other legislative trends forced a change in the concept of contract.

49. On the question of whether the state should do for a man what his forebears did for themselves, it is interesting to compare the views of an early American pioneer of sociology, William Graham Sumner of Yale. He held to the frontier individualist notion that the state has no obligations beyond peace, order and the guarantee of rights. See his *What Social Classes Owe to Each Other* (New York: Harper & Brothers, 1920). A foremost American follower of Spencer, his views were diametrically opposed to those of Hobhouse.

50. *The Metaphysical Theory of the State, a Criticism*, p. 83. While this is a broad generalization, it is hard to deny that it contains an appreciable degree of truth. Hobhouse had already made his profound analysis of comparative morals before expressing this generalization.

51. *C. P. Scott, 1846–1932, The Making of the 'Manchester Guardian'* (London: Frederick Muller, 1946), p. 41.

5 Two Conflicting Theories of Progress

One contribution of Hobhouse to social thought relates to his study of human progress. What he did, specifically, was to set forth a norm of progress in the concept of 'harmony' and to bring out some of the ramifications of that term. A second contribution lies in his criticism of the biological and individualistic view of progress that was current in his day and which still occasionally appears in contemporary thought. A lesser contribution is seen in his exposition of what might be termed a 'prolegomena' to progress. Throughout the works of Hobhouse are scattered various points which, taken together, form an illuminating set of prerequisites to social advancement.

One of these relates to the individual and society. Hobhouse showed that it was fallacious to consider individuals as abstract entities independent of each other, and he early insisted upon the fact of interaction in society. Every individual is the centre of an indefinite number of relations and cannot be considered except as a component of the social groups to which he belongs.

A second point concerns the need for a reasoned theory of social progress. He noted that the apostles of revolution always have an underlying theory, and an obligation to be similarly equipped is laid upon the advocates of peaceful and constructive change. He also showed that a theory of progress would, of necessity, have to include a reasoned standard of value.

In connection with theory, Hobhouse suggests the need to study the history of ideals of progress so contemporary views may be seen with greater perspective and insight.

Similarly, another prerequisite is that human beings should display unity of aim and will, expressed in common action. Efforts on behalf of social reform often lack a clear statement of aims and manifest little rational consistency. Hobhouse makes the following significant comment:

> To promote unity of aim among men of goodwill and lay a basis of co-operation between those attacking different sides of the social problem is a practical problem of the highest importance.[1]

The mere fact that action can conflict with action is not a ground for taking no action at all. Hobhouse notes that if the only course open to man were to accept social trends as he found them, science would become fatalistic. The idea that inevitable forces will nullify all efforts at social amelioration was, for him, a false view. Such effort suggests a further consideration, namely, a concern for present-day problems. Progress is in one sense dependent on the number of persons who have a concern for the things of social value.

The ideals of such persons, however, must bear some relationship to actual conditions—a point on which he was insistent. This suggests what was, in his view, the main defect of Utopian schemes: that they were Utopian. Similarly, they often presuppose some revolutionary change and overlook the dynamic character of social affairs.

He also indicated that the inherent spirit of a culture or civilization is more important to its future than the external course of events. The moral and psychic forces of society are more important than social machinery, though it is through such machinery—law, organization—that they have to work. For example, he made the generalization that 'every association that works is founded on a bedrock of trust and mutual goodwill'.[2] This statement referred to a league or federation of nations, though it obviously has wider application. His study of progress involved the importance of the individual and the harmonious expression of individual capacity, together with humanitarian concepts and a criticism of contrary theories.

Harmony and the individual

Society consists of individuals in a state of interaction. Hobhouse brings forth an important point when he says that it is insidiously easy to forget individuals and deal in abstractions. For example:

We talk of the conservation of energy without thinking either
of masses, or of molecules, or of the spirit of the British
constitution without thinking of British men and women.
Yet what is energy apart from matter, or a constitution apart
from human minds ?[3]

He therefore insisted that any sound political or social theory would
emphasize the importance of the individual, his freedom and his
happiness. For, no matter how the common good may be defined,
it cannot be opposed to the good of individuals. Conscious efforts
to ameliorate the life of humanity can only work through the
humanity that is in every individual. When collective achievements
do not embody the deep-seated needs of the individual human
being, they become 'utterly sterile and illusory'.[4] He further
pointed out that, in the execution of great national purposes, there
is a tendency to forget and ignore individuals, as is evidenced by
the mass misery caused by governments at war. He regarded as
false those aims and purposes that do not have the effect of further-
ing the fulfilment of human power and happiness; and, on this
criterion, national glory, power and territorial aggrandizement
would be suspect.

Similarly, while Hobhouse did not underestimate the importance
of institutions, he raised a fundamental point when he made the
following statement:

Appraised in themselves by abstract logic, with no living
sense of the men and women whom they so intimately affect,
social institutions, collective wealth, power and magnificence
become bloodless and inhuman, and yet have something of
the glamour which for many minds attaches only to the
unreal.[5]

Collectivities have the power to force destructive sacrifice from
human beings. On this premise lies a condemnation of the state
system which is based on a perpetual military serviture, and of the
industrial system which reduces workers to automatons.

Hobhouse gave the concept of a harmonious fulfilment of
individual human capacity as one norm of progress, and showed the
social value that inheres in individuality. He pointed out that the
common life is fuller and richer for the great variety of types that

it includes; a further point of emphasis is that the good, however defined, must be of a type in which all members of the group can share so that its pursuits by one will promote its pursuit by another.

It may be asked whether, on this view, there is only one type of ideal citizen. But Hobhouse refutes this by showing that it is in the nature of constructive individual divergences that they contribute to the social harmony which makes use of them.[6] He has also made it clear that one condition of this harmony is that all individuals should contribute to it. He insisted on the importance and worth of constructive individual differences, and showed the inclusive character of democratic humanitarianism. He indicated that differentiation is an essential element in all high organization, and showed that this does not consist in any autocratic subordination, but in the willing co-operation of free human beings.

Herein lies one difference between civilization and barbarism. Hobhouse notes that, in primitive societies, custom has tyrannical force and individual divergences find little scope, while the conception of a common good is narrow. In more developed societies, individuality finds greater scope for expression. In fact, 'civilization is distinguished from barbarism, not more by the order which it establishes than by the many-sided development which it allows'.[7]

A related point in his theory of harmony is that harmony does not lead to repression, nor is it based upon repression. On the contrary, it involves directions for human capacity in which this may work to produce a social life that is fuller and richer. Hobhouse has insisted that any enrichment of society in one direction which involves repression in another does not represent harmony. This point appears in his writings in several connections.

For example, personal morality may be looked upon as self-control, and good government as the maintenance of order, but, in either case, harmony is not mere order based on repression. Impulses which are held down remain as sources of inner conflict, while the repression of a subordinate class or race is incompatible with social harmony.

The distinction made by Hobhouse between a unity of harmony and a unity of control may be briefly summarized. For the unity of control, it is sufficient that an impulse, an individual or a group be made subject by any possible means, including extinction, if necessary. For the unity of harmony, it is essential that the element be developed and enjoy the fullest expression in a form compatible with a corresponding expression of other elements. In individual life, this involves self-control as a rational acceptance of the social harmony, while harmony depends on the free growth of character. Conversely the subjection and impoverishment of the masses in any culture represent the principle of repression as opposed to that of harmony.

For Hobhouse, progress lies not in repression but in the free expression of individual human capacity, despite the conflicts to which this may give rise. He expresses the underlying thought as follows:

> The spirit of man does not develop equally from a single centre, but wells up with irregular profusion in thousands of distinct individuals, groups and interests. Each centre pursues its own life and fights for its own hand. The anarchy may be ended by the steam roller, but such is not the method of permanent progress. Progress lies in convincing the separate centres that within and below their differences there is something common by the service of which they can best express themselves.[8]

Judged by this viewpoint, the 'steam-roller' method of government which is hidden under the labels of 'efficiency' and 'expediency' often tends to reduce the individual to a mere industrial functionary. The conditions of human welfare are apt to be forgotten, and perfection of governmental machinery comes to be regarded as more important than human beings. To follow the rule of expediency would, for Hobhouse, imply the ignoring of conceptions of right and justice. It would involve the dangers of crushing individual spontaneity.

Against the view of government that is inherent, for instance, in Machiavelli's *Prince*, Hobhouse would contend that good government is of social value in terms of the life that it makes possible. The free growth of divergent capacities, and the spontaneous co-operation of elements which maintain their independent life, are, for this sociologist, preferable to governmental repression and mechanical organization.

Harmony may appear to have an abstract and Utopian aspect. To this charge, Hobhouse would reply that it can only be reached by a highly developed community, since it is drawn from the experience of such communities and formed by the selection of that which actually operates harmoniously in group life. For example, progressive statesmanship deals with the disharmony at hand, since to remove one source of conflict without exciting another is to remove repression without weakening respect for law.

The concept of harmony has many sociological implications of significance. For example, how far does a society or group promote the individual capacities of its members in their fulfilment? How far is a social order based upon repression, as distinguished from harmony? Hobhouse avers that the demands of the present should not involve the sacrifice of qualities that are necessary to a more complete development. The immediate necessities of order should not, on this view, be allowed to crush the attitude of independence. Bureaucratic socialism, with its 'experts' and its officialdom, may tend to do this. Similarly, collective achievement on the part of a 'superior' class may have repressive consequences for the weaker majority, in which case subordination of the many will exert a high price in the lack of potentially greater cultural achievement. The repression of woman is another community loss, since the group thereby loses the particular contribution of the woman's mind.[9]

Further implications accrue for cultural sociology. In the harmonious fulfilment of human capacity lies the substance of a creative social development, and the societal system that gives larger scope to human faculties is preferable, for Hobhouse, to the system that gives less scope. A social tradition may be the means of repressing capacities in art, industry, politics and religion. In these four areas, the spontaneous expression of personality may become deadened by academies, division of labour, bureaucracy and ecclesiasticism. Hobhouse makes a significant comment on this subject when he says: 'Tradition preserves principles by canning them. Society may eke out life upon the tinned goods, but the vitamins are gone.'[10] This is not to imply any radical conflict between culture and individual vitality, since, if this were the case, permanent progress would be impossible. It does, however, suggest that one criterion of cultural advancement is seen in the degree to which individual capacities find free expression.

The concept of harmony implies that a constructive social system calls forth the creative capacities of individuals in such a way that they further and promote those of their fellows. Every form of social life that maintains itself contains some element of this harmony, for if it were dominated by conflicting tendencies it would disintegrate. Hobhouse saw as an ideal society one in which growth occurred through the harmonious development of the parts, one in which the development of various parts tended to further the development of others.

An example may be cited in the case of the happy family life wherein the love of husband and wife, parent and child, is expressed without any repression of personality development for any member. In the larger social groups, this condition is only gradually realized because of the clash of forces and human needs and the demands of the social order. If progress simply consisted in the growth of order, the process would be much simpler, for whatever did not meet its demands would be suppressed. The liberation of human energies brings problems of a vast scale and variety, and social changes involve loss as well as gain, but in the theory of Hobhouse there is no irreconcilable conflict between social solidarity and the liberation of human capacity. In so far as fundamental human needs find satisfying expression, harmony in social relations may be said to exist. In this condition mutual development takes the place of subjection or repression, and there is a realization of the concept of community as something actually shared by all the members in the participation in a common life. Basic to this is a concept of freedom as a harmony in development:

> The problem of freedom is not that of dispensing with all guidance and all restraint, but that of finding the lines upon which the manifold social qualities of man can develop in harmony, with the result that the restraints involved are voluntarily accepted and self-imposed.[11]

In the theoretical system of Hobhouse, freedom becomes so important a condition of harmony as to be identical with it. Constructive freedom is not the freedom of one individual gained at the expense of others, but something that becomes, under the principle of harmony, the mainspring of progress and cultural advancement. Hobhouse sets forth the idea that liberty is the condition of mental and moral expansion, and is the foundation of science and philosophy, religion, art and morals.

The validity of this contention will be apparent when it is realized that the periods of outstanding cultural expression in history have been those when the human mind was free to discover, invent and enter upon fresh territory. In this growth of mental power lay societal development. Says Hobhouse: 'The foundation of liberty is the idea of growth.'[12]

He further maintained that any valid conception of social welfare would include a place for the abstract ideas of rights and duties. Equality, for example, is not the sole end and object of society, but in some form it is an essential part of any ethical ideal, standing as it does for the common humanity that underlies superficial distinctions. In 1898, forty years before the Second World War, Hobhouse expressed the idea that any society in Western Europe which wholly ignored the principle of liberty or equality would be doomed to disintegration.[13]

Similarly, economic equality involves the opportunity of all members of society to fulfil their capacities. Economic progress in itself does not lead to cultural advance, but it is one necessary condition of such advance. Although *economic* equality is not the whole of societal progress, the concept of equality is a basis for social and political reform. It naturally lends itself to considerations of justice in which the human being is seen to have certain basic rights *as* a human being. This is a revolutionary idea that cuts across the traditional distinctions of race, nationality, sex and class. Allied to it is the view that progress is dependent upon the maintenance of fundamental human rights.

Hobhouse has also shown the relation between co-operation and harmony; the harmony principle is clearly one of co-operation. Harmony constitutes a 'standard of value to which the actions of man and the institutions of society may be referred for judgement'.[14] It is 'the rational good'. On one side it is happiness, on another it is 'the fulfilment of vital capacity as a consistent whole', while in both aspects together it is happiness found in this fulfilment.[15]

The humanitarian principle

It is basic to the nature of this rational good that it should be universal in the sense of being shared by all. What are the implications of this condition of universality? The concept of humanity was basic to the theory of Hobhouse, and an insistence upon the importance of human rights runs all through his writings. For Hobhouse, any ideal has to have a universal aspect; that is, it must be a good in which all can share, whether this good be freedom, equality or some other ideal. Social development consists in finding adequate expression for the basic needs of *all* individuals in a coherent working scheme. This is to say, the 'rational good' must be participated in by all. By this criterion any system in which one class shares a development at the expense of other classes is incomplete in its growth. A *common* good is the foundation of the rights of all the individuals in a group. For Hobhouse, as for Goethe, there is ultimately only one group, humanity.

Throughout the pages of his *Morals in Evolution* there is the underlying view that, in so far as the principle of humanity is expressed and applied, the distinctions of group-morality have been transcended and societal advancement has occurred. He notes that there are two meanings to the term 'humanity'. In the first place, humanity may refer to a certain quality that is in each individual; and secondly, it can be an expression for the whole race of men. There is a close relationship between these two meanings, for 'humanity' as a whole is the group to which, by reason of the 'humanity' in each of them, all individuals belong.[16] For Hobhouse these two concepts are central to the development of ethico-social codes.

It would be a truism to point out that, as one ultimate community, humanity has never found organized expression. Rights and duties are dependent, as always in the past, upon group-membership rather than pertaining to human beings *qua* human beings. Hobhouse showed that in the modern period humanitarianism is associated with such social and political changes as the abolition of slavery, the breaking down of class privilege and the establishment of equality of opportunity. He also showed that the humanitarian principle is not negative or destructive, but positive and creative. Again he has pointed out that the principle would give free play to the constructive aspects of nationality, in that it would not reduce divergent types and characteristics to a lifeless uniformity. Under the principle of humanitarianism, each national state would represent a part of one greater community in which a common human heritage would be realized without loss of national vitality.

In conclusion, Hobhouse stressed the principle of humanity as antithetical to the group-morality which makes distinctions and raises barriers between individuals. He has shown how harmony has to be universal to be complete in its development, and that it is essentially connected with the idea of constructive societal growth and development. Within the modern period, however, another view of society and progress has arisen which is opposed to the humanitarian outlook.

The biological view of progress

Some of the social consequences of the Darwinian theory have already been described in Chapter 1. Its application to social questions has provided a theoretical obstacle to schemes of social progress. Darwin's followers did not study him sufficiently to recognize that his theory gave a place to co-operation as well as the 'struggle for existence'. The idea arose that scientific justification underlay the view that 'might makes right'. Progress was thought to come about through a conflict in which the fittest would survive; therefore any interference with the struggle was undesirable. To aid the weak would only be to preserve inferior biological stocks.

In sociology, the stress upon biological factors was a retarding influence for a time in that all sociological issues came to be judged in the light of biological principles rather than anthropology, history and culture.

But it was with the social, political and economic consequences of the biological view that Hobhouse was more particularly concerned. The popular misinterpretation of Darwin was well described as follows:

> . . . more and more as the formulae of evolution became
> popular, and gathered about them all the loose and
> unscientific accretions that belong to the language of a half-
> educated society, they spread the belief that for 'science'
> progress was the child of strife, and, therefore, of self-
> assertion, hardness, and moral anarchy. Science was deemed
> to have slain not merely the Christian God, but the
> Christian ethics . . .[17]

According to this biological theory, the highly developed forms of living species were evolved from simpler types by the continual emergence of small variations, of which the fittest survived. It was held that the process of selection went on among human beings as elsewhere; in every population were some individuals who were better fitted, and others who were worse fitted, to face the conditions of existence. Progress, then, was automatically provided for, since the relatively fitter would maintain themselves and reproduce themselves, while the least fit would perish. No further factors in human progress were required.

Here, apparently, was a sound scientific basis for sociology and the formulation of social policies. The problem of social amelioration was reduced to that of determining the conditions under which the best qualities were enhanced and the worst eliminated. On this question, biology spoke with an unequivocal answer. The best was that which survived, and its survival was assured by the progressive elimination of the unfit. Hobhouse expresses this viewpoint in terms of a biblical paraphrase as follows:

Whatsoever soul is hard, whatsoever is unlovely, what there is of self-assertion, if there is any ruthlessness, if there is any unimaginative self-centred push, this type shall prevail, for of such is the process of evolution.[18]

Involved in this outlook is a condemnation of any aid to the weak and the economically powerless. William Graham Sumner was a foremost American exponent of this individualistic outlook, and a contrast can be drawn between his perspective and the humanitarianism of Hobhouse.

A further feature of the evolutionary viewpoint is its fatalistic implication. The human mind tends to be reduced to a glorified reflex action without any special significance in the evolutionary scheme. Man is powerless to control his future, since in the cosmic process the human will and intelligence play a subordinate and unconscious part.

Moral considerations are unlimited, since the right is simply that which is most conducive to survival, and nothing more. The 'rights' of man become the rights of the highwayman or robber baron while social legislation is seen as a retarding factor, since it aids the weak and stifles the qualities of enterprise and self-reliance.

Other implications of the theory are that acute commercial competition can be justified as the process whereby the fittest reach their height of success; bad housing conditions among the poor represent a natural environment for the unfit, and are the means of their elimination. Excessive infant mortality may be vindicated as another means of ridding a society of weaklings; the same applies to pestilence and famine. Tuberculosis acts as a beneficent selection agent, thereby reducing the number of those with weak and unhealthy tissues. Finally, war can be regarded as the method whereby the strong nations claim their just deserts.

The above may seem an exaggerated interpretation of the biological viewpoint, but Hobhouse maintained that it was necessary to draw out the ultimate implications of this outlook for the arguments put forward by the school to be seen with greater clarity for what they were worth. The criticism that Hobhouse gave of these arguments will now be presented and analysed.

Criticism of the biological view

In several realms the theory of evolution had been used to justify unrestricted competition and block the sense of collective responsibility, to justify war and conquest, and to silence the claims of personal justice and international right. Success came to be justified in its own right. In short, the theory of natural selection became 'the great intellectual stand-by of all opponents of social justice'.[19]

Such a view of progress was irrevocably opposed to the ethical-humanitarian outlook of Hobhouse, who attacked it on the grounds that it was logically impossible and would result in the opposing of all types of help and service on behalf of human beings; secondly, the theory gave no valid norm or standard of social progress whatever; thirdly, mutual aid was for Hobhouse a more potent force than hostility. These and other of his arguments will be considered in some detail. According to Morris Ginsberg, the refutation of social Darwinism made by his predecessor has not received the notice that it warrants.[20]

The first point to be recognized in the contribution of Hobhouse is his portraying of the confusion of terms inherent in social Darwinism. The biological view confused evolution with progress. It implied that they were synonymous terms. Hobhouse contends that progress is only one among many possibilities of social evolution. He defines evolution as 'any sort of growth', but progress is 'the growth of social life in respect of those qualities to which human beings attach or can rationally attach value'.[21]

If the concept of progress as a change to something better had been clearly kept in mind, the idea of progress as involving an unrestricted struggle for existence would not have maintained itself for long. Hobhouse has set forth the difference between the two terms, noting that evolution in general is the working out of what there is in things, the coming into actuality of that which existed in potentiality, the bringing to maturity of that which existed in germ.[22] But there is no inherent 'upward' tendency in evolution in so far as it is dependent on a blind struggle for existence. There is nothing to decide whether the new types that arise are capable of a life that is richer or more worth having than the older types. In this connection, the following statement is significant:

> The justification of any breach of ethics by the 'laws of evolution' ceases to be valid as soon as it is understood that those 'laws' have no essential tendency to make for progress.[23]

The next argument brought forth concerns the ambiguity of the term 'fitness'. If it is true that the fittest survive, the question arises, fittest for what? Hobhouse shows that although the term 'fittest' suggests the possession of desirable qualities, as judged by human valuations, the suggestion is not warranted by the assumptions of the argument. An individual may win in a struggle with others because he is harder or more selfish; he may get the better because he is braver or more honourable. The determinant factor is the environment. Only in an environment embodying some measure of justice and humanity will these qualities tend to survive.

The conception of survival of the fittest, then, gives no guarantee of progress in any humane or socialized sense. If the fit are those best adapted to their environment, then the ruthless and unsocial qualities will prevail. Although the simplest way to maintain a position is the primitive way of the strong man armed, it is incompatible with organization in social life. It is, of course, the way to ensure the survival of the types most fitted to survive by that method. This raises another argument against the theory of evolution as applied to social questions, namely, that social organization is by its very nature opposed to the struggle for existence. The mere fact of survival does not prove that a type is in any way 'higher' except in the sense of being able to adapt itself to conditions of unrestricted struggle.

The biological view presupposes that survival constitutes an end in itself. But if one type of social life is regarded as inherently higher and more developed than another, new questions arise which the biologist is not qualified to answer. Fitness to survive does not constitute evidence of superiority in other respects.

Hobhouse has raised a fundamental point in insisting that there is nothing to prove that those who conquer others in the struggle are in any way 'higher' in the sense which human beings attach to that word. Judged by any humane criterion, it is often the worst type that survives, as the fields of competitive commercialism and politics often testify.

Hobhouse has also noted that the claim of aristocracies to biological 'superiority' rests on dubious foundations; by the same token, he pointed out that poverty cannot be regarded as proof of unfitness. Qualities making for economic success are not necessarily the truly social qualities. The terms 'higher' and 'lower' cannot be defined without reference to a reasoned standard of value, and that the biologist has no such standard, other than that of mere survival, is very evident.

Hobhouse also revealed the illogicality of the argument that mutual aid is the great enemy of progress. With Kropotkin, he observed that mutual aid is operative, even in the animal world, and that as the level of life is ascended and the human stage reached, mutual aid increases; certainly, for example, in the parent-child relationship. Since the highest human values are generally supposed to be those involving mutual sympathy and the most highly developed social life, two alternatives present themselves. These valuations are either absolutely false and concepts of higher and lower are meaningless, or progress does not depend on the unmitigated struggle for existence.

The social Darwinian view, as he showed, involved a 'barren tautology'. Progress results from the survival of the fittest, because it is the process in which the fittest survive. Similarly it is always the fittest who survive because their survival proves their fitness. Hobhouse maintained, with reason, that this constitutes a mere playing with words. He clearly demonstrated that when the term 'fit' is used without any attempt to determine what is of value, and what is not, the problem is completely misrepresented.

Nor does his criticism end here. He challenged the biological viewpoint with the fact that the species which are higher—that is, those which show the greater degree of individual development and social co-operation—come relatively late in the course of evolution and tend to dominate the lower types. Social Darwinists modified their theories to meet this kind of rejoinder by substituting the idea of a struggle between groups, according to which war is 'natural' and the means of progress.[24] That this view is untenable need not be emphasized. The group-morality concept as an outcome of a modified biological theory of conflict is incompatible beyond a certain level of social development. The most advanced communities have been those in which the relative anarchy of hostile groups or military domination has been replaced by the widest forms of human association. The self-contradictory character of group-morality is exposed by Hobhouse in the following statement:

> We cannot deliberately and with our eyes open mutilate ethical principles and preserve the portion of them which we wish to cherish, unaffected by that operation. We cannot, for example, refuse the elementary rights of humanity to those who are not of our nation or race, and yet retain the conception of these rights in all their full, living vigour for use amongst ourselves. The obligations recognized under group-morality are never so complete as those which are founded on the conception of common morality. Nor lastly, can we justify aggressive war and conquest as methods of securing race-domination, without thereby laying our own social structure open to serious reactions. If we are to wage war, we must be organized as a military society.[25]

Although written in 1911, the above passage has an obvious applicability to recent world conditions. Hobhouse's conclusion was that 'the uncritical application of biological principles to social progress results in an insuperable contradiction'.[26]

He also expressed a valid contention in insisting that the most eugenic of agencies is not a blind condition of struggle for life, but an atmosphere of justice, equality of opportunity and humaneness. For this reason, the use of eugenic arguments against social legislation to mitigate struggle is seen to be unfounded. Hobhouse rendered a service by demonstrating that social legislation should not be motivated by the aim of accommodating institutions to the survival of the stronger, but rather that it should aim to bring the societal structure in line with principles of social co-operation. In this type of social system, the 'fit' would be those who were capable of becoming useful members of a co-operative society.

Hobhouse was not unaware of the element of competition in social interaction. On the contrary, his writings reveal that he was fully cognizant of this factor in life. He makes an important distinction between what might be termed social and unsocial competition, just as he distinguished between social and unsocial freedom. For he maintained that competition should be a stimulus to action, and was justified as long as the contests were governed by rules embodying justice. If competition represents the improvement of a standard rather than the suppression of individuals, it can become 'an imperfect incarnation of the enthusiasm for progress'.[27]

His contention is based on the distinction between the rivalry of the keenly contested game that is subject to rules of sportsmanship, and the rivalry which is unconcerned with means and quick to plunder and destroy. Social organization tends to limit the competitive struggle, a fact of which the biologist often is unaware.

For Hobhouse, progress is dependent upon the extension of social co-operation, and this involves the organization of life rather than unregulated struggle. The evolution of new types through such a struggle cannot genuinely be considered a permanent condition of progress, for as higher types emerge they tend to emancipate themselves from the struggle and substitute principles of social co-operation and rational organization. Progress in evolution, or the development of higher types, is regarded by Hobhouse as identical with the advance of organization. According to this view, history is a record of a process by which elements of value and rational purpose have come to make themselves felt by organized coherence.

Hobhouse reached these conclusions only after a long and

careful study of history and subhuman evolution. Anarchical struggle is incompatible with organization, and if any social harmony is possible—that is, if society is capable of developing to a more rationally valuable life—the principle of harmonious co-operation, rather than the unmitigated strife that the social Darwinians espoused, will be fundamental.

It is an important consideration that, with the advance of organization, struggle for existence tends to be suppressed. Even in the animal world, the *lower* the species the keener is the struggle for existence; and on the human level, this struggle is at every stage curtailed by a developing civilization. It is the savage who lives in a state of frequent war and blood-feuding, yet it is the savage who has not progressed. In fact, the research of Hobhouse reveals that, from the lowest levels of organic life to civilized man, there is an increase in integration which constantly substitutes, in place of the struggle of isolated atoms, the harmonious concurrence of interdependent parts. At any stage, social life represents some degree of organized structure, and it is in the development of organization that progress consists. Hobhouse has made it abundantly clear that competition is the law of unorganized, co-operation the law of organized, life.

He rejected the egoistic view of man and noted that in several fields of endeavour, including medicine, religion, education and public service, motives other than egoism are found. The phenomena of parental care also tend to refute the egoistic doctrine.

The development of social organization was found by Hobhouse to be correlated broadly with the growth of mind in society. On this view, a just conception of evolution justifies the idea that progress consists in the development of mind, interpreted as an order of ideas by which life is guided.[28]

It may be asked whether the growth of organization does not restrict individual enterprise and initiative. To this the theory of harmonious growth gives an answer, as does the distinction between social and unsocial freedom. In the nineteenth century, the teachings of the laissez-faire school had come to represent what Hobhouse termed 'an unlovely gospel of commercial competition', in which mutual aid and benevolence were decried as preservation of the weak, in accordance with the prevalent scientific opinion.[29] The social and industrial conditions to which this outlook in nineteenth-century England had given rise were such as to demand the introduction of social legislation. A curtailment of the freedom of some individuals was necessary to ensure a greater degree of liberty for a larger number. When free competition for employment involved a working day of twelve to sixteen hours, the liberty of the employing class had to be restricted in favour of the well-being of all workers.

Such social legislation, however, does not preserve inferior types, as the laissez-faire individualist would maintain. It is, of course, perfectly possible that a social type which thrives in a society founded upon principles of justice, freedom and humanity might easily succumb under conditions of barbarism, religious tyranny, anarchy or military despotism. Hobhouse makes a fundamental point when he notes that many who are physically weak may yet possess strong minds that can contribute more to society than strong bodies. He maintained that the best society is, on the whole, that which provides the best environment for those of the most social capacity—that is, those with the highest psychic and intellectual endowments.[30]

Throughout his writings on this topic runs the recognition that, in a keen struggle for existence, the most humane and social types may be vanquished. Humane qualities may well be a disadvantage to their possessor. In periods of re-barbarization, such as war, it is the humane elements and qualities that are in danger. But Hobhouse is equally insistent that it is the humane and creative types which are most valuable to a society. The higher intellectual and moral qualities may be a disadvantage in a competitive régime, yet they are ultimately of high survival value to society. Hobhouse shows a shrewd insight into human nature when he says:

> The greatest offence a man can commit against society is to be in any respect better than society. For such the criminal law has always reserved its worst tortures. But these germs of higher qualities, so dangerous to their possessors, are destined in their fuller development to carry human life to a higher level. What was a short time ago a struggling ideal, is now placidly accepted as normal.[31]

The more advanced social qualities are dependent upon political and other institutions for their survival and growth. They require an environment in which their growth is not impeded, and to which they can contribute.

Hobhouse has made it clear that a system of free competition does not provide such an environment. Nor is it true that the best egoistic desires and impulses of each individual, when left unrestricted, would lead to the harmonious development of all. If this were so, it would constitute a miracle of predetermined harmony. The theory of free competition presupposes freedom, enlightenment and equality of opportunity. Hobhouse showed that these are only obtainable through a system of restraint on the destructive utilization of personal or class ascendancy. The theory assumes organized action for the general welfare; it makes a pretension to a harmony theory of society, but in actuality it is a conflict theory. Hobhouse makes a keen differentiation between a harmony based upon and developing out of social impulses, and a harmony based upon 'a mechanical coincidence of self-centred desires from which the social interest is eliminated'.[32] In the type of society based on the second of these, the destructive types find opportunities offered them by the social institutions and values that are ready at hand. Throughout the writings of Hobhouse there is an emphasis upon the environmental or cultural factors that can make for progress or decay. He showed the importance of culture at a time when this was not so widely recognized and understood as it is today; it is through cultural phenomena that great social changes can occur in the course of a few generations without any change in the average hereditary individual capacities of the members of the group. The 'rugged individualist' and the 'self-made man' are apt to forget that the cultural environment was waiting for them and enabled them to achieve. It is often forgotten by the biologically orientated that culture modifies the form in which native impulses and urges are expressed.

The contributions of Hobhouse on this general theme may be summarized as follows: he set forth some 'prolegomena' to social progress; he showed the ramifications of the concept of 'harmony' as a norm of progress, and applied the principle to contemporary problems; he pointed out the importance of cultural factors in progress; he expressed a humanitarian outlook that was antithetical to the ethos of his time; he gave a reasoned criticism of social Darwinism, pointing out the confusion, weaknesses and false assumptions of this biological viewpoint; he distinguished between social and unsocial competition, and showed that 'free competition' does not provide a favourable environment for those who are most likely to benefit society; finally, he undermined the fatalistic implications of the evolutionary biological point of view.

This last point occupied much of Hobhouse's time and attention, and will be dealt with separately. An analysis of his interpretation of the possibility of social progress will form the subject of Chapter 6.

Notes and References

1. *The Elements of Social Justice*, 1922, Preface, p. iii.

2. *The World in Conflict*, pp. 94, 95.

3. *The Theory of Knowledge*, p. 194.

4. *Social Development, Its Nature and Conditions*, p. 245.

5. ibid., p. 76.

6. *Social Evolution and Political Theory* (1911), pp. 91, 92. See also *Social Development, Its Nature and Conditions*, p. 243.

7. *Democracy and Reaction*, p. 111.

8. *The Rational Good*, pp. 180, 181.

9. *Democracy and Reaction*, pp. 227–9; *The Elements of Social Justice*, pp. 132, 133; and *Liberalism*, p. 112.

10. *The Elements of Social Justice*, p. 24.

11. 'Sociology', *Encyclopaedia of Religion and Ethics*, XI: 663, 1921.

12. *Liberalism*, p. 122.

13. 'The Ethical Basis of Collectivism', *The International Journal of Ethics*, 8: 140, 141, January 1898.

14. *The Rational Good*, p. xxi.

15. ibid., pp. 156, 157.

16. *Morals in Evolution* (1919), pp. 357, 358.

17. *The World in Conflict*, pp. 36, 37.

18. *Development and Purpose*, p. 12.

19. *Social Development, Its Nature and Conditions*, p. 328.

20. J. A. Hobson and Morris Ginsberg, *L. T. Hobhouse, His Life and Work*, pp. 123, 124.

21. *Social Evolution and Political Theory*, p. 8.

22. 'The Roots of Modern Sociology', pp. 22, 23.

23. *Democracy and Reaction*, p. 101.

24. ibid., pp. 86, 87. See also *Social Evolution and Political Theory*, pp. 22–6.

25. *Social Evolution and Political Theory*, pp. 27, 28.

26. ibid., p. 28. In fairness to more recent biological conceptions, it should be noted that revisions of outlook have occurred, and reasoned conceptions of social values have come to assume more importance, as seen in the views of the eugenic school.

27. *The Rational Good*, p. 180.

28. *Democracy and Reaction*, pp. 115, 116.

29. ibid., p. 227.

30. *Social Development, Its Nature and Conditions*, p. 107.

31. *Mind in Evolution* (1926 edition), p. 433.

32. 'Sociology', loc. cit., p. 662.

6   Purposive Social Development as an Aspect of Progress

Mental factors in cultural evolution

It has been seen that, for Hobhouse, progress takes place through harmonious co-operation and rational organization. This is in direct opposition to the biological view, which, stressing natural selection, regards mind and purpose as of minimal significance.

The Hobhouse approach is one that regards progress as the result of the application of intelligence to the conditions of life. To this the biologist of Hobhouse's day would have replied that mind is non-existent, and that man is a reacting mechanism, the product of blind forces. The contemporary behaviourist would express much the same viewpoint. But, for Hobhouse, mind is all-important. His refutation of the mechanist theory was considered in connection with science (pages 31-37), and need not be repeated here. It is noteworthy, though, that his main conclusion is that man unquestionably possesses both mental power and the freedom of will to make us of it.

Indeed, for Hobhouse, evolution represents a development of the power of mind, from the earliest strivings of cortical activity on the subhuman level to the highest contemporary manifestations of mind in science, philosophy and cultural systems. Speaking of this remarkable growth of mind, he says:

> This development is the outstanding feature of the main or 'orthogenic' line of evolution from the Protist to the highest ideals of philosophy and religion. Mind peeps out first in disconnected centres, feebly adjusting impulse to momentary requirements. As it advances in articulation and scope its elements come into relation with one another. The underlying conditions of its activity are brought into consciousness. Ideas dominate action and ideas in turn are brought under

criticism. The very structure which gave rise to mind, and even, one may say, is mind, becomes an object to mind and falls within the grip of its reconstructive energy—a structure that can remake itself.[1]

On this view, mind has its first manifestations on the lowest levels of life and can be traced upwards from its vague impulses to purposes of increasing clearness and scope, in which, even on the subhuman level, the relation of the individual to its fellows plays a role. In man, as co-operation overcomes its early limitations, mind in society develops towards a unity in which can be seen a developing harmony. There is thus an evolution of mind from the dawn of life to the rise of modern thought. In fact, Hobhouse showed empirically[2] that evolution 'upwards' consists in the growth of mind.

Evolution in other directions simply represents the growth of qualities that assist survival. In so far as it determines the behaviour of the individual, and thereby the life and growth of the species, mind becomes a factor in evolution. An animal may give evidence of intelligence to the extent that it utilizes experiences for the achievement of ends or purposes, though, on the lowest levels of animal organisms, intelligence reaches a vanishing-point. On those levels, as Hobhouse showed, purpose is very hard to discern.[3]

He indicated how, with the growth of mind in animals, and later in man, purpose comes into view. In fact, mental development is for Hobhouse a process in which the growth of purpose can be traced. As it emerges, however, the organization of life changes in character and scope. From the lowest levels, where purpose is merely an organization of behaviour directed to the maintenance of the type, it passes to organization directed to the attainment of ends relating to the control of conditions. An evolution of mind, then, is seen from the groping of unconscious effort to the clarity of conscious aims of societal self-direction.

Hobhouse's research indicated that mind is basically teleological in character. Even in its mechanical interactions, there is often found some element of conational adjustment. Natural selection does not explain mind or its origins, nor can it account for developments that have no survival value. Mind can be traced back to the very beginnings of organic life; there is evidence of conative

activity among unicellular organisms. In so far as living phenomena deviate from mechanical principles, the cause may be regarded as conation in some elementary phase, and conation, for
Hobhouse, is the activity of mind, as a mode of behaviour.

Mind constitutes the moving force in all development, on this
view, for 'where there is mind there are order and system, correlation and proportion, a harmonizing of forces, and an interconnection of parts'.[4] Hobhouse saw mind as a purposeful activity that
correlates phenomena, brings elements together, systematizes
them and interconnects them. Mind seeks to interpret and organize
experience. In its highest levels, as in logic and philosophy, it
analyses its own workings. A vast advance is represented, Hobhouse showed, between an animal's first dawn of consciousness
and the human synthesis of the sciences and philosophical analysis.

In this advance, Hobhouse saw the possibility of indefinite
growth and the extended control of mind over the conditions of
life. This extension of control has not been continuous in the past,
but it has proceeded by successive stages of great significance. The
growth of mind runs through the entire history of mind and its
environment. Hobhouse put forward the hypothesis that the conditions making this growth possible are permanent, or are certainly
of very broad range.

In the development of mind there is a self-conscious evolution,
and this determines both the method of advance and the rate of
movement. The entire life-span of the human species is a very
small fraction of the millions of years of organic evolution. But,
in that period, the extension of the scope of mind and its power to
direct natural forces is as great and significant, if not greater, than
all that took place in the far longer era before the emergence of
man. Hobhouse noted that the greater part of man's antiquity
consists of the lowest stage of culture. It was only in the last
6,000 to 8,000 years that the great civilizations arose, and even
these were a very stationary type. Only with the emergence of
Greek civilization did a forward movement begin.[5]

Hobhouse traced the rise of this movement, in support of the
view that control by mind is basic to social and cultural advance.
A study of history is necessary for any guidance of the human
future. Although it is not possible to know the future simply by
reviewing the past, yet control of the future presupposes an
understanding of the present and how it came into being. The

problem is not one of fatalistic prediction, but rather a question of 'focusing racial experience in a way that will throw clear and dry light on the permanent human problems'. Hobhouse saw this as the task of *inductive sociology*. This involved methods of describing and distinguishing the successive stages through which societies had actually passed. In history, and its philosophical interpretation, lay the answers to many vital questions regarding human development.[6]

Hobhouse has given a useful frame of historical reference in the function of mental correlation as seen in its socio-cultural products. The collective stock of knowledge in a group or a culture, the equipment of method and dominating conceptions which make up the working intellectual capital of a particular society, furnish a means of ascertaining the level of development reached.

The growth of mind in society may be considered in several aspects. There is, for instance, man's growing power over nature, as seen in the rise of industrial arts, leading up to modern scientific discoveries. There is his religious and ethical development, as evidenced in the rise of religious and moral concepts and practices, allied with man's dawning comprehension of his place in the universe. A third area of mental development revolves around the growth of communities from the earliest primitive groupings to present-day efforts to evolve a world-society.

The work of Hobhouse in tracing the rise of material culture may be briefly summarized. This rise represents the growth of mind as a control over environmental conditions.

In the development of material culture, Hobhouse distinguished four main stages. The first is that in which primitive man adapts materials from nature to his own uses—for example, the pointing of bones and the stitching of skins. He relies on his own physical strength and gains his food directly from natural products. He is almost entirely dependent upon nature. His dwellings consist of caves and crude huts, health and disease were subjects beyond his range of knowledge, and natural death was attributed to witchcraft. Such was the culture of the lowest hunting tribes, and, apparently, of the Palaeolithic Age.

In the second stage, formless materials are shaped by man to his own purposes, as in the case of the potter's vessel, and spinning and weaving. This, in general, represents the level of contemporary barbarism when not influenced by contact with a more developed culture. Hobhouse notes that it also applies to the more advanced peoples between the close of the Ice Age and the start of recorded history. There is seen the development of specialized industries.

In the third stage, use is made of partly artificial materials. Natural forces, wind and water, are utilized through mechanical devices; agriculture becomes intensive, and species are improved by breeding and grafting. Writing and the use of metal are basic elements of the advance to this stage; they accelerate the formation of settled states. Writing was still ideographic in the middle of the fourth millennium B.C., though the Babylonian script lost this form before 3400 B.C.

The fourth stage that Hobhouse distinguishes may be said to have begun in the middle of the thirteenth century with a series of inventions that led to a new epoch. They included gunpowder, printing, the microscope and the telescope, in addition to the barometer and the thermometer. Iron smelting with coal and the steam engine should also be noted.

In this last stage, substances are decomposed and reconstructed from their elements, as in electrical science and chemistry. The modern period is one in which industry, aided by science, employs the forces of nature for human purposes in engineering, medicine, chemistry and hygiene.

In this control over the natural environment, the role of mental development has affected the whole cultural and social structure.[7] It is contended that Hobhouse has brought forth empirical evidence in support of his argument that human development takes place through the action of mind when applied to problems; the inventions, discoveries, and cultural advances outlined above were essentially intellectual achievements, as is all culture.

Hobhouse revealed a third advance, namely, man's developing power to reconstruct his mental universe and to inquire into the causes of phenomena, as a means of control leading to societal self-direction. He noted that in early society the power of tradition is reflected in the dependence upon magic. Spells and charms are used to bring about desired results in the objective order, and supernatural causes are regarded as omnipotent. Mind is attributed to inanimate objects, and emotional superstition dominates thought and action. Indeed, the main texture of thought for primitive peoples is constituted by magical and animistic ideas.

The 'checks of truth' are lacking, as is the ability to grasp certain distinctions—for example, those between image and object. Experience for the savage has been narrow, and he thinks and acts practically only in relation to the teachings of that narrow experience. At this stage, the elements of articulate thought are still in the process of being formed.

What Hobhouse did in this connection was to indicate the type of thought-patterns current at this primitive level. Among these peoples, differences of culture and economy could imply an extension of organized experience, and so of organized thought. But, among primitives generally, there is a great confusion of categories, as evidenced by animism. Ideas have not yet acquired a definite outline or a permanent and recognizable identity. With the advance of the industrial arts, simple wisdom is enlarged. In this advance, commonsense ideas are used in their normal application, as are observation, comparison and practical tests. 'Commonsense ideas' in the earliest groups are exemplified by the case of the savage who sharpens a spear-point.

The emphasis in this study of ideas was laid upon the stock of knowledge in a group or culture. For Hobhouse, this stock of knowledge—the dominating conceptions, the thought-ways, presuppositions, inventive gains and religio-philosophical outlook—constituted the 'working intellectual capital' of the group. He furnished an interesting frame of reference which might be utilized in the sociology of knowledge. The fact that the contribution of Hobhouse along this particular line is little known is no indication of its relative value and potentialities.

One important advance that Hobhouse indicated centred around the invention of writing. This made records possible; intellectual achievements could be preserved, communicated and handed on. The work of the past became a foundation for future thinkers. In written work, statements and ideas are capable of being seen in relation to each other, and systematic thought is enabled to develop. Hobhouse supported this claim with material drawn from the history of Egypt, Babylonia, China and India. He named this era as that of 'proto-science'. It was marked by reflective theories of life, resulting in a religion, a metaphysics and an ethics.[8]

Similarly, he noted that a new epoch arose with early Greek philosophy. Nature was interpreted by the Greeks on the basis of crude but intelligible generalizations of experience. Later efforts constructed reality by means of an examination of thought and its products. For example, Socrates attempted to criticize thought-products themselves, and this involved the accurate definition of meanings and the referring of concepts to the experience they appeared to formulate, or to comparison with other concepts. On these methods, Plato and his followers constructed their theories, working out the fundamental categories of experience.

Hobhouse analysed the work of Aristotle and Euclid. He concluded that the main effort of the Greek thinkers lay in the construction of the conceptual order rather than the formulation of valid hypotheses. But, with philosophy, went the development of mathematics in Euclid, mechanics in Archimedes and astronomy in Ptolemy.

Hobhouse pointed to Greek thought as a stage in human development. It represented the rise of a systematic, critical method involving inquiry and proof, in which the early sciences were dependent upon the analysis of common ideas or elementary data of experience. Similarly, the Socratic method involved the critical examination of concepts. This was an advance over the loose ideas of 'common sense', and involved a basic reconstruction both in method and in data.

The world of common sense advanced on uncritical lines and built up an order of ideas which had practical value but did not reflect the objective order accurately. Higher developments consisted of more critical methods of organizing experience, including the recognition of the processes by which results are obtained. In the ancient world, this began in the demand for a logical treatment of concepts and with attention being given to considerations of unity, system, accuracy and interrelation.

Hobhouse showed that, in the modern world, this movement is carried further by the systematic application of critical methods to the extension of empirical data. Controlled experiment replaces crude observation, and instruments of calculation are invented and perfected. The subjective factor is recognized and taken into account, while experimental assumptions and axioms are utilized and criticized. Thought itself is seen to be a growing structure—a point emphasized by Hobhouse himself—and its first principles are brought under examination in order that the results of mental activity may be refined and extended.

From the lowest stages, then, in which the difficulty of forming any conceptions prevents the full distinction of the familiar categories of experience, there is an advance to the level of concrete ideas in which categories are grasped and concrete experience is reflected fairly distinctly in mental pictures and images.

The more accurate reflection of the objective order, through the use of instruments of measurement and keener definitions of ideas, makes up the later stages of mental development. An important distinction is that it is only in the latest stages that the mind grasps the conditions and possibilities of its own growth, and sees the opportunity for self-direction.

Hobhouse calls this last stage the level of 'experiential construction'. It is one in which the human mind interprets and enlarges the range of its experiences through methods of calculation and instruments of measurement which increase the power of human sense-organs. 'Experiential construction', then, depends on the logic of observation and experiment, mathematical analysis and instruments of measurement.

An essential feature of this stage is that measurement alone is not sufficient as a means of interpreting the objective order. Calculation and instruments are only aids in the interpretation of reality. The human mind still has to use powers of reflection, reasoning, analysis and comparison, without which scientific instruments are in themselves insufficient.

To summarize this evolution of mental power, four stages appear to be dominant. They will be given in Hobhouse's own words:

In the development of thought we distinguished four phases, in the first of which we supposed general ideas to be in process of formation, leading up to a second stage in which they become sufficiently definite to form the elements of that which we call the commonsense order. In the third, they were so analysed and interconnected as to establish conceptual systems, deductive sciences, physical and metaphysical theories, leading to the fourth stage, the critical reconstruction of experience which we hold to be the problem of thought in our own time.[9]

Other stages were posited by Hobhouse[10] on the basis of the growth and extension of the mental function of correlation, but as this lies in the field of comparative psychology rather than the sociology of knowledge or the history of culture, it will not be given in this study. It should be noted, however, that Hobhouse was aware of the hypothetical character of the divisions he discerned.

He concluded that there is a rough and indirect, but nevertheless real and far-reaching, connection between intellectual and social development. This connection is rough and indirect because social organization represents the work of many minds in interaction, and this interaction involves both conflict and co-operation. The life of a civilization nevertheless tends to reflect the level of mental growth that has been reached by that civilization. Although mental development is only one side of social growth, Hobhouse has rendered a service to social science by emphasizing the place of intellectual factors in evolution and by outlining certain historical stages in cultural advance that presupposed the developing power of mind in society.

Non-linear social development

Hobhouse insisted upon the non-linear nature of social development. Since the later nineteenth century saw the rise of many linear or 'straight-line' theories of progress, this point is important. He was one of the early writers who showed the error of this type of thinking. Through his study of history and comparative institutions, Hobhouse clearly recognized that 'progress' had not been continuous, as some of his contemporaries maintained. Throughout his writings there is seen an awareness of the fact that development on one side of society may bring repression or retardation on another side.

Hobhouse emphasized that any culture is made up of many interacting strands. Although the development of thought is a strand that can be discerned to proceed with regularity, on account of tradition, yet even here there is no straightforward continuous movement. In no area of social or cultural development is there any automatic forward movement towards 'progress'. Judged by certain criteria, it is possible to aver that past epochs represent an advance over the present in their religion, social organization, individual happiness and industrial objectives.

The development of machinery is cited by Hobhouse[11] as an advance on one side of life that brought retrogression on other sides. Although man's control over nature was aided, the rise of industry lowered the living conditions of the working classes and accelerated man's ability to destroy.

A final consideration regarding social development and progress is put forward by Hobhouse. He notes that it is unscientific and illogical to conclude, on the basis of false comparisons, that present-day society has made no progress over the past. For example, the view was sometimes put forward in England that contemporary English society did not represent any advance over some favoured epoch in history, such as the time of Euripides. This viewpoint involves the failure to see that the British people are not Greeks, but Teutons and Celts, and that their 'progress' or lack of it should be measured by what the Teutons and Celts were at the time, rather than the Greeks.[12]

Some thinkers who would admit the validity of this point would still maintain that the interaction of social and cultural forces precludes the possibility of control by mind. To this Hobhouse would reply that, behind culture, lies the mind that produced culture. Further, what appears to be the blind march of events is in actuality the interplay of many human wills and purposes, and mind is at work in all these individual purposes.

Although social change may begin in an unconscious way, it later nevertheless comes under the dominion of mind as rational control extends its sway. Hobhouse maintained that it is in the nature of mind to bring life under its control. This control over the conditions of life is a basic element of the theory of progress put forward by Hobhouse. The remainder of this chapter will deal with this view of mind as a factor in social advance, and with its implications for man's future.

Mind as an agency of rational control

In opposition to such thinkers as Bury, who maintains that the question of progress is one that lies beyond man's power to affect, Hobhouse contends that there is no cause of progress outside the human mind and will.[13] On this view, it is the application of mental power to social problems and relations that underlies social development in the normative sense.

The research of Hobhouse showed, however, that it is only in its most developed form that intelligence becomes a significant factor in the evolution of higher types. On the animal level, intelligence is only one of many qualities which a species uses to maintain itself. On the human level, for Hobhouse, a forward movement takes place only in so far as the mind widens its scope and forms general conceptions of social welfare, religion and science. Civilization does not proceed in a steady general advance, but, with the rise of a new conception, or a fresh application of mental power, new movements develop, and from a combination of many new movements social evolution proceeds.

The function of intelligence is, for Hobhouse, one of correlating experience, and the development of intelligence involves a widening of the scope of this function, and a perfecting of its execution. On this view, the organization of life, both in individual and social experience, rests upon intelligence. Indeed, 'without intelligence, the race is not master of its fate'.[14] It is, then, intelligence that makes evolution possible. When man's evolution in the past and present is seen as the beginning stage of a further growth, and when the comprehension of this growth operates in the realm of social standards and concepts, evolution becomes conscious and capable of being directed towards an end.

Hobhouse attempted to disprove the view that the human mind and will had played no part in the movement of society. The sketch of cultural development given previously is testimony to the extension of mind as a purposeful force. A conclusion that Hobhouse reached was that 'a scientific analysis of individual and social life leaves us with no doubt as to the reality of human purpose as an agency in the movements of life'.[15]

It was one of Hobhouse's main efforts to portray the development of purposeful intelligence in evolution and social growth.[16]

Individual and social purposes have to act, though, within a cultural milieu that involves a tradition. The writings of Hobhouse portray tradition as a force that can make for progress. Civilization is an intellectual achievement, and he portrayed how the cumulative growth of knowledge and mental power can be explained, at least in part, through the existence of tradition. Through tradition each mental acquisition becomes the basis for further advance. Past gains become foundations for future achievement, despite the fact that tradition can, as a conservative force, make for retardation.

It is through tradition that human mental power is allowed to develop. Hobhouse goes so far as to declare that:

> The underlying truth of history is the opening out of the
> power of mind in man. This is pre-eminently a social
> process . . . and it operates through tradition, mutual
> stimulus, selection and co-operation.[17]

The growth of mental power, made possible by tradition, is also revealed in the development of religion. Hobhouse traced certain aspects of this growth, from the early attempts to satisfy human needs by constructing a world of magic and spirits, to the most advanced conceptions of religious philosophy and ethics. Mind is seen in the building of religious theories of nature and life, theories which act as controls over conduct. Religion for Hobhouse is a 'system of conceptions built up by the aid of imagination out of inward and outward experiences', and in this it is like art and science. Religion represents one form in which human experience is organized, and this organization is essentially the work of mind.[18] In religion is seen one means of social control, by which action is shaped and guided by the conception of a personal or social good.

Similarly, the vast research of Hobhouse in comparative ethics testified that the existence of codes and religious beliefs makes possible the guidance of life by principles which can be taught, and later criticized. This constitutes one method by which society has in the past indirectly sought to control its own future.

Hobhouse has portrayed how the development of ethical control is essentially the work of reason. In becoming rational, man became moral, and, indeed, 'progress has consisted in the realization of the conditions of full social co-operation and in the extension of the rational control of life'.[19]

This control is both scientific and ethical; it extends over the realm of human conduct as well as the conditions of external nature. For Hobhouse it is in this rational organization of life that progress is to be found. The application of ethical principles to the social and political structure represents for him rational social guidance. In this view, human evolution is based not on conflict, but on principles of co-operation and rational organization. The formation of a peaceful order involves the recognition of rights and duties which make for social solidarity, and the extension of this recognition represents the development of the humanitarian principle.

Hobhouse saw ethical progress as, essentially, a progress of ethical conceptions, working through tradition and expressed in social relations. Advancement, on this side, consists in the rationalization of the moral code, which becomes more coherent and clear, and more consistently and universally applied, as society develops.

It is granted that, in the evolution of social codes and traditions, non-rational factors play their part, but, as the mind uses its powers, codes are rationalized and their underlying principles are brought to light and criticized, and in this process the great ethical and religious systems are born. They aim at the rational guidance of life.

Hobhouse would maintain that ethical conceptions and their development represent the work of rational intelligence. The force of custom, human needs and interaction is not to be overlooked, but the rise of new ideas of human right and welfare is attributed to the mind of man. Progress is made possible, on this view, through the rational organization of life, under ethico-humanitarian principles.

Morals in Evolution would appear to support the view that ethical history has largely consisted in the growth of the intelligent guidance of life through codes and concepts which become more rational and humane with social evolution. In connection with this ethical development, Hobhouse has said:

> It is the history of the transformation whereby the blindly-
> followed custom arising like an animal instinct, and with
> little more understanding than the instinct of the animal,
> in response to the hard and narrow conditions of early
> social life, becomes transformed into the instrument of a
> clear and comprehensive intelligence envisaging the total life
> and happiness and development of humanity.[20]

It is this later control of conditions by rational intelligence that Hobhouse emphasizes, as a means of joining the social and the ethical in development. The rational urge, he points out, lies behind the work of the intellect and the ethical consciousness, and the expansion of mind in one direction involves a development in another, in breadth of view, more rational method and clarity of thought and insight into the place of man in the world order.

With the growth of this ideal in rationality, and the control by mind over its own conditions, social and ethical development become one.

In conclusion, it may be noted that Hobhouse has shown how human evolution represents a rise of the power of mind in man, as a consequence of which life becomes more organized, rational and humane. He posits a further stage in which the future of the race will become 'the all-embracing purpose of action'. Although this ideal organization may be remote, he suggests that the trend of theoretical science is towards the discovery of the conditions of human development, while the trend of the ethical spirit is towards making that development the supreme object of action'; and, in this union, 'knowledge of the underlying conditions of development would become the basis of a system of conduct designed to promote development'.[21]

There is validity in Hobhouse's claim that the concept of social progress as a conscious movement towards the reorganization of society in accordance with ethical ideas is not contradictory or disharmonious. The claim is one based on the facts of man's evolution, and it is itself the outcome of higher evolutionary tendencies.

Progress represents a growth in the rational control of life-conditions, under the guidance of mind, leading to a harmony of individual and societal development. The possibility of such progress in the human future will form the topic of the next section, with some consideration of Hobhouse's analysis of the modern contemporary situation. The arguments for a telic view of mind will be analysed.

The present and the future

Hobhouse made a thought-provoking analysis of his contemporary world-situation during the years just before his death in 1929. While the view of rational co-operation as the means of progress may seem an over-facile optimism, it should be noted that Hobhouse was fully aware of the existence of conflict in social evolution. He wrote about the mood of Europe in the months and year prior to August 1914,[22] and in his study of social development took account of the modern problems of reconciliation that centred around class antagonisms, racial hatreds, colour prejudices and national rivalries. The following statement, written in 1924, is pertinent here:

> The world almost against its will has become one vast
> society in which all communities are members one of another,
> seeing that any one of them may be vitally affected by that
> which is most remote, but it has neither the spirit of unity,
> nor the clear sense of a common interest, nor an adequate
> mechanism which might at least maintain the externals of
> orderly peace.[23]

Nevertheless, despite the enormous complexity of modern problems, Hobhouse contended that their very complexity was evidence of a richness of social organization that earlier societies lacked. Very often the social harmony existing in primitive society was only maintained because that society was not capable of higher organization. More modern conflict, on the other hand, gives evidence of a higher development and the potentiality of a greater and fuller harmony.

In addition, the growth of the power of mind has enlarged the sense of possibilities in human achievement. Herein lies Hobhouse's main reason for the contention that progress may reasonably be expected in human affairs: namely, the fact that the conditions of life are now being brought under man's control. This view is set forth in a striking passage:

> The distinguishing characteristics of our time are that
> civilization for the first time has the upper hand, that the
> physical conditions of life have come and are rapidly coming
> more and more within human control, and that at least the
> foundations have been laid of a social order which would
> render possible a permanent and unbroken development.[24]

With this increase of human control, societal self-direction becomes possible. Only when mind assumes a stage of development in which it can control all life-conditions is the danger of cultural extinction prevented. For Hobhouse, it is here that modern culture has made its main advance: namely that, through science, the control of physical life is being made possible, while in ethics and religion concepts of world-unity are being formed.

This constitutes a more recent statement of the Comtean conception of a self-directing humanity, the view that the race is now at a level at which it understands its past development and is becoming self-directing. Hobhouse also expressed a point of some significance when he said that the very idea of progress is a product of modern times. It is only since the middle of the eighteenth century that it has become prominent. As an object of human endeavour, progress is a late arrival.

Although Hobhouse lived before the era of atomic energy, he expressed the pertinent view that psychic energy, even as revealed in war, was not likely to be forever used for destructive ends. He regarded this outcome as 'inherently improbable', since partial social organization, despite its dangers, was the means through which greater unity was made possible. A further significant claim is that, even if internal violence were to result in the disintegration of modern culture, something would remain. Just as the breaking-up of ancient civilization did not bring about a complete cultural finale, so present-day civilization would bequeath ideals of humanity, liberty and the control of nature. These represent modern achievements.[25]

The highest stage of mental development is one in which humanity understands the conditions underlying its own growth and the end of its action. The theory of mind put forward by Hobhouse suggests an affirmative answer to the question of whether the race is capable of forming an inclusive ideal of the end desired, and of bringing itself to this destination. For the analysis of the growth of mind supports the theory that mind in society is gradually becoming master of the conditions of its own growth and life. From this it follows that if past conditions which have dominated human development can be rationally controlled, they will not in the future dominate this development in the same way. The future course of events will therefore not be like that of the past.

Because man is a purposeful being, he can participate in the direction of his own evolution to the extent of controlling his racial future. Self-evolution becomes the *human* responsibility. Hobhouse suggests therefore that control over conditions by the human mind is likely to increase in the future. When the growth of mind is regarded as the main fact of human progress, the past appears as a period of preparation. It was basic to Hobhouse's study of knowledge that thought is a growing structure, as is knowledge. Thought extends its domain and refashions its conceptions. With growth in knowledge goes a corresponding growth in control. A greater, rather than smaller, degree of rational control can be expected.

The telic view of mind presupposes a faith in the power of human reason, with the implication that it will ultimately triumph over partial views and half-knowledge.[26] In this rationalistic perspective, knowledge is a dynamic growing element in a larger whole, rather than a closed circle. While the consequences of knowledge-expansion cannot be predicted, it may be asserted that the more territory mind brings under its control, the larger the unconquered region beyond appears. Says Hobhouse:

> We stand on the edge of illimitable, unexplored regions,
> into which our vision penetrates but a little way. But at
> least we can dismiss as foolish the fear that science will
> exhaust the interest of reality, or peace destroy the excitement
> of life, or the reign of reason cramp imagination.[27]

Hobhouse here expresses a point that is often overlooked: that progress, like knowledge, is not an end but a beginning. It is a harmonious growth, not a fixed destination. The ideal of self-direction is itself a dynamic concept, not a static symbol. It is also apparent, as Hobhouse and others showed, that society is a growing phenomenon, and in so far as the sociologist understands its laws he can hope to modify it intelligently. It was upon this idea of a self-directing humanity that Comte based his ethics and his religion.

The influence of Comte is plainly revealed in Hobhouse's writings dealing with societal self-direction. Comte showed that the significance of the history of science lies in its portrayal of a developing control over life-conditions—a view that was shared by Hobhouse. In this ascending mastery by man over his environment, there is first seen the dominance by him of physical nature, then organic nature, and finally the various conditions of human life and development. Rational guidance of life is increased with every advance in this scientific mastery.

A further argument in favour of the telic view of mind is, for Hobhouse, that, in the past 150 years, there has taken place a revolution in man's rule over physical nature; and there have been signs, both before and since Hobhouse's death in 1929, that the next 100 years will bring an even greater control in this area. The scientific treatment of health and disease, and laws of physical life generally, is not more than a century old. The knowledge gained in that time regarding disease and physical heredity is greater than all that had gone in the preceding 2,000 years.

It is significant that, though Hobhouse lived in England, a country which during his lifetime produced little work of a strictly sociological nature, he nevertheless predicted that this new science would be the means of accelerating the betterment of human relations. This was partly due to Comte's influence. Speaking of sociology, Hobhouse said:

> Here . . . we have a science in its infancy, but the mere attempt to deal with public questions in the spirit of science implies an advance ethical as well as intellectual. At any rate it is on the possibility of controlling social forces by the aid of social science as perfectly as natural forces are controlled at present by the aid of physical science, that the permanent progress of humanity must depend.[28]

Herein lies another implied argument for the telic view of mind that he set forth, and the possibility of societal self-direction. At the outset of his teaching career at the University of London, Hobhouse said that 'the demand for sociological knowledge is itself a feature of modern social evolution, and its growth is intimately related to other processes of social development'.[29]

The conclusion may be reached that, in orthogenic evolution, there is a constant growth of mind in scope and therefore in power, culminating in man's ability to control his own future. The development of mind gathers speed and finally becomes a steady onward movement whose goal is the control by the human intellect of the conditions of its life and growth.

Hobhouse stresses the fact that the actual degree of harmonious development reached by any group represents 'the available amount of moral wisdom' current in that society. The social structure is 'the proffered solution of a problem' that varies around the theme of man and his world, and the solution reached is a further reflection of the amount of this wisdom. He notes that it is only through an advanced growth of this wisdom that the more profound human problems become recognized. The survival of civilization, and the problem of world-organization, are for Hobhouse dependent upon this 'available moral wisdom' among the peoples of the world. The phrase indicates the concern of Hobhouse for ethical as well as intellectual self-direction.[30]

His works would suggest the conclusion that upon an inductive theory of evolution the growth of mind in society is a reality, and that this growth is the condition of progressive harmony; further, that where this control is lacking, progress is retarded; the range of control today is greater than at any previous period; and finally, that this mental growth has proceeded sufficiently to indicate that the possibility of developing harmony in social life is a reality to which all evolution points.

Although the future cannot be predicted, the fact of a self-conscious evolution of humanity is in itself of vast significance, for it points to the possibility of a greater social harmony than any known in the past. Hobhouse concludes one of his works with a passage that describes this harmony in striking terms:

> The rational harmony contemplated here means neither more
> nor less than the more perfect adjustment and co-ordination
> of the permanent forces that make for betterment in the
> movement in the world, and which, slowly gathering vitality
> as civilization advances, now mainly require a fuller and
> more adequate expression to secure to them the ultimate
> control of the movement of social life.[31]

Chapter 7 will compare the contributions of Hobhouse with the work of other sociologists in showing the significance of mind in the human past, in pointing out the implications of a telic view of mind, in describing progress in terms of a rational organization in which the concept of harmony is dominant and in criticizing contrary views of progress.

Notes and References

1. 'The Philosophy of Development', pp. 174, 175.

2. *Mind in Evolution* (1901).

3. *Democracy and Reaction*, pp. 103, 104.

4. *Mind in Evolution* (1926), p. 6.

5. ibid., p. 441.

6. See F. Muller-Lyer, *The History of Social Development* (London: Allen & Unwin, 1920), translated by E. C. Lake and H. A. Lake, with Introductory Note by Hobhouse, pp. 5, 6.

7. *Development and Purpose* (1927), pp. 194–9.

8. *Social Development, Its Nature and Conditions*, pp. 230, 231.

9. op. cit., p. 194.

10. See *Mind in Evolution* for a treatment of this topic.

11. *Development and Purpose*, pp. 193–233.

12. ibid., p. 235, note. See also *Social Development, Its Nature and Conditions*, pp. 333, 334. Ample indications of Hobhouse's insistence on the non-linear character of social evolution are to be found in *Social Development*, pp. 90, 305–8, 311; *Development and Purpose*, xxiii–xxiv, 190, 191; *Morals in Evolution* (1919), pp. 31, 32; *Social Evolution and Political Theory*, p. 160; and *Liberalism*, pp. 136, 137.

13. *Social Development, Its Nature and Conditions*, pp. 337, 338. See also J. B. Bury, *The Idea of Progress* (London: Macmillan, 1920).

14. *Mind in Evolution* (1926), p. 429.

15. Review of J. S. Mackenzie, *Lectures on Humanism, with Special Reference to its Bearings on Sociology* (London: Swan, Sonnenschein, 1907), in *Sociological Review*, I: 306, July 1908.

16. The more distinctly philosophical side of his work was concerned with the ultimate implications of the concept of purpose in interpretations of reality. Herein lies one of the elements of his theory that distinguished him from Comte, for the Positivist approach to ultimate questions was one of scepticism. The Comtean positivist would maintain, however, that progress is a genuine possibility for human endeavour, and to this extent Hobhouse is in agreement with Comte. They would both hold that progress is to be brought about through the activity of mind as a controlling power. To this Hobhouse would add that an increased application of mental power will be necessary, if past achievements are to be transcended, for the harmony of society rests on the control of conditions by man's mind. This control involves both human conduct and the external environment.

17. *Social Development, Its Nature and Conditions*, p. 314. For further references to the cumulative power of tradition, see ibid., pp. 184, 185, 309. Also *Social Evolution and Political Theory*, p. 154; and *Morals in Evolution* (1919), p. 635.

18. *Mind in Evolution*, p. 346.

19. *Social Evolution and Political Theory*, p. 156.

20. Review of Edward A. Westermarck, *The Origin and Development of the Moral Ideas* (London: Macmillan, 1908), in *Sociological Review*, II: 405, October 1909.

21. *Mind in Evolution*, p. 394.

22. *The World in Conflict*, 1915. See also 'The Social Effects of the War', *Atlantic Monthly*, CXV: 544–50, April 1915.

23. *Social Development, Its Nature and Conditions*, p. 30. See also *Development and Purpose*, pp. 225, 226.

24. *Social Evolution and Political Theory*, p. 163.

25. *Development and Purpose*, pp. xxxv, xxxvi.

26. *The Theory of Knowledge*, pp. 607, 618–20; see also p. 602.

27. *Morals in Evolution*, p. 611.

28. ibid., p. 634.

29. 'The Roots of Modern Sociology', in *Inauguration of the Martin White Professorships of Sociology, 17 December 1907* (London: John Murray, 1908), p. 7.

30. See *Social Development, Its Nature and Conditions*, pp. 69, 305; *Development and Purpose*, p. 232. See also 'Democracy and Civilization', *Sociological Review*, XIII: 125, July 1921.

31. *The Rational Good* (1921), p. 234.

7 Comparisons with Other Sociologists

How are Hobhouse's contributions to sociology related to the work of other sociologists? The present chapter will deal with this question, noting both the similarities and differences of viewpoint between Hobhouse and other writers. The main emphasis will centre upon the specific contributions made in the particular areas under review.

Criticism of mechanism

The first of these contributions concerns Hobhouse's criticism of the mechanistic approach to society and behaviour. The background from which this criticism arose was mentioned in connection with the influences upon Hobhouse, and in the chapter that dealt specifically with mechanism. What have other sociologists said on this subject?

What Hobhouse did was to analyse the principles and assumptions underlying mechanism and trace their historical roots back to Newtonian physics and the dominance of the mathematical outlook of the seventeenth and eighteenth centuries. He pointed out that it was not the object of science to reduce everything to matter, and that the 'scientific' attitude did not consist in the elimination of the non-material. Further, he analysed behaviour on the animal level and showed that some forms of behaviour bear no likeness to machine processes. On the basis of this empirical research in comparative psychology, he drew a clear and valid distinction between the categories of mechanism and teleology. His contribution, in effect, is that he undermined the theoretical bases of a viewpoint which underlay much physical and social science. He also pointed out the emasculated quality of any sociology founded on mechanistic or behaviourist principles. But his central conclusion related to the fact that human behaviour is not mechanical, but teleological or purposive. Human beings interact on the basis of thought, feeling and will, and the element of conscious purpose runs through these interactions as an integral element. As a result of observation and empirical investigation, Hobhouse showed that mechanism and behaviourism are invalid in their basic presuppositions, and that they result in an inadequate interpretation of societal phenomena.

The first sociologist who will be contrasted with Hobhouse in this field is Pitirim A. Sorokin. Sorokin's essential contribution in this connection is two-fold. In the first place, he has described and analysed the sociocultural manifestations of the mechanistic outlook on human life. In two of his works,[1] he has in particular expressed the view that present-day society is mechanistic in its approach to values and in its denial of certain psychic values. Sorokin uses the term 'sensate' to describe contemporary culture, and he has studied this culture in relation to past epochs that were 'sensate' or non-sensate in varying degrees. He finds that modern culture is mechanistic in its sensatism, its concern for material things, and its denial and repudiation of intellectual and psychic values. This conclusion is reached upon the basis of an extensive culture-history in which a cyclical theory of cultural evolution plays an interpretative role.

What Sorokin has contributed has been essentially a study of the mechanistic aspects of culture, including a denunciation of this mechanistic or 'sensate' element. This is by no means the same as a reasoned criticism of mechanism *per se*. This latter was the contribution of Hobhouse. Although Sorokin did not look with favour upon mechanism, he did not make a detailed analysis of its basic assumptions. He rather dealt with its manifestations in contemporary culture—twentieth-century emphasis upon the material aspects of human association, behaviouristic and nihilistic views on life, lack of concern for what he regarded as enduring values, and a resultant disorganization in society. At the same time, he sees the solution to this present dilemma in the gradual evolution of an 'ideational' culture, in which the main values will centre upon intellectual and psychic values rather than upon the material aspects of life.

While Sorokin and Hobhouse both wrote concerning the mechanistic outlook, they attacked the problem from different angles and viewpoints. Hobhouse went to the roots of mechanism, and Sorokin dealt with its socio-cultural consequences. A further contribution of Sorokin that should be mentioned consists in his historical account of mechanism as a school of thought. He has noted that the essential characteristic of mechanism is a monistic conception of the universe as a whole, and the universal application of all natural law. He points out that mechanism can be traced back to Thales, who believed that all was water in essence; since the time of Thales, periods of marked advancement in mathematics and physics have resulted in their conclusions being transported to the field of social life, and mechanistic interpretations have resulted therefrom. This was particularly true of the seventeenth century.

Sorokin further notes that serious misinterpretations may arise from carrying the laws of mechanics and physics into the realm of social phenomena. Such a transference is apt to result in inadequate views of the social reality; people are seen merely as physical phenomena. The Italian sociologist, Pareto, is criticized by Sorokin in this connection. Pareto had the conception of a 'social physics', and involved in this was a confusion between the categories of the mechanical and the distinctively social.[2]

This particular aspect of Sorokin's writing is more akin to the criticism of mechanism made by Hobhouse. Sorokin's criticism, however, is more in the nature of a historical evaluation of mechanistic theories with special stress upon those of Pareto. His remarks about the tendency of mechanism to reduce societal phenomena to material phenomena are only incidental to his historical account of this school of thought. He does not write, as did Hobhouse, in terms of the purposive and the organic. Nor has he analysed mechanism from a psychological angle, as did Hobhouse in his investigation upon animals.

Another sociologist who has given a criticism of mechanism is Clarence Marsh Case. Although his writings upon this topic are not as extensive as those of Hobhouse or Sorokin, they are worthy of note for their anti-mechanistic and anti-materialistic tone. Case points out that, according to the naturalistic conception of the world, nothing in the universe possesses any enduring value or meaning whatsoever. For the mechanist, there is no such thing as progress. Indeed, Case claims that mechanism lacks the logical basis for the conception of progress.

Writing in 1931, Case observed that there had taken place a change of outlook in science and philosophy. A 'post-Newtonian' brand of science had arisen, of which Sir Arthur Eddington and A. N. Whitehead were outstanding exponents. The mental climate had changed, partly on account of the breaking-up of the Newtonian ideas of matter as a hard substance. Matter had come to be regarded as a form of energy, and the philosophical consequences of this change of thought were such as to allow room for religious faith and values. Biology, similarly, had been freed from the tyranny of mechanism, while in psychology the Gestalt school represented a corrective to a sterile behaviourism.[3]

Case's contribution to the literature of this general topic consisted in his recording the change in scientific thought. Although no originality can be claimed for this, there is evidenced an awareness on his part of the philosophical assumptions of science. What Case did was to note that the foundations of crude philosophical materialism had been discredited as philosophy and undermined as science.

Hobhouse was partly responsible for this change in thought. He was one of those actually to examine and criticize the foundations of mechanism at the turn of the century. The behaviouristic claim that mind and purpose are non-existent received a challenge from his empirical studies, and the materialistic view that reduces human progress and values to meaninglessness were similarly attacked in a later statement of the contrary outlook.[4]

It would be unfair to dismiss Case as simply having recorded a change in thought-fashion and as having done nothing more. All through his writings runs an emphasis on the point of view that is opposed to mechanism. He stressed human values, the concept of progress and the function of religion in progress, as did Hobhouse. Case noted that psychological behaviourism involves the carrying of physical science methods into a field where they are certain to miss the essence of the phenomena under investigation.[5] In fact, 'the more mechanistic we become the more we miss the rich meaning and significance of the concrete realities of the living world'.[6]

Hobhouse and Case shared the same general viewpoint in their opposition to mechanistic interpretations of man and society. Hobhouse was more prolific in his writings on this topic, but he was closer in time to the issue of mechanism and materialism in the scientific ethos of the later nineteenth century. He was studying behaviour empirically in these years in an attempt to undermine the current viewpoint. What Case had to say about mechanism came later, but in its essential stand it was in accordance with Hobhouse's findings.

This would also apply to the contribution of another American sociologist, Charles A. Ellwood. Ellwood was cordial to the outlook of both Hobhouse and Case, though there is more of an affinity between him and Hobhouse. Ellwood's year of study in England under Hobhouse (1914–15) influenced his sociological outlook considerably, and throughout the pages that follow it will be seen that they were very close on many points. Ellwood seemed to have more in common with Hobhouse than probably any other writer on sociological subjects, with the one exception of Morris Ginsberg.

Ellwood dealt more with applications of mechanism in psychology and sociology than did Hobhouse. He made vigorous attacks upon behavourism and the interpretation of human society derived therefrom. He noted that behaviourism does not describe societal phenomena in the totality of its aspects, but gives a grossly inadequate view of human interaction. Ellwood was a cultural sociologist, maintaining that values were the product of the human mind and culturally transmitted. He rejected absolutely the view that they were merely speech-reactions, and argued that the mechanist had no right to assume the metaphysical theory of materialism at the outset of his investigations. Since the mechanistic view ignores the attitudes, values and purposes that arise in the course of human interaction, Ellwood describes it as 'a major methodological error'.[7] It springs from the attempt to carry natural science methods over into social science, a tendency to which Ellwood was strongly opposed.

Further criticism made against mechanism and behaviourism by Ellwood related to the extreme use made of technical terms and behaviourism's moral effects. Ellwood maintained that behaviourism dehumanized the social sciences by taking away all meaning from the higher values of life and culture, and its enthusiastic reception in Soviet Russia confirmed the worst apprehensions as to its ethical consequences.[8] How does this criticism compare with that made by Hobhouse?

Ellwood was fully aware of the assumptions and implications of mechanism. For example, writing in 1913, he said:

> If it is true that 'natural science rests finally upon the assumption of mechanism (i.e., rigid determination of all processes through the operation of mechanical causes) and excludes all other conceptions', then there can be no scientific treatment of religion, morality, or any other phase of the mental and social life of man. Upon this assumption there can only be physical and biological sciences, and we must give up the hope of having mental and social sciences . . .[9]

Such nihilistic implications were repugnant to Hobhouse, as they were to Ellwood. Hobhouse, though, was led to make actual investigations, both philosophical and scientific, into the bases of mechanism. Ellwood did not examine mechanism in this way, nor did he engage in empirical research regarding this subject. It would not appear that Hobhouse's distinctive contribution here has been matched by similar research by sociologists. And it is noteworthy that his criticism of mechanism was upheld in the main by the British scientist, J. S. Haldane.[10]

The methodological aspects of mechanism and behaviourism have received more attention from Ellwood. In the 1920s, problems of social science methodology were more in the forefront of academic attention in America rather than England, and Ellwood's contribution has been in the area of criticizing methods. He showed what he considered to be the inadequate and 'emasculated' sociology that emerges from mechanistic assumptions, and he criticized the carrying of natural science viewpoints and methods over into the social sciences. Hobhouse was equally aware of the fallacy of 'reductionistic mechanism',[11] but he made a more thorough analysis of its foundations than did Ellwood. Ellwood attacked the mechanistic viewpoint as a methodology and as a destroyer of social and religious values. Hobhouse, equally cognizant of its implications for sociology and religion, gave more attention to showing the weakness of its scientific and philosophical foundations.[12]

Another sociologist who took an anti-mechanistic position was Robert M. MacIver of Columbia University. Although MacIver's training and outlook were philosophical, he did not undertake a philosophical criticism of mechanism, since his interests lay more in political philosophy. But he authored a work that analyses causality in social affairs and has described what he termed 'the mechanistic fallacy'. This consists in a type of thinking which treats interacting factors that result in a phenomenon as independent homogeneous units, each of which produces a measurable portion of their joint result. He says:

> This crudely mechanistic assumption vitiates those investigations that seek to assess, often in precise quantitative terms, the role of the various components of a causal complex.[13]

MacIver goes on to note how this fallacy regards the various components of a social situation, or of any organized system, as though they were detachable, isolable and independently operative. He points out that even a slight knowledge of mechanism would correct this view, for even a mechanism works as an organization of parts that are independent in their functioning.[14] This criticism, which has important implications for social re-research, is an original contribution of MacIver to the discussion of mechanism. Together with Hobhouse, Ellwood and Case, MacIver did not fall into the 'mechanistic fallacy 'of isolating the interdependent and interacting factors that work to produce a social phenomenon. Each of these writers was sufficiently aware of the organic nature of society to realize that no such isolation of factors was practically justifiable. Hobhouse's writings on the interdependence of societal phenomena are worthy of note in this connection.

MacIver also dealt with some of the methodological aspects of mechanism, but Hobhouse set forth a scientific and philosophical criticism of the mechanistic viewpoint at a time when this type of thinking was very dominant. It had been denounced in less scientific terms by religious leaders, while from the ranks of philosophy had come opposing theories.[15] But sociologists have been reluctant to criticize it, partly because of the popularity of behaviouristic conceptions and principles. Hobhouse is noteable for having attacked this theory, not only from a philosophical point of view, but also upon the basis of scientific research. This combination gives him a prime place as one of the few sociologists who have made such an attack upon the foundations of the mechanistic approach.

The importance of theory and assumptions

Hobhouse's early training was in philosophy and logic, and he made a contribution by indirectly showing the importance of logic and theoretical analysis in sociology. His whole work attests to the importance of theory. He showed that reason, judgement and comparison are needed in the social sciences, in addition to observation and techniques of calculation. He was also one of the few social scientists to point out the limitations of science and scientific method. He noted, for example, that science cannot offer a criterion of the validity of its own methods. These criteria transcend science; they are philosophical, and most of the important questions in the social sciences cannot be answered by scientific methods alone, since they are questions of theory and logic. Hobhouse pointed out that theory underlies all science, and that science is not simply a quest for facts. On the contrary, its advance has been due to the revision of its theoretical foundations, as well as to discoveries of empirical data. In pointing out the prime importance of logical analysis and theory, Hobhouse has clearly shown that sustained and reasoned theoretical analysis is not to be equated with vague speculation.

He stressed the fact that presuppositions and assumptions exist and play an important role in scientific endeavours. The existence of assumptions would appear to be a truism, were it not for the fact that many social scientists frequently appear to be oblivious to them. The open-minded attitude that is the ideal of science is often identified with a state of mental presuppositionlessness. Hobhouse has shown that this is a false concept, and that the human mind is not 'open' in this sense. He has pointed out that the derivation and analysis of facts is always made upon the bases of assumptions. It is in the light of these assumptions that the selection of facts is made, and their meaning understood. Hobhouse has also called into question the assumption that science represents the one road to valid knowledge, but his main contribution in this connection has lain in his emphasizing and bringing into the open the existence and role of assumptions and presuppositions. He has shown that these underlying principles need to be recognized and criticized, and that if they are invalid, the results of science will be invalid. The work of criticizing assumptions properly belongs to logic, and here is seen a main example of the need for logic and theory in social science.

Hobhouse also stressed the experimental attitude. This point is mentioned only in passing, because the need for a scientific attitude in sociology is generally assumed from the start. What

Hobhouse specifically said was to note that there is no finality in knowledge, that the scientific temper consists in realizing the tentative character of conclusions and that human knowledge at any stage only represents a stage and not a termination. He emphasized the importance of holding an experimental attitude to the methods employed. Scientific methods, he thought, should be held liable to criticism, and the knowledge already gained by science should not be regarded as final, for a developing experience and improved techniques might bring many types of changes. An objective attitude should be adopted towards science itself, instead of a slavish devotion to any one set of techniques or tools. Truth, for Hobhouse, was a dynamic process, not a fixed mould. No partial knowledge was to be looked upon as the 'last word' on any subject, no concept was to be exempt from further revision, and no method to be regarded as the one gateway to complete and final truth.

Which other sociologists have stressed the function of social theory and the importance of assumptions, and how are their various contributions related to those of Hobhouse? Social theory has not enjoyed a great popularity among sociologists until recently, partly on account of a preoccupation with empirical data and the prevalent distinction between social science and social philosophy. There has also been in evidence a lack of concern with assumptions and their analysis. However, some writers have attested to the importance of theory in social resarch. For example, before the Second World War, Barnes and Becker noted that research would be doomed to failure if not allied with theory.[16] Another writer who shared this viewpoint was Eduard C. Lindeman, who says:

. . . it is my belief that social scientists who are not also sound theorists will never be capable of formulating or utilizing workable principles for a dynamic sociology. In fact, they will not even be able to produce relevant units of research. A chemist or a physicist may be able to operate successfully without philosophical accompaniments, but when a social scientist attempts to do so his work loses its dynamic content. In order to become effective the social sciences must serve as a bridge between the physical and biological sciences on the one hand and the humanities on the other, and I include philosophy as a humanistic study.[17]

A statement such as the foregoing is to be expected from a social philosopher. Among sociologists, the need for more theoretical orientation has been briefly noted by C. M. Case, who said, forty years ago, 'it may not be unprofitable for sociologists to recognize, as is all too seldom done, the logical implications and philosophical boundaries of their discussions'.[18] Although Case did not make any study of the role of assumptions or first principles, or the logic of the social sciences, he was aware of the existence of first principles, as shown in his criticism of mechanism. He also noted that scientific canons demanded that the social scientist approach his subject with a minimum of presuppositions.[19]

Contributions to the history of social theory have been made by Sorokin, who has evaluated and classified various theories. Sorokin is aware of the power of assumptions and the way in which they intrude into even the most 'scientific' thinking. He cites Pareto as an example of a sociologist who espoused 'logico-experimental method' in an attempt to base sociology on 'the facts', forgetting that assumptions underlay the facts.[20]

Sorokin is the author of the statement that the contemporary emphasis on fact-finding is largely responsible for the lack of outstanding leaders in social science, compared with the leaders of the nineteenth and early twentieth century. He has shown that the history of science represents an alternation between periods of fact-finding and periods of synthesis. The former periods are, he finds, unfavourable to broad generalization, original synthesis and marked originality. Fact-finding is apt to cause pure thought to be regarded with suspicion. Sorokin found, though, that the fact-finding periods are actually marked by fewer discoveries of relevant new facts than are the synthetic periods.

Ellwood has said that Sorokin brilliantly exhibits the possibility of combining fact-finding with philosophical synthesis, and he recalls with approval how Albion W. Small of the University of Chicago emphasized the need for sociology to be philosophical as well as scientific. Ellwood is also sympathetic to Sorokin's insistence on the need for more training in systematic thinking, logical principles and philosophical methods.[21] Sorokin's contribution lay in his historical analysis of theories and in his claim for synthetic analysis.

Ellwood's general agreement with this viewpoint has been noted. He has pointed out the need to combine theory with facts and broad synthesis with minute investigation. He has noted that narrow scientific methods cannot solve the larger problems in social evolution. These are problems of values, and the discussion of values falls to philosophy. Ellwood also pointed out that philosophy is not to be identified with mystical speculation. On the contrary, empirical methods are being utilized in modern philosophy. The facts of experience are being studied, rather than *a priori* principles.[22]

Ellwood held that sociology should embrace social theory, and not confine itself to the description of social data. He looked upon sociology as a philosophy as well as a science, in that the term philosophy designated the more general and speculative aspects of all the sciences.[23] Philosophy for Ellwood, though, should be empirical in its approach, and therefore the methods of philosophy and science should overlap—a view in which Hobhouse concurred.

Ellwood regarded the social sciences as essentially reasoned sciences, on account of the nature of their subject-matter. For this reason he stressed training in systematic thinking, logical principles and philosophical reflection rather than in mere techniques of fact-finding. Ellwood's emphasis upon logic and theory is brought out in the following passage:

> What . . . shall be the regulative discipline of the social
> sciences? Manifestly, it must be logic, which, as the science
> of right reasoning, is fundamentally the regulative discipline
> of all the sciences, including mathematics itself. Logic has
> a peculiarly close bearing upon the psychical sciences,
> including sociology, inasmuch they must look to logic, rather
> than mathematics, for the validation of their reasoning, since
> their phenomena, for the most part, will not submit to
> measurement. In order to perfect an adequate scientific
> method, therefore, the sociologist must have recourse to the
> principles of logic at every step.[24]

Ellwood predicted that the social sciences would turn to philosophical methods of logical reasoning, synthesis and the logical criticism of theories. Ellwood looked upon the current stage of science as merely transitional, and felt that in its final development sociology would be not just statistical and quantitative but synthetic and philosophical.[25] To date, more than twenty-five years after his death, this stage has not been reached.

Another contribution that is worthy of note was made by Simmel, who gave a critical exposition of the presuppositions of the social sciences. Simmel pointed out, for example, that science is based upon the assumption that the world is a unitary and coherent totality, and therefore is intelligible. This represents an assumption, an axiom, and one that will stand although the greater part of the world's phenomena may remain unknown. It is not necessary, Simmel noted, to wait for a faultless knowledge of the world's factual content before proving the validity of this axiom.[26] Spykman, in giving his interpretation of Simmel, notes that philosophy was the mother of all sciences; philosophy gives the first approaches to knowledge which is later tested, confirmed or rejected by methodological empiricism.[27]

What Simmel did was to inquire into the basic concepts, the fundamental presuppositions, and the *a priori* categories of the social sciences. Such inquiries cannot be settled within the field of inductive empirical investigation, since they form the basis on which that investigation rests. Simmel called these problems the epistemology of society. The philosophical aspects of Simmel's work will not be dealt with here, but it may be noted that he made a contribution to social theory with his concept of 'socialization'.

Other writers who have dealt with theory and assumptions can be briefly considered. Howard Becker has said that 'nothing is more practical than theory',[28] and has pointed out the desirability of carefully framing hypotheses. MacIver has dealt with causal hypotheses and has raised the question of the universality of the conditions of phenomena that are allegedly causal. He sees the need for a closer definition of the causal nexus. The role of the statistical test is seen here, for it does not provide any positive proof but gives exact formulations of the correlations of variables, thereby furnishing important clues as to where causal connections should be sought. MacIver notes that statistics may lead to greater knowledge as to the universality of a hypothesis, and he uses as an example, the causal relation between an economic depression and the number of marriages taking place. He showed the necessity for good logic in the matter of social causation.[29]

More recently, since the Second World War, theory has received greater attention in sociology. In particular, Talcott Parsons of

Harvard has contributed to its literature, as has his pupil Robert Merton. Parsons has noted the fallacious tendency to think of scientific advance as consisting entirely in the 'discovery' of 'facts', with the attendant view that theory consists in the modification of generalizations that arise from the new facts gained. Allied with this error is the view that all facts are essentially independent of theory.

Another perspective noted by Parsons is that scientific theory is an independent variable in scientific development; it is a body of logical interrelated 'general concepts' of empirical reference. Parsons points out, however, that there is an interaction between facts and theory. All empirically verifiable knowledge involves systematic theory, although certain writers strongly deny this. But, says Parsons, to deny that one is theorizing is no reason for this denial. It simply represents a failure to investigate the theory involved in expressed statements.[30] What Parsons has attempted to do is to expound the thesis that the changes in empirical interpretations of society have been intimately associated with changes in the structure of theoretical systems. This development, according to his hypothesis, has largely been a matter of the reciprocal interaction of new facts and changes in the theoretical system. Both, for Parsons, are mutually interdependent.

The importance of assumptions and theory may be once more noted, in that Comte based his whole system upon an assumption regarding the impossibility and undesirability of knowledge of causes and first principles. It may be pointed out once again that Einstein, who has been called the Copernicus of the twentieth century, expounded a *theory* of relativity based upon a criticism of the *assumptions* of physics.

The experimental approach, as one of Hobhouse's contributions, will not be considered at length as it was an indirect contribution. Hobhouse simply stressed the need for keeping a tentative point of view in science and logic. The experimental approach is allegedly espoused by most social scientists, though not all of them actually maintain it in practice. Hobhouse allied his tentative approach with a study of the logical principles underlying human knowledge. Perhaps the writer who has come closest to this point of view is John Dewey in his instrumentalism. For both Dewey and Hobhouse, there were no absolutes in the kingdom of knowledge. Dewey has also in his various works shown how theory underlies all action. He has tried to set forth a reasoned theory of social progress.[31] In conclusion, Hobhouse was one of the first to stress the importance of theory in social science, the role of as-sumptions, and the dangers that surround hypotheses when not allied with careful theory and logic.

Empiricism and measurement

The next point to be considered is his insistence upon the empirical approach in science and logic, in contrast to the method that would set up *a priori* dogmas, and regard these as above criticism. It is contended that Hobhouse stressed a point of prime importance for societal theory when he wrote of the worth of empirical method. He held that no principle should be regarded as axiomatic and self-evident unless reasoning demonstrated it as valid. This is allied with the criticism of first principles. He pointed out the inadequate interpretations of society that would accrue from narrow views of the meaning of experience. He demanded that no type of human experience be ignored in social and philosophical interpretations and that any approach which limited the concept of experience at the start would result in erroneous conclusions. To limit empirical data to the observable or the measurable, for example, would only result in an extremely restricted type of science.

Involved here is a criticism of the Comtean assumption that knowledge should be limited to the factual, to 'phenomena' and its 'laws'. Hobhouse showed that Comte's positivism was based upon an assumption for which positivism offered no grounds. A related point is Hobhouse's distinction between science and mere measurement. This is central to his criticism of mechanism, since mechanism rests in part upon the postulate that all data must be made to lend themselves to mathematical treatment. Hobhouse insisted that mathematics could not be looked to for a compre-hensive interpretation of human experience in the totality of its aspects. Statistics might form a useful sociological tool, but had their limitations.

Which other sociologists have written of the empirical approach and the dangers of a narrow view of experience? Which writers have shown the limitations inherent in the identification of science with measurement and the attempt to reduce all experience to mathematical terms? These questions will be dealt with as a means of throwing light on Hobhouse's specific contribution in this area.

His pupil, Charles A. Ellwood, has noted the limitations of statistical methods in social research, as part of a larger criticism of the use of natural science methods generally in social sciences. Ellwood has emphasized the view, only briefly mentioned by Hobhouse, that natural science methods are inadequate and unsuitable in social study and that an 'emasculated' sociology will result from the attempt to use natural science techniques exclusively. He also criticized the school that would limit science to the measurement of factual data. Ellwood espoused the empirical approach, but supported it with broad generalizations of a philosophical nature. He did not, however, analyse the concept of experience itself, nor did he provide, as Hobhouse did, a criticism of Comtean positivism as a metaphysics, except to say that Comte 'made grave mistakes in his early phenomenalism and objectivism'.[32]

Similarly, Sorokin has criticized the taking over of methods, terminologies, principles and laws from the natural sciences into the social science field. Sorokin cites Lundberg, Dodd, Chapple and Coon as writers who have no understanding of the principles and theories of mathematical and physico-chemical sciences.[33] Sorokin's theme of ideational-idealistic-sensate culture is implicit testimony to a broader concept of 'experience' than that of the mechanists and behaviourists. Sorokin's sociology deals with religious and psychic experience and embraces some consideration of moral values.[34] Nevertheless, while Sorokin does not fall prey to a narrow view of empiricism, he has not analysed as did Hobhouse the concept of experience philosophically. Finally, although Sorokin is a foremost exponent of the school that looks askance at the wholesale importation of natural science techniques into the field of social relations, it would appear that he has tended to use statistical methods in the area of culture-analysis with a minuteness of detail that would itself seem to invalidate the conclusions reached.

C. M. Case has written that measurement in the physical science mode is a modern tendency which is hailed as 'scientific'. Case is aware of its discarding of philosophical considerations. He noted that science involves a minute analysis and abstraction with little thought for the wholeness of phenomena. Science, says Case, deals with the countable, the separable, the measurable, but he goes on to say that measurement in itself will not make a science out of sociology.[35]

As was noted in connection with mechanism, Case, like Hobhouse, was opposed to narrow views of human experience, but he did not write as prolifically as Hobhouse regarding the concept of experience and the empirical approach. Nor did he engage in a criticism of Comtean positivism.

Talcott Parsons gives a good statement of the need for the empirical approach. He writes as follows:

> It would lead to the worst kind of dialectic sterility to treat the development of a system of theory without reference to the empirical problems in relation to which it has been built up and used. True scientific theory is not the product of idle 'speculation', of spinning out the logical implications of assumptions, but of observation, reasoning and verification starting with the facts and continually returning to the facts.[36]

This quotation is very closely akin to Hobhouse's own position on this topic. It is in line with the view that theory is not to be equated with 'idle speculation', but is made up of empirically based observation, reasoning and verification. Parsons's distinction between scientific theory and mere speculation is reminiscent of Hobhouse's differentiation between the positivistic and the 'dialectical' methods of approach to society and its problems.

The last sociologist to be compared with Hobhouse on this topic of empiricism is R. M. MacIver, whose distinction between 'the range of the measurable' and 'the range of the knowable' has often been cited. MacIver amplifies this point as follows:

> There are things we can measure, like time, but yet our minds do not grasp their meaning. There are things we cannot measure, like happiness or pain, and yet their meaning is perfectly clear to us. Perhaps, after all, we can measure only the external, the unknown, and can know only the internal, the conscious state, the incommensurate . . . It is

only quantity we can measure, but it is only quality we can experience.[37]

MacIver shares with Hobhouse a view of science that is broader than that which reduces it to measurement, and he avers that quantitative relations are inadequate as a means of revealing the nature of social facts.[38] He sees a distinction between obtaining factual data and interpreting that data. MacIver also notes the fallacy in examining the responses to a series of questions to determine the degree of such intangible qualities as the 'happiness', or the 'adjustment', of human beings. Such terms, he points out, are ambiguous and do not lend themselves to mathematical treatment. He writes of the '*cul-de-sac* of operationalism', meaning the treatment of certain items, traits or data that can be counted and measured. The complete operationalist, says MacIver, defines his subject by his measurements or operations. Intelligence, for example, becomes defined as that which intelligence tests test, without further definition. MacIver cites Lundberg as one who rejects the commonsense assumption that a phenomenon can be recognized and approximately identified before its nature is investigated or 'measured'.[39]

As for statistics, MacIver notes that this method has its value but that, following his statistical analysis, the sociologist must re-invest himself with his own role as social agent. If the sociologist does not do this, 'though he may learn how much a war has cost in men and treasure, he will never learn why men fought the war, what passions and persuasions moved them, what they sought'.[40] MacIver states a point similar to that made by Hobhouse—namely, that the verification of hypotheses by statistics or other methods can never be complete, but only approximate. Hobhouse would agree with MacIver's statement that 'what we cannot fully apprehend is that which is intrinsically dynamic'.[41] He would also concur with MacIver that 'social relations can never be adequately stated in quantitative terms or understood as expressions of quantitative laws'.[42]

Both Hobhouse and MacIver were aware of the imponderable and intangible factors in human association, and of the errors of attempting to reduce all experience to the measurable. It may be added that they both approached the study of society with a broad background of learning in political economy and philosophy, and neither of them has fallen into the particularistic errors of any one sociological 'school'. It is also interesting to note that most of the criticisms of the school that lays undue stress on measurement in sociology have come from writers who enjoyed a reputation for wide scholarship and philosophical reflection. This is true of Hobhouse, MacIver, Ellwood, Case and Sorokin. It also could be said of Charles Horton Cooley, who held that physical science methods in sociology were inadequate.[43]

The dangers of overspecialization

In his exposition of a synthetic view of social science, Hobhouse pointed out the dangers of academic divisions and departmentalization. He held that an organic unity, society, required a synoptic treatment. He stressed the dangers that would accrue from over-specialization in sociology; his warnings expressed in 1908 have been vindicated by developments since that date. Hobhouse urged the need for a greater co-operation among social scientists. He used the term 'General Sociology' to denote a synthesis of the social sciences, and illustrated this by pointing out the ideal functions of a sociological journal. He criticized partial views that saw one aspect of social interaction as though it constituted the whole. Briefer criticisms related to undue use of particular sociological methods and the imposition of a narrow method upon a dynamic subject-matter.

Hobhouse's insight into the need for a broad view of social science, with the attendant criticism of the tendency to over-specialize, was related to his clear portrayal of the historical and philosophical backgrounds of modern sociology. He distinguished the principal roots of sociology in their growth and interaction—political philosophy, the philosophy of history, physical and biological science and the modern movement towards specialization. He showed the influence of these four background trends, and their positive and negative effects. In this he was one of the early (1907) portrayers of modern sociology in relation to its historical and philosophical origins. Since Hobhouse came to sociology from a training in both science and philosophy, and was in a favourable position to analyse the philosophical trends that underlay the more scientific study of society, he could differentiate the more clearly between the two approaches. He portrayed the two approaches, the scientific and the philosophical, and insisted on their separation. He clearly and categorically insisted that while both the study of facts and the study of values were necessary and legitimate, they should not be fused. He denounced the mixing of the 'is' and the 'ought', the value-approach and the scientific approach. He also contended that values were an intrinsic feature of the subject-matter of sociology, and that they belonged to the realm of 'social facts'.

How do these emphases compare with similar points expressed by other writers? In connection with Hobhouse's early portrayal of the dangers of overspecialization, the writings of Spykman may be noted. In his interpretative work concerning Simmel, Spykman pointed out that 'single-cures' have been offered by eugenics, psychology, economics, political science, law and religion. All these particularistic remedies for social ills come, says Spykman, from scholars of long standing, and 'the results would be humorous beyond all measure were it not that they throw a light on the very sad conditions existing in the social sciences'.[44] This 'single-formula thinking' arises, according to Spykman, from the desire for unity and simplicity; simple formulas have appealed to human beings. The search for the all-sufficient single formula will not furnish scientific knowledge. Indeed, sociology was born in part from a dissatisfaction with the fragmentary character of the knowledge gained in the various social sciences. Sociology arose from the desire to see life whole, and to find a technique of social improvement.

Spykman goes on to point out that neither of these two needs can be satisfied by science. A social philosophy is required if a synoptic view of social life is to be gained, and a technique of social amelioration requires an integration and co-ordination of the knowledge of all the social sciences. Confusion has arisen, in Spykman's view, on account of sociology's being applied indiscriminantly to social philosophy and to a body of knowledge labelled 'social engineering'. 'Sociology' was applied to anything that had to do with social life, from social metaphysics to public sanitation. For Spykman, this confusion regarding sociology indicates a lack of a clear understanding of the basic presuppositions and the mutual relations of the social sciences. No advancement in theoretical inquiry can be expected, on this view, until the relation between sociology and other social sciences is definitely determined. Spykman espouses specialization in theoretical inquiry, holding that a common method and consensus of opinion is required regarding the relations of the science of sociology to the other social sciences.[45]

Spykman's contribution here would seem to lie in his criticism of single-cures and single-formulas in social thought, and in his statement of the need for redefining the subject-matter of sociology and the various social sciences. Sociology in the early years of the century was in the hands of broad systematizers—Sumner, Ward, Giddings, Ross, Small—and their type of thinking has been continued by such men as Sorokin, Ellwood and MacIver. Of these writers, Ellwood is closest to Hobhouse in his criticism of overspecialization and the dangers in this trend. Ellwood insisted that sociology must be a synthesis of both science and philosophy in its outlook and methods. No single method or approach in sociology is sufficient; knowledge must be gained from all reliable sources. In 1912, Ellwood said that one-sidedness or partialness of view was the bane of the sociologist,[46] and he continued to hold this outlook in his later writings. He expressed the view that breadth of scholarship, including command of facts and principles of interpretation, is more important than methodological techniques and specialities. For Ellwood, narrow methods in science, such as stem from narrow outlooks regarding the scope of science, are inadequate for the understanding and solution of human problems. His viewpoint is well expressed in the statement that 'synthesis of all methods that will yield truth is alone adequate for the purpose of the social sciences'.[47]

In comparing the work of these two sociologists on this particular topic, it would appear that Ellwood's contribution lay in his criticism of *methodological* specialization, while Hobhouse's writings laid more stress on specialization of *subject-matter*. Hobhouse warned of the dangers of excessive narrowness of interest within the social sciences generally, while Ellwood noted the dangers of a too great concern for specialized methodological tools within the field of sociology itself. On this particular topic, he wrote more prolifically than Hobhouse and continued to plead for a synthetic approach until the end of his life. He also wrote with vigour upon the dangers of trying to carry natural science methods into the social science field, a point which Hobhouse mentioned only incidentally.

Hobhouse's contribution in stressing the synthetic point of view has been cited by Ginsberg, who himself urges greater co-operation with anthropologists, historians and students of comparative law and comparative religion.[48] Ginsberg's emphasis on the need for an organic view of society may be ascribed at least in part to the influence of his late teacher.

Perhaps it is a truism to note that since Hobhouse first wrote concerning specialization and its dangers American sociology has become a collection of specialisms. As early as 1938, Barnes and Becker said:

> Of recent years American sociology has more and more abandoned the older effort to work out a comprehensive system covering all phases of social life. Not only are there few younger contemporary synthesists such as Ward, Small, Giddings, Ross, Bernard, or Ellwood, but even the attempt to set forth a comprehensive frame of reference for analytic purposes has but a small body of supporters. MacIver, Park and Burgess, Thomas and Znaniecki, and Sorokin have many admirers but few real followers.[49]

The same writers observe that there has been a marked trend towards specialization, or even compartmentalization. However, a few years before the above was written, Read Bain and Joseph Cohen noted that the need for an organic concept of social life was evidenced by much of the new literature in sociology. They cited Hobhouse, together with Cooley, Dewey and Barnes, as writers who illustrated the plea for a realization of the inter-dependence of all social and physical science.[50]

Howard Becker has also suggested that there is evidence of a trend in the opposite direction. In a review of sociological developments as early as the year 1946, Becker saw a tendency towards a more synoptic view of societal phenomena. He wrote as follows:

> Tendencies long apparent in U.S. sociology became very obvious in 1946. These tendencies were toward the merging of sociology, social and cultural anthropology, social psychology and social psychiatry in what was coming to be called the science of social relations. Harvard brought the trend into the open by establishing a department of social relations,

but essentially the same state of affairs existed at Chicago, Wisconsin, Yale, Columbia, and a number of other universities.[51]

It would appear that this merging of several disciplines into a science of social relations bears a resemblance to the Hobhousian conception of sociology as a synthesis of the various social sciences. Hobhouse put forward this concept in 1908. The modern trend, as described by Becker, would make sociology one speciality among others.

The early plea made by Hobhouse for greater co-operation among specialists in social science has also been set forth by Emory S. Bogardus in connection with co-operative research. Bogardus defines this as 'the working together at the same time of a number of persons upon a single research project',[52] and he notes the advantages that will accrue. Participants can stimulate each other in unique ways, and a variety of approaches are given to the research problem. Bogardus cites the need for seminars in which two or more university departments attack a research problem together, and he suggests 'inclusive seminars' in such fields as the physical sciences, social sciences and philosophy combined with religion. There is evidence of a trend in the direction of the synoptic viewpoint that Hobhouse emphasized in the early days of sociology, and since 1950 this trend towards 'team research' scientific studies has gained momentum.

With regard to Hobhouse's indication of the historical background of sociology, what he did was to show, briefly and succinctly, four roots of sociology that extended from Greek times to the modern period, all of which had been trends of thought influencing sociology in its modern development. The historical approach to sociology has been dealt with by many writers who have given histories of social thought, dealing with the contributions made by specific individuals and schools. Hobhouse, on the contrary, showed how sociology had arisen from, and been influenced by, four main currents of thought.

The place of values in sociology

Hobhouse's insistence upon the separation of the two approaches— the scientific and the valuational—has been noted. He was one of the early sociologists to make this distinction. The mixing of facts and value-judgements has long been a hindrance to the development of the science of sociology. Numerous instances from early sociological literature could be cited in which the inclusion of value-judgements rendered a piece of research less useful than it might otherwise have been.

Another sociologist who has distinguished between the scientific approach and the value-judgement approach to social phenomena is Max Weber. Bogardus says of Weber that he insisted that these two approaches should not be allowed to mix in the study of society, and that 'in his own way he laid a foundation for the development of a science of sociology'.[53]

Spykman has noted[54] that many sociology texts contain a combination of social philosophy and social ethics, while others consist of anthologies of the masterpieces of literature pertaining to social affairs and handbooks for social reformers. They represent a mixture of facts and value-judgements.

MacIver has pointed out that sociology should not be value-free in the sense that it leaves values out of account, or in the sense that they should be treated as facts, lacking operative significance. It should be value-free, says MacIver, in the sense that in dealing with value-facts the sociologist should never allow his own valuations to intrude into, or to affect, his presentation of the valuations which are registered in the facts themselves. MacIver notes the difficulties of excluding value-judgements and cites their use by Leopold Von Wiese and Pareto, both of whom had denounced their introduction into social study.[55]

In pointing out the necessity for avoiding the confusion of the 'is' and the 'ought', MacIver comes very close to Hobhouse. It is also worth noting that MacIver adopts a position very similar to that of Hobhouse regarding the importance of values as objects of sociological study.

The concept of 'value' is found in several fields of endeavour and not merely in sociology, but on account of its philosophical and ethical connotations sociologists have fought shy of the term. Under the influence of behaviourism, there has been a tendency to forget that values are an integral part of human life, as distinct from mere 'speech-reactions'. Despite this trend, however, certain sociologists have attempted to treat values sociologically. Hobhouse's *Morals in Evolution*, first published in 1906, may be regarded as a sociological investigation of human values in their development through the centuries and in different cultures. Other sociologists who have paid attention to values include Thomas and Znaniecki, whose epoch-making *Polish Peasant in Europe and America* analysed values in relation to corresponding attitudes.[56] C. M. Case also concerned himself with social values as 'meaningful group objects',[57] and C. A. Ellwood regarded them as important sociologically, noting that values are essentially cultural. For Ellwood, every social value constituted a social fact.[58] Similarly, P. A. Sorokin has noted that every process of meaningful human interaction involves human beings, and meanings, values and norms for the sake of which individuals interact.[59] Morris Ginsberg, under the influence of his former teacher, insists on the separation of facts and values but maintains that values are not at the same time social facts and that a synthesis of the scientific and philosophical approaches to sociology is needed for a complete study of social life.[60]

MacIver has said that, in the life of society, every physical and organic factor of human association becomes transformed into a value: consanguinity comes to mean pride of race or family; marriage comes to mean all the values and satisfactions of home life. Says MacIver: 'All society depends on the recognition of facts as values'.[61]

In his early insistence upon recognizing values as an integral part of the subject-matter of sociology, Hobhouse was ahead of his time. Although Hobhouse did not himself engage in a particular sociological study of values as such, with the exception of *Morals in Evolution*, his recognition of the importance of values as subject-matter is now shared by later sociologists. Two further examples of this recognition may be given. As early as 1933, Howard E. Jensen wrote that '. . . every social situation . . . is shot through and through with value, in the light of which our external observations and measurements get whatever cultural significance they have'; and, Jensen further stated, perhaps John Laird had been right in believing that 'the concept of value might prove the key that would release human sciences from a position of pathetic, if dignified, futility'.[62]

A later statement by Howard Becker indicates that the significance of values in human life became more apparent to sociologists during the ten-year period ending in 1946. During these years, according to Becker, behaviourism declined in influence, and the sociological 'white-rat' behaviourism was found inadequate, as was the view of values as more 'speech-reactions'.[63]

The recognition of the valuational quality of social interaction that Hobhouse expressed in the early years of the present century is reflected in the writings of later sociologists, where considerably more attention is being paid to this element of human association. Since 1945, the reality of values as social facts is being admitted by social scientists. It is seen that values can be empirically studied and different value-systems compared.

Hobhouse's emphasis upon values was related to his recognition of human purpose as a fundamental social force. His contribution in this connection lay in his analysis of the role of the human will and human purpose in relation to the possibility of making sociological laws. He gave reasons for the view that the existence of will and purpose does not render valid laws impossible, or make sociology unscientific. Hobhouse similarly pointed out the fallacies in the fatalistic assumption that sociological law renders the human will of no account. On the contrary, he showed how the mere knowledge of a law may be sufficient to modify the effects of tendencies operating in connection with that law.

He noted the importance of sociological laws as early as 1908, and wrote of the conditional character of laws and the difficulty of applying them in the field of human relations. He pointed out the error of the idea that a scientific law could ever be 'broken', and gave a more accurate interpretation of the ways in which a law might be believed to fail. Hobhouse emphasized the importance of purpose in social interaction, showing that individuals are purposive beings and not just mechanical robots.

Lester F. Ward made central use of man's ability to direct purposefully his own activities towards a goal. Similarly, Charles A. Ellwood has pointed out that social interaction is based upon thought, feeling and will,[64] though Ellwood only indirectly treated the concept of purpose in society.

W. I. Thomas's theory of the 'four wishes' constituted a study in motivation, but was not related to the possibility of setting up sociological laws. It would appear that the sociologist who comes closest to Hobhouse on this theme of human purpose is R. M. MacIver. MacIver sees purpose as implying power and choice, which constitute liberating factors. He says:

> It is as men purpose in relation to one another that they build the great structures of community. Purposive activity is a cause of causes, yet neither mingles with nor abrogates other causes . . . The law of purpose runs through all life, it is the revelation of life. To know what a being seeks is to know what that being is.[65]

In addition, MacIver decries the view that unless social laws can be formulated with the same exactitude as laws of physics, sociology is not a science.[66] His study of social causation showed an awareness of the role of purpose among human forces, and the inapplicability of the physical-science concept of 'law' to the social sphere.

Hobhouse's specific contribution in this connection is related to his study of mechanism. He emphasized the role of purposive conduct as shown by empirical research, and related this to the concept of sociological law in addition to clarifying the particular nature of this concept.

Kinship, authority, citizenship

In these three principles, Hobhouse gave a theory of political and social evolution. Hobhouse sets forth the theory that these three types of social bond can be traced in history, and he supports his contention with data drawn from past epochs. They provide a hypothesis for research into the historical factors underlying the growth of the state.

Sorokin has said that Hobhouse's three principles are an example of the linear type of trend that was so extensively manufactured by social scientists of the nineteenth and early twentieth centuries. He regards Hobhouse's theory as comparable to other examples of 'the dozens of historical trends manufactured by sociology and anthropology, law and history, concerning the evolution of the family, marriage, and kinship, all of them with uniform stages of development . . .'[67]

According to Sorokin, sociologists and social scientists in the nineteenth century saw their central problem as one of discovering and formulating the linear trends that were believed to be unfolding in the course of time. In the area of socio-cultural change, the task was simply one of drawing a unilinear or spiral main line from primitive man and society to the present time. Sorokin uses the modern college curriculum as an example to explain his point; primitive man was regarded as a college freshman who subsequently passed through stages that brought him to the class of positivism or 'freedom for all', or any other final stage that appealed to the scholar in question.[68]

This criticism, when applied to Hobhouse, appears to be unjustified and unsound. In the first place, Hobhouse has made it abundantly clear that social evolution has not proceeded in any straight-line fashion.[69] Throughout the pages of his *Social Development*, *Morals in Evolution*, and *Social Evolution and Political Theory* runs a repeated emphasis upon the existence of cultural lag, one-sided development, reversals to barbarism, and the general view of man's evolution as a winding curve, made up of several interacting strands, rather than of one unilinear and direct course from primitive times to the present. Nor did Hobhouse foresee any straight line of development so far as man's future was concerned. He pointed out, both in the years prior to and following 1918, that future reversals to barbarism were perfectly possible and could not be ruled out of account.

Hobhouse possessed too wide a knowledge of history to regard man's past as having proceeded in one straight line, or as representing one direct march towards 'progress'. His three principles of kinship, authority and citizenship throw light on social evolution and constitute a useful hypothesis upon which further research might be profitably directed.[70]

Morals in evolution

The study of the evolving customs and conduct-rites of mankind constituted another area in which Hobhouse made a contribution. What he did, specifically, was to analyse a vast amount of literature pertaining to the development of moral rules and practices, and to describe the leading customs in several areas of social life. The value of his book *Morals in Evolution* lies in its being a fine historical survey, a careful collection of data. It is true that Hobhouse has given criteria by which to judge ethical progress, but the work constitutes primarily an outline of the developing moral ideas and customs of mankind. It is one of the first (1906) such works to possess scientific value. One reviewer said of the book that 'one must ascribe to it a unique value as a collection of the facts upon which any interpretation of morality must be based'.[71] Along with the facts went Hobhouse's careful interpretation of the facts; he was not unmindful of the pitfalls that exist for the interpreter of historical data.

His particular contribution is perhaps best illuminated by the words of the Preface to *Morals in Evolution*. Here Hobhouse says:

> The purpose of the present work is to approach the theory of ethical evolution through a comparative study of rules of conduct and ideals of life . . . The attempt made in these volumes is to ascertain the main features of development, and by piecing them together to present a sketch in which the essentials of the whole process will be depicted in outline.[72]

This passage throws light on the merits of the work, but it also gives an indication of the limitations. Hobhouse has avoided the dangers of mere conjecture that is unsupported by empirical historical evidence, but it could not be expected that two volumes would give more than a 'sketch' or 'outline' of so vast a theme. Nevertheless, one of the main strengths of Hobhouse's study lies in the fact that, in two volumes (later brought into one), he has given an excellent summary of the main trends of development in human customs and conduct. The work is divided into two parts, the first dealing with the evolution of custom, laws and institutions, and the second with the rise of religious concepts, moral theories and theological doctrines, from early times till the modern period. Hobhouse was one of the first writers to depict in sound outline the evolution of the ethical consciousness in man, as evidenced not only in religious and moral theories but in actual customs and rules of conduct through the centuries. Based upon a careful study of historical factual data, it covers a vast amount of material within a reasonable space. During the period 1906 to 1925, Hobhouse revised the work to take account of research done by various scholars in the field.[73]

How does Hobhouse's work in this area of ethical evolution compare with that of other writers?

A famous and early contribution in this field was by W. E. H. Lecky. His *History of European Morals from Augustus to Charle-*

magne[74] has received much attention and has often been quoted. Some of its limitations, however, are seen in the title: it deals with Europe, and is restricted to a particular historical period. Lecky makes many wide generalizations and value-judgements. The work gives some consideration to ethical theory, notably the Utilitarian and Intuition schools, but its historical survey is limited largely to the period of and following the Stoics, the Roman Empire and the Byzantine Empire. Topics covered include Neo-Platonism, the conversion of Rome, the persecution of the Church, Christian teachings, asceticism and the life of the monasteries. It does not give the wide historical survey attempted by Hobhouse, and the dates of its publication (1869 and 1877) bear witness to fewer advantages of historical scholarship than those enjoyed by the author of *Morals in Evolution*. Nevertheless, despite its difference in scope and a less scientific approach to problems of moral evolution, Lecky's work did at the time represent a landmark and still possesses value in throwing light upon the rise of Christianity in the Greco-Roman era. Coming at a later period in the development of historical research, Hobhouse was able to build upon Lecky's foundations.

Another work that is worthy of note in this connection is the *Descriptive Sociology* of Herbert Spencer. This consists of 'atlases' or tables, exhibiting historical facts collected by Spencer and his assistants. They aimed to set forth in description the institutions and customs of the principal peoples of the world. The work is divided into three questionable divisions, or sets of tables, relating respectively to uncivilized societies, civilized societies that were extinct or decayed, and civilized societies of recent date or still flourishing. A statement from the Preface, however, is suggestive of the weaknesses in Spencer's work. In calling attention to scientific standards, Spencer brings to mind some of the ways in which he failed to meet scientific requirements. He wrote as follows:

. . . before there can be reached in Sociology, generalizations having a certainty making them worthy to be called scientific, there must be definite accounts of the institutions and actions of societies of various types, and in various stages of evolution, so arranged as to furnish the means of readily ascertaining what social phenomena are habitually associated.[75]

It is now recognized that Spencer did not produce generalizations 'worthy to be called scientific', and that there are many difficulties in the path of sociologists who attempt to find 'what social phenomena are habitually associated'. One valid criticism that may be expressed regarding Spencer in this connection is that his selection of facts was somewhat arbitrary. Secondly, the work in question involves sharp divisions; for example, one of his divisions ends with the Reformation, another with the Norman Conquest, another with the year 1688, and a fourth with the year 1850. It would be unfair, perhaps, to charge Spencer with having no recognition of the artificial character of these divisions, but the work is nevertheless arranged in this manner. A further criticism relates to the authorities cited, upon which Spencer bases his 'facts'. They are of the nineteenth century, before 1875, and some even date back to the eighteenth century. The scientific worth of such authorities is open to question.

It is true, of course, that Hobhouse relied upon nineteenth-century sources, particularly in the first edition of his work. Nevertheless, he did have the advantage of the work that had been done during the years following the publication of *Descriptive Sociology*. The scientific approach to history and morality did receive some impetus during those years. A further point relating to the superiority of Hobhouse over Spencer lies in Hobhouse's greater grasp of the evolutionary frame of reference. It is contended, therefore, that Hobhouse was theoretically and empirically superior to Spencer in the study of human development,[76] and that his work in comparative ethics constitutes a more scientific contribution.

The writer who may be most closely compared with Hobhouse on this topic is his colleague, Edward A. Westermarck. In his Preface, Hobhouse says:

> Dr Westermarck's important work on the *Origin and Growth of the Moral Ideas* would have been of immense value to me had it appeared a little earlier. It is particularly satisfactory to me to find that so far as we cover the same field my results generally harmonize with his, and this notwithstanding a material divergence in ethical theory.[77]

The first comparison that may be noted between the two works, apart from the difference in theory mentioned above, relates to the topics they cover. Westermarck deals with the emotional origin of moral judgements, the nature of moral emotions, the will as the subject of moral judgement, motives and character, in addition to murder, sacrifice, children and family morals, and slavery. His second volume embraces property rights, truth and deceit, good faith, politeness, gratitude, altruistic sentiments, suicide, dietary mores, asceticism, marriage and celibacy, duties to the dead, and duties to the gods. Although Hobhouse's work was broader than its title indicated—it dealt with the development of law, government and social institutions—it did not consider all of the specific topics covered by Westermarck's chapters. Nevertheless, Melvin J. Williams avers that *Morals in Evolution* was as equally extensive as Westermarck's volume, more precise and perhaps more valuable.[78]

C. Wright Mills notes that Westermarck relied upon psychological and biological theory for his ultimate explanations of moral data. For Westermarck, according to Mills, 'cause' and 'origin' were biologically much the same.[79]

Hobhouse and Westermarck approached their subject from different ethical viewpoints. For Westermarck, moral concepts were mere generalizations of inner emotions. On this view, emotional differences were made to account for the ethnographic fact of a variety of moral judgements. Westermarck found moral ideas to have their origin in the 'moral emotions', whereas Hobhouse saw a rational element at work. His own comments on this difference of viewpoint are illuminating. He held that, though there is an emotional element in all genuine ethical experience, to identify the moral consciousness with emotion is to narrow it unduly. Emotion constitutes an integral element in the moral consciousness but there is no inductive proof, says Hobhouse, that the essential nature of morality is emotional.[80]

Other theoretical deficiencies in Westermarck's work are noted by Mills, who points to an uncritical and indiscriminating use of historical material, a charge that was made against Spencer. Lowie is cited in support of this view regarding Westermarck. The charge is also made that Westermarck used illustrative evidence as a means of supporting his theory, especially in connection with primitive promiscuity. And W. I. Thomas is cited for the view that Westermarck's strength lay in his wealth of material rather than in his theory.[81] On the other hand, Hobhouse did approach his subject with a solid foundation of theory. He was aware of the fallacy of possessing an *a priori* theory and supporting this with the convenient facts. It can be claimed that he did give a 'prolegomena' to the study of morality.

Westermarck's rank as an empirical researcher, however, was upheld by Hobhouse, and he did undertake field investigations in the pursuit of his factual data. He spent several years in Morocco and wrote concerning the folkways and mores of that land.

Of the two, it would appear that Hobhouse has exerted more influence, judging by footnote references to his works. Mills is the author of the statement that Westermarck has not been of 'any real importance in the actual work of American sociologists',[82] and he further remarks that Westermarck did not possess the type of synoptic mind that can extract from masses of data the analytically characterizing sentence. The literary quality of *Morals in Evolution*, on the other hand, suggests an interesting comparison on this point.

A final statement by Barnes concerning Hobhouse's volume throws more light on these two students of comparative morality. It is one in which the present investigator concurs. Barnes says:

> This work is probably the most notable single contribution to the study of the mental and cultural evolution of humanity. This estimate is made in full knowledge of the bulky volumes of Frazer's *Golden Bough* and Westermarck's *Origin and Development of the Moral Ideas*. The former is no longer taken seriously in its theoretical aspects by any scientific student of ethnology, and the latter, while infinitely better, partakes of many of the faults of classical anthropology and manifests a far less subtle insight into the nature of human cultural evolution than Hobhouse's volumes.[83]

In conclusion, while both works represent pioneer attempts to place the empirical aspects of comparative morality on a firmer basis, Hobhouse's effort possesses greater scientific value, manifests more compactness and rests upon a stronger basis of theory. This judgement is corroborated by the scholars previously cited.

A final comparison can be drawn in connection with another monumental work in the sociology of morals, William Graham Sumner's *Folkways*,[84] published in 1906. What Sumner did however, was not entirely akin to the work of either Hobhouse or Westermarck; as his title indicates, he analysed folkways and mores as such, defining them and pointing out their role in society. Sumner showed the bearing of the mores upon social interaction, and stressed their great power and influence as agents of social control and conditioning. As the subtitle of *Folkways* indicates, Sumner was concerned with showing the sociological importance of usages, manners, customs, mores and morals. His contribution is a treatment in social psychology rather than in historical evolution. As Barnes says, *Folkways* is 'essentially an attempt to explain the origin, nature, value, and persistence of certain of the most important and characteristic group habits'.[85] The difference between this treatment and that given by Hobhouse is readily apparent. It should be noted that Sumner's volume is not devoid of historical references, for the author makes use of much data from the human past to explain or amplify his contentions. But *Folkways* is primarily a social-psychological work. It covers a wider range of cultural data than does *Morals in Education*, since the folkways are broader in scope than the mores. Sumner's work embraces the artifacts of culture, especially early material culture, and also deals with the folkways of sport, drama, labour and education.

Floyd N. House says that probably no writer of the past has contributed more to the systematic and objective sociology of morals than Sumner. He regards *Folkways* as the first book to study moral practices and ideals in an objective manner that involves a freedom from propaganda where any particular code of morality is concerned.[86]

The objectivity of *Folkways* has, however, been called into question. For example, Barnes considers it as being not entirely free from the tone of the preacher, along with other writings of Sumner.[87] Nevertheless, *Folkways* is probably unrivalled as a study of mores and customs from a social-psychological rather than a historical approach.

The resultant conception of social evolution as an automatic process, beyond man's power to affect, will be considered in a comparison of Sumner and Hobhouse on the subject of human progress. Before this topic is analysed, some of the specific contributions in Hobhouse's study of morals may be listed briefly.

Hobhouse insisted upon an empirical basis for the study of

morality, and upon the distinction between historical facts and value-judgements regarding the facts.

He pointed out the distinction between rules of conduct that possess binding force, and rules and precepts that are mere statements of ideals—an important distinction for the historian of morals, bearing as it does upon early codes and the development of law.

He clearly indicated the non-linear character of moral and social evolution, and he brought together the conclusions of many specialists from the fields of history, ethics, anthropology and ethnology. He analysed the growth of law and justice,[88] and showed the close relationship between culture and family organization.

In studying the relations between communities, he gave an exposition of the slow evolution from 'group morality' to broader ethical principles in which the dawning concept of 'humanity' appeared.

Hobhouse exposed patriotism as 'group morality' and noted the difference between that and internationalism. He stressed the application of moral principles to international relations, and gave a criticism of the German view of the state as an entity transcending moral principles. He showed the influence of religion in relation to war and its mores, and studied the different attitudes of historical religious groups towards militarism. He traced the rise of the concept of human rights within the group, as well as in intra-group relations, and gave a historical account of slavery as an institution.

Finally, Hobhouse traced the evolution of ideas and practices relating to property, and analysed the concept of 'freedom of contract', in which he gave a differentiation between social and unsocial freedom. He pointed out that property has come to represent power over persons as well as over things.

This last point, concerning ideas of freedom that spring from different conceptions of society and its well-being, leads up to a related contribution of Hobhouse, dealing with social progress.

Humanitarianism and Social Darwinism

What Hobhouse did in this connection was to expound the concept of the harmonious fulfilment of individual human capacity. This harmony was one in which divergencies of character and person-

ality would find constructive expression. It represented a democratic conception based on the view that individual differences
should contribute to a richer common life. In the scope for many-
faceted development which it allows, civilization differs from
barbarism. Hobhouse pointed out the ramifications of 'harmony',
showing that it is not a condition based upon repression. Harmony
is a philosophical concept, and as 'the rational good' it constitutes
a criterion of societal advancement. For example, to what extent
does group-life thwart or enhance the harmonious fulfilment of
individual human capacity?

Hobhouse gave a sound theoretical base to the humanitarian
outlook that characterized the British Liberal Party at the turn of
the century. He substituted the concept of 'harmony' for Bentham's notion of 'pleasure', and set forth the implications of the
harmony concept for religion and morals.[89]

Other sociologists who have made similar contributions to
theories of harmonious co-operation include Bentham and J. S.
Mill, who modified Bentham's theory by introducing quantitative
distinctions between pleasures. The common nature of all human
groups was emphasized by Vico, another member of the 'co-
operation' school, who saw the 'natural sociability' of man as the
basis for the co-operative spirit. Bogardus describes him as 'one
of the first persons to work out a systematic interpretation of co-
operation',[90] though Vico's emphasis differed from that of Hobhouse.

Ratzenhofer was another writer who, though a social Darwinist,
considered co-operation as *one* element of the social process, and
he influenced Albion W. Small, who analysed the 'interests' or
unsatisfied capacities of human beings, noting a conflict of
interests and the consequent need to direct all interests towards
social amelioration. Small stressed co-operation, though, as an
integral element of the social process; it represented a civilizing
factor, and one that played an increasingly important role.[91] His
view of the social process as a movement from a maximum of
conflict to a minimum, and from a minimum to a maximum of
helpful reciprocity, is comparable to Hobhouse's concept of a
developing harmony. It should be noted, though, that while the
theory of harmony set forth by Hobhouse is plainly one of co-
operation, yet Hobhouse gave little attention to the concept of co-
operation as such but dealt rather with the theoretical ramifications

of harmony. This is a concept that has not received great attention from sociologists, partly because of its normative and philosophical nature. Even Hobhouse's pupil, Charles A. Ellwood, did not devote much space in his writings to the term. He noted it as one of three norms of societal progress, the other two being social survival and social efficiency, but he did not deal with the concept philosophically, as did Hobhouse.[92] The term 'socialization' is more descriptive, though it also has an evaluative sense which renders it comparable to 'harmony', for it involves a condition that is essentially one of harmony in which conflict and competition are diminished.[93]

A further point stressed by Hobhouse, allied with his 'harmony' concept, was his combination of the scientific and humanitarian outlooks upon societal organization.[94] Comparisons here may be made with his successor, Morris Ginsberg, who reflects the thought of his former teacher when he says that moral progress involves the rationalization of moral judgement and the moralization of religion.[95] Here, as in other writings, Ginsberg expresses the influence of Hobhouse. The humanitarian strain that runs through Ellwood's works may also be ascribed in part to the effect that Hobhouse had upon his outlook. For Ellwood, humanity was the ultimate group; it transcended all national boundaries.

Allied with this humanitarian outlook is the criticism that Hobhouse gave regarding the biological view of progress, as exemplified in the individualistic laissez-faire philosophy of Spencer. Hobhouse provided an exposition of the sociological, racial, political and economic implications of social Darwinism, pointing out how it had constituted a 'reaction' in sociology; it had also been made to justify economic exploitation and rampant imperialism. He analysed 'evolution' in relation to progress, and critically examined the supposedly scientific doctrine of 'the survival of the fittest'. Complementary to this criticism was a plea for social and economic democracy and a denunciation of militarism and imperialism.[96]

Other sociologists who have given further criticisms of social Darwinism include Emory S. Bogardus, who notes that it is false to Darwin's own principles, and that Darwin himself pointed out the existence of co-operation between animals.[97]

Similarly, Kropotkin, in his *Mutual Aid*,[98] has shown that Darwin's account of evolution gives a place to co-operation as well as conflict. Kropotkin interprets the outcome of evolution in terms of human co-operation that leads to control over physical force and selfishness. Like Hobhouse, he studied animal life extensively and found 'struggle for existence' at a minimum between animals of the same species. Bogardus terms Kropotkin as one who 'led the way in defining the law of co-operative individualism'.[99] In comparison, Hobhouse's specific effort lay in his examination of the theoretical foundations of social Darwinism and in the resultant presentation of a humanitarian viewpoint, in relation to the social and politico-economic situation in Britain and the British Empire at the turn of the century.

A brief criticism of one aspect of social Darwinism is given by C. M. Case, who considered economic success in the competitive and exploitative field to be a poor test of 'fitness' or superior ability. Case declared that superiority of socio-economic position could not be identified with superior characteristics that were biologically transmitted.[100]

In conclusion: Hobhouse was one of the first writers to give a sociological and philosophical criticism of the theoretical foundations of social Darwinism and its varied social manifestations. He showed clearly that it was based upon false assumptions and confused thinking.

Purposive social development

The idea of societal advancement and control through the application of man's mind goes back a long way in the history of thought. In the modern period it is usually thought of as beginning with Saint-Simon and Comte. As one of the influences upon Comte, Saint-Simon saw progress in terms of the development of man's scientific intelligence applied to the problems of his society. According to Comte, this mental development had gone through three historical stages, a theory which Hobhouse criticized. Nevertheless, Comte's great contribution lay in the concept of man's directing his own future by means of applied social intelligence.

The sociologist who is the most well-known for expounding this viewpoint is Lester F. Ward. Ward strongly affirmed the possibility of social progress through applied intelligence, and he laid the foundations for a scientific, educational and political meliorism.[101]

According to Ward, man has readapted his social environment, moulding it to fulfil his purposes. By means of creative intelligence and scientific knowledge, man can perfect his environment. In Ward's view, intelligent purposes can be made to control, modify and direct human affairs to progressive ends. Mind is the controlling factor in evolution. It has been said by Barnes that:

> . . . Ward's outstanding contributions to sociology were his grasp of the relation between cosmic and social evolution and his doctrine of the superiority of the conscious to the unconscious control of the social process. In neither of these respects has he been surpassed by any other sociologists.[102]

Ward also secured recognition for the psychic factors in social evolution at a time when Spencer's influence was very strong. Ward opened an attack against the mechanical world-view of Spencer, based on the attempt to show that mind has the power to control the conditions of life.[103]

How does Hobhouse compare with Ward on this topic of 'telic' progress? What Hobhouse did was to provide a refutation of the mechanistic view of life and mind. He gave a statement of evolution in anti-Spencerian terms, in which mind was seen to play a dominant role. Ward's contribution was very similar, though Hobhouse refuted the laissez-faire philosophy of Spencer and pointed out its social consequences in England and the British colonies.

Hobhouse showed that society had advanced through the application of mental power to human problems. He set forth the concept of 'development' as revealed in historical ethical growth, and in mental and material culture. He traced the growth of mind in society, as seen in man's increasing power over nature. He portrayed the role of purposeful intelligence in social evolution and set forth the hypothesis that the increasing harmony of society has been dependent upon intellectual control of life-conditions.[104] He showed that, by means of social guidance through tradition, science, religion and ethics, life becomes more organized, rational and humane. He gave an exposition of the concept of progress in terms of the rational control of life-conditions, leading to a harmony of individual and social development. Hobhouse pointed out that the nature of mind is to grow and develop. Mind, like the knowledge that it produces, is not static but dynamic, and this fact has important implications for man's future.

Of the two sociologists, it would appear that Ward exerted the more widespread influence. Although their outlooks were essentially similar on the points mentioned above, and though they both furnished a refutation of Spencer's philosophy, yet the writings of Ward aroused a greater interest and received more attention. Ward had been a Spencerian in his philosophical viewpoint. He had rejected Spencer's conservatism and laissez-faire individualism, but had accepted the mechanistic view of evolution in his younger days. As noted by Ellwood, here was a Spencerian refuting Spencer, and *Dynamic Sociology* (1883) 'at once produced a sensation among Spencer's followers'.[105] Ward had a temporal priority over Hobhouse, since it was not until 1901 that *Mind in Evolution* appeared, in the Preface of which work Hobhouse mentioned his obligations to Ward.

Other later sociologists who have contributed to this general topic include Clarence M. Case, who furnished the term 'societal self-direction', referring to the ability of a society to select a goal and move towards it. He also set forth three criteria in this respect: (a) *utilization* of natural resources, (b) *equalization* of distribution of natural resources and social values, and (c) *appreciation* of social values. Case saw political regeneration, education, religion and eugenics as means of societal self-direction. He restated the faith of Comte and Ward in man's power to direct and accelerate social evolution, and suggested a combination of means for this end.

Charles A. Ellwood had the telic emphasis of Comte, Ward and Hobhouse, and was influenced by all three, particularly by Ward and Hobhouse. Ellwood saw progress in terms of a socialized and ethical science, education and religion.

Finally, Robert Briffault has tried to answer the question of how human progress has come about in man's evolution. He sees the answer in an increased control by man over the conditions of his life. For Briffault, whatever enhances the expansion of that control is good, and whatever frustrates it is bad. He regards this control as having developed through a process of 'rational causation', and has ably summarized the rise of civilization in a work entitled *The Making of Humanity*.[106]

In his general sociological outlook and method, Hobhouse may be most aptly compared with Ellwood, Ginsberg, MacIver and Cooley.

Notes and References

1. See Pitirim A. Sorokin, *The Reconstruction of Humanity* (Boston: Beacon Press, 1948), and *The Crisis of Our Age: the Social and Cultural Outlook* (New York: E. P. Dutton, 1941).

2. Pitirim A. Sorokin, *Contemporary Sociological Theories* (New York: Harper & Brothers, 1928), Chapter 1.

3. Clarence M. Case, *Social Process and Human Progress* (New York: Harcourt Brace, 1931), pp. 260–71.

4. See *Mind in Evolution*, also *Development and Purpose*. It is not implied here that Hobhouse was either the first or the only critic of mechanism. Spencer's materialistic world-view was attacked by several writers. See, for example, James Ward, *Naturalism and Agnosticism* (London: Adam, 1903).

5. Case, *Social Process and Human Progress*, p. 260.

6. ibid., p. 34.

7. Charles A. Ellwood, 'The Struggle over Method in the Social Sciences', *Social Science*, 5: 137–40, 1930. See also Ellwood's *Methods in Sociology, a Critical Study* (Durham: Duke University Press, 1933), pp. 21, 52.

8. See Ellwood, *Methods in Sociology*, pp. 53, 65, 66.

9. Charles A. Ellwood, 'Scientific Method', letter to the editor of *Science*, 37: 412, 14 March 1913.

10. J. S. Haldane, 'Are Physical, Biological and Psychological Categories Irreducible?' in *Life and Finite Individuality* (London: Williams & Norgate, 1918), pp. 73, 74.

11. See *Social Development, Its Nature and Conditions*, pp. 240, 241.

12. It is not possible to state the extent to which Hobhouse was actually responsible for Ellwood's anti-mechanistic outlook. That Ellwood took this viewpoint before his First World War contact with Hobhouse is evidenced by the date (1913) of the above quotation (see note 9) from *Science*. The hypothesis is put forward by the writer that the effect of Ellwood's contact with Hobhouse in this connection was to strengthen and confirm the anti-mechanistic elements already shown in Ellwood's thinking. It is interesting to note that an earlier teacher of Ellwood in Berlin, Simmel, gives an implied criticism of mechanism when he says that there are many forms in which mental life reconstructs and shapes the content of its world, apart from empirical investigation. Art and religion represent categories by means of which experience is reformulated. Philosophy and the world of values represent other fundamental categories—fundamental in the sense that they cannot be derived from each other or from simpler elements. See Nicholas J. Spykman, *The Social Theory of Georg Simmel* (Chicago: University of Chicago Press, 1925), pp. 16, 17. This would appear to be in direct antithesis to the mechanistic view that reduces all phenomena to the physical and material.

13. Robert M. MacIver, *Social Causation* (Boston: Ginn, 1942), p. 94.

14. ibid., pp. 93–5.

15. See J. S. Haldane, *The Philosophical Basis of Biology* (Garden City, N.Y. Doran, 1931), and *Mechanism, Life and Personality: an examination of the mechanistic theory of life and mind* (New York: Dutton, 1921). See also Joseph Needham (ed.), *Science, Religion and Reality* (New York: Macmillan Company, 1925), and C. E. M. Joad, *Guide to Modern Thought* (New York: Frederick A. Stokes Company, 1933).

16. *Social Thought from Lore to Science*, 1938, Vol. II, pp. 997, 998.

17. Eduard C. Lindeman, 'Sociology Synthesized', a review of Howard W. Odum, *Understanding Society: The Principles of Dynamic Sociology* (New York: Macmillan Company, 1947), *Saturday Review of Literature*, XXX: 13, 27, December 1947. Lindeman's statement, and especially its last sentence, may be compared with one by Hugh Carter to the effect that Hobhouse had made 'a colossal attempt to bridge the distance between philosophy and a science of society' (*The Social Theories of L. T. Hobhouse*, 1927, p. 132).

18. *Social Process and Human Progress*, p. 33.

19. ibid., p. 61.

20. Sorokin, *Contemporary Sociological Theories*, pp. 40, 41.

21. See Pitirim A. Sorokin, 'Improvement of Scholarship in the Social Sciences', *Journal of Social Philosophy*, II: 237–45, April 1937, quoted in Ellwood, *A History of Social Philosophy* (New York: Prentice-Hall, 1939), pp. 555–8.

22. Ellwood, op. cit., pp. 557, 558.

23. Ellwood, *Sociology in its Psychological Aspects* (New York: D. Appleton-Century Company, 1912), 66.

24. ibid., pp. 92, 93.

25. *Methods in Sociology* (Durham, North Carolina: Duke University Press, 1933), pp. 83, 84.

26. See Nicholas J. Spykman, *The Social Theory of Georg Simmel* (Chicago: University of Chicago Press, 1925), p. 12.

27. ibid., p. 14.

28. See Harry Elmer Barnes, Howard Becker and Frances Bennett Becker, *Contemporary Social Theory* (New York: D. Appleton-Century Company, 1940), p. 541.

29. MacIver, *Social Causation*, pp. 259, 260, 385–7.

30. Talcott Parsons, *The Structure of Social Action, a Study in Social Theory with Special Reference to a Group of Recent European Writers* (New York: McGraw-Hill, 1937), pp. 6–10.

31. See John Dewey's *Logic* and *The Quest for Certainty*. For a good statement of the role of assumptions in modern science, see Arnold Nash, *The University and the Modern World* (New York: Macmillan Company, 1944), Chapter III.

32. Ellwood, *A History of Social Philosophy*, p. 405. In this connection, it is interesting to note that Ellwood regarded as 'probably the best psychological criticism of Comte's law of the three stages' the one given by Hobhouse (see Ellwood, op. cit., p. 383). Ellwood also cites the saying of Albion W. Small that 'students of sociology should always keep both feet on the ground', and he interprets this as meaning that 'sociology should be based upon all of the facts of human experience, past and present, tangible and intangible, objective and subjective' (ibid., p. 558). On this interpretation, then, Small stands very close to Hobhouse.

33. P. A. Sorokin, *Society, Culture, and Personality, their Structure and Dynamics, a System of General Sociology* (New York: Harper & Brothers, 1947), p. 25.

34. See, for example, *The Crisis of Our Age* and *The Reconstruction of Humanity*.

35. Case, *Social Process and Human Progress*, pp. 33–5, 270.

36. Parsons, *The Structure of Social Action*, pp. v–vi. It may be noted that both Hobhouse and Parsons use the word 'dialectic'. Hobhouse employed this term in connection with the German school of thought, based on Hegel, which he criticized so vigorously in *The Metaphysical Theory of the State*. Similarly, Parsons's quotation is from a work that deals with German thinkers, written after ts author had studied in Germany.

37. R. M. MacIver, *The Elements of Social Science* (London: Methuen, 1944)' seventh edition, pp. 15, 16.

38. ibid., p. 18.

39. MacIver, *Social Causation*, pp. 156–8.

40. ibid., p. 388.

41. ibid., p. 392.

42. R. M. MacIver, *Community, a Sociological Study* (London: Macmillan, 1917), Preface, p. ix.

43. See Charles Horton Cooley, 'The Roots of Social Knowledge', *American Journal of Sociology*, 32: 59–79, July 1926.

44. Spykman, *The Social Theory of Georg Simmel*, p. x.

45. ibid., pp. x–xiii. Spykman would appear to be in agreement with Hobhouse regarding the need for a social philosophy in the search for a synoptic treatment of social phenomena. But Spykman apparently had a narrower concept of sociology than Hobhouse, who included social philosophy in his broad domain. The general American viewpoint is nearer to Spykman's and holds that he is correct in denouncing the indiscriminate use of the term 'sociology'. Hobhouse is more typically European (and English) in his broader use of the term. He

would probably agree with Spykman, though, regarding the need for defining sociology's relations to other disciplines.

46. Ellwood, *Sociology in its Psychological Aspects*, p. 84.

47. Ellwood, *Methods in Sociology, a Critical Study*, p. 82. In this same volume, Ellwood says that the work of Hobhouse and Sorokin constitutes good examples of adequate scholarship in the social sciences. Ellwood also claims that there is a need for more sociologists like Hobhouse and Cooley, who are trained in the spirit and methods of modern science, yet combine this with a philosophical approach to the problem (ibid., pp. 7, 26).

48. Morris Ginsberg, *Reason and Unreason in Society, Essays in Sociology and Social Philosophy* (London: Longmans, Green, 1947), p. 56.

49. Barnes and Becker, *Social Thought from Lore to Science*, Vol. II, p. 990.

50. George A. Lundberg, Read Bain, and Nels Anderson (eds.), *Trends in American Sociology* (New York: Harper & Brothers, 1929), p. 370.

51. Howard Becker, 'Sociology', *Britannica Book of the Year*, 1947, p. 704.

52. Emory S. Bogardus, 'Cooperative Research', *Research News* (University of Southern California, Graduate School), XI: 2, October 1946.

53. Emory S. Bogardus, *The Developnent of Social Thought* (New York: Longmans, Green, 1940), p. 479.

54. Spykman, *The Social Theory of Georg Simmel*, p. xii.

55. R. M. MacIver, *Society, a Textbook of Sociology* (New York: Farrar & Rinehart, 1937), pp. 518–20; and *Society, its Structure and Changes* (New York: Ray Long & Richard R. Smith, 1931), pp. 407, 408. MacIver contends that Hobhouse did not always keep facts and values separate in his own work, and that Hobhouse's criteria of value tend to conflict. On the other hand, Ginsberg has maintained, in conversation with the present writer, that this charge is unfounded and that Hobhouse's use of the term 'development' did not involve ethical colouring.

56. W. I. Thomas and Florian Znaniecki, *The Polish Peasant in Europe and America* (New York: Alfred A. Knopf, 1927).

57. C. M. Case, *Essays in Social Values* (Los Angeles: University of Southern California Press, 1944), pp. 37–9.

58. C. A. Ellwood, *Methods in Sociology*, pp. 24, 64; and 'Emasculated Sociologies', *Sociology and Social Research*, 17: 219–29, January 1933.

59. P. A. Sorokin, *Society, Culture, and Personality*, p. 41.

60. Morris Ginsberg, *Sociology* (London: Oxford University Press, 1947), pp. 24–37.

61. MacIver, *Community*, pp. 20, 21.

62. Howard E. Jensen, Introduction to C. A. Ellwood, *Methods in Sociology*,

p. xxxiv. For a classical portrayal of the significance of values in human inter-action and the social sciences, see Radhakamal Mukerjee, *The Social Structures of Values* (London: Macmillan, 1950).

63. Howard Becker, 'Sociology', *10 Eventful Years, a record of events of the years preceding, including and following World War II, 1937 through 1946* (Chicago: University of Chicago and Encyclopaedia Britannica, 1947), Vol. 4, p. 113.

64. See C. A. Ellwood, *The Psychology of Human Society, an Introduction to Sociological Theory* (New York: D. Appleton-Century Company, 1936).

65. R. M. MacIver, *Community*, p. 19.

66. ibid., p. iv. See also *The Elements of Social Science*, pp. 14–19.

67. Sorokin, *Society, Culture, and Personality, their Structure and Dynamics, a System of General Sociology*, p. 679.

68. ibid., p. 680.

69. Hobhouse clearly points out (*Morals in Evolution*, 1919 edition, pp. 31, 32' and *Social Development*, p. 207) that social evolution presents a winding curve rather than a linear process. Any particular culture shows the interaction of many social forces, and it is very apparent that Hobhouse did not believe in any linear type of social evolution (see *Development and Purpose*, 1927 edition, pp. 191, 235).

With reference to the three principles of kinship, authority and citizenship, Hobhouse states categorically that they do not represent successive stages in serial order. They merely involve types of the social bond that appear to be predominant in social development. They may be blended, or exist co-tem-poraneously, in varying degrees. Hobhouse's recognition of the fact that 'we cannot say of humanity as a whole that it began with the system of kinship, passed into that of authority, and ended with that of citizenship' (*Social Evolution and Political Theory*: New York, Columbia University Press, 1922, p. 148) would seem to show the inapplicability of Sorokin's criticism. On pp. 149–54 of the above volume, Hobhouse gives further amplification of his position regarding the non-linear character of social evolution. Sorokin mentions numerous other theories put forth by Toenies, Durkheim, Buckle, Spencer, Novicow, Gobineau, E. de Roberty, Karl Marx, Sir John Lubbock and other writers, and makes the same general criticism of them all, in addition to Hobhouse's theory of kinship, authority and citizenship. Actually, Hobhouse was more empirical in his approach than most of the above writers, and he had greater command of the relevant facts. He was not a mere subjective theorist who proclaimed pet fancies regarding 'laws' of social evolution. On the contrary, he went to the *facts* of mental life to show that the growing power of mind is the underlying force of historical development.

Since the three principles mentioned above illuminate the rise of the state, it may be noted that he has influenced the thought of Harold Laski. In a con-versation with the writer, Professor Ginsberg set forth the view that many of the ideas in Laski's *A Grammar of Politics* reflect the thought of Hobhouse.

70. Harry Elmer Barnes makes a pertinent statement to the effect that 'Professor Hobhouse's survey of the origin and historic development of the state is one of the best summaries of that subject to be found in any language'. See Harry Elmer Barnes, *An Introduction to the History of Sociology* (Chicago: University of Chicago Press, 1948), pp. 626, 627.

71. Norman Wilde, in *Journal of Philosophy, Psychology, and Scientific Methods*, 4: 183, 28 March 1907.

72. L. T. Hobhouse, *Morals in Evolution, a Study in Comparative Ethics* (New York: Henry Holt, 1925), p. v.

73. Dr. Radhakamal Mukerjee has made a contribution to this field with *The Dynamics of Morals, a Sociopsychological Theory of Ethics* (London: Macmillan, 1951), but the approach is more psychological than historical.

74. W. E. H. Lecky, *History of European Morals from Augustus to Charlemagne* (London: Longmans, Green, 1920), 2 vols.

75. Herbert Spencer, *Descriptive Sociology: or Groups of Sociological Facts Classified and Arranged* (New York: D. Appleton, 1873–81), Preface, p. iv.

76. Spencer has been subject to criticism for many years. The main criticism of Spencer in this particular connection is that, compared with Hobhouse, he made little intelligent use of the historical method. His approach was deductive rather than inductive. His theory tends to order his data, and it is noteworthy that Albion W. Small characterized Spencer's method as 'speculation fortified by illustration', a judgement which Ellwood regards as not altogether unfair. See Charles A. Ellwood, *A History of Social Philosophy*, p. 442.

77. *Morals in Evolution*, Preface, p. vii.

78. Melvin J. Williams, 'Representative Sociological Contributions to Religion and Ethics', in Harry Elmer Barnes and Howard Becker, *Contemporary Social Theory*, p. 860. Hobhouse's own comments on Westermarck's volumes are pertinent. He praised the book, saying that 'Professor Westermarck's book as a whole is a contribution of first importance to the work of removing sociology from the region of more or less plausible theorizing and establishing it once for all as an inductive science' (see Hobhouse's review in *Sociological Review*, II: 402, October 1909). He mentioned the lucidity, comprehensive knowledge and amazing industry represented in Westermarck's contribution, declaring that it made it possible for the first time to move securely on the lines of evolutionary interpretation.

79. C. Wright Mills, 'Edward Alexander Westermarck and the Application of Ethnographic Methods to Marriage and Morals', in Harry Elmer Barnes, *An Introduction to the History of Sociology*, pp. 661–2.

80. Hobhouse, *Sociological Review*, II: 403, 404, October 1909. In this review of Westermarck, Hobhouse criticizes the concept of an emotion 'felt by the community at large', and inquires as to the source of agreement among individuals which it implies. He also points out that Westermarck's definition of religion as 'a belief in and a regardful attitude towards a supernatural being on whom man

feels himself dependent and to whose will he makes an appeal in his worship' would exclude Buddhism. However, although Hobhouse differed markedly from his colleague in the analysis of the ethical order, he found himself in broad agreement with Westermarck in the general summary of ethical development with which the *Origin and Development of the Moral Ideas* concludes.

81. Mills, in Barnes, *An Introduction to the History of Sociology*, pp. 659, 660. In fairness to Westermarck, it should be noted that the charge of uncritical use of historical material has been made against Hobhouse. See Harry Elmer Barnes, *Historical Sociology, Its Origin and Development, Theories of Social Evolution from Cave Life to Atomic Bombing* (New York: Philosophical Library, 1948).

82. Mills, in Barnes, *An Introduction to the History of Sociology*, p. 661. This statement could apply with almost equal force to Hobhouse, yet Hobhouse's contributions have been recognized in America, and he has been cited in many sociological works; e.g. Ellwood makes many references to him and L. L. Bernard's *Social Control in Its Sociological Aspects* (New York: Macmillan Company, 1939) contains many quotations, often of length, from *Morals in Evolution*, which may itself be regarded as a study in social control in its historical features. Mills makes the significant statement, though, that 'a sociology of morals, worthy of the name, cannot be said to exist among American social thinkers' (ibid., p. 662). This is still the case in 1974.

83. Harry Elmer Barnes, 'Some Typical Contributions of English Sociology to Political Theory, (II) Leonard T. Hobhouse and the Neo-Liberal Theory of the State', *American Journal of Sociology*, 27: 448, January 1922.

84. William Graham Sumner, *Folkways, A Study of the Sociological Importance of Usages, Manners, Customs, Mores, and Morals* (Boston: Ginn, 1906).

85. Harry Elmer Barnes, *An Introduction to the History of Sociology*, p. 158.

86. Floyd N. House, *The Range of Social Theory, A Survey of the Development, Literature, Tendencies and Fundamental Problems of the Social Sciences* (New York: Henry Holt, 1929), 253–5.

87. Barnes, *An Introduction to the History of Sociology*, p. 156. Despite this criticism, Barnes (p. 170) attests to the worth of *Folkways* by describing it as 'the outstanding sociological analysis of the origin and nature of moral codes and social customs'.

A further work on the subject of evolutionary ethics is J. H. Breasted, *The Dawn of Consciousness* (New York: Charles Scribner's Sons, 1939). This book only deals, however, with the early human period and gives little treatment of the post-Hebrew era. It is not specifically factual, but gives a useful study of early religion, myth and worship. Hobhouse's pupil, Charles A. Ellwood, has furnished a study of cultural growth which is not dissimilar in its conclusions from *Morals in Evolution*. Like *Folkways*, however, it deals with topics other than those specifically considered by Hobhouse, as its title indicates: *Cultural Evolution, a Study of Social Origins and Development* (New York: The Century Co., 1927).

88. Harry Elmer Barnes has written of Hobhouse's 'masterly excursion into historical jurisprudence', and has declared that 'nothing to equal it exists in any language within the same number of pages'. See 'Some Typical Contributions of English Sociology to Political Theory, (II) Leonard T. Hobhouse and the Neo-Liberal Theory of the State', p. 463.

89. Hobhouse has applied the principle of the rational good to modern problems in the practical fields of economic and political life, industrial organization and social affairs generally. In *The Elements of Social Justice* (New York: Henry Holt, 1922), he has shown some of the implications of the principle of harmony in society. In the view of most contemporary sociologists, this would be regarded as a contribution to social ethics rather than to social science.

90. Bogardus, *The Development of Social Thought*, p. 381.

91. Albion W. Small, *General Sociology, an Exposition of the Main Development in Sociological Theory from Spencer to Ratzenhofer* (Chicago: University of Chicago Press, 1905), pp. 369–70, 433ff.

92. See Charles A. Ellwood, *The Psychology of Human Society* (1936), pp. 426–7. Ellwood's use of the concept of harmony as a social norm probably came from the influence of Hobhouse. A more differentiated set of norms or tests of progress is provided by C. M. Case, in his analysis of utilization, equalization and appreciation. See his 'What is Social Progress?', *Journal of Applied Sociology*, XI: 109–19, November–December 1925, and *Social Process and Human Progress*, pp. 61–71.

93. See R. E. Park and E. W. Burgess, *Introduction to the Science of Sociology* (Chicago: University of Chicago Press, 1921), p. 496.

94. Hobhouse's emphasis upon humanitarianism, like the 'telic' emphasis of Lester F. Ward, may be questioned by some sociologists as not constituting a contribution to science. In this connection, C. M. Case makes a pertinent comment when he speaks of 'the marked tendency of many professional scholars to suffer a distortion of perspective wherein "academic" values loom bigger than the *human* values of which they are merely a highly specialized aspect . . .' (*Social Process and Human Progress*, p. 259).

95. Morris Ginsberg, *Reason and Unreason in Society*, Chapter XVI.

96. Barnes notes that William Graham Sumner was 'the outstanding American sociological opponent of militarism and imperialism, comparable in this way to L. T. Hobhouse in England', and he refers to Sumner's *War, and Other Essays* in this connection (*Introduction to the History of Sociology*, p. 170). But it may be asked whether Sumner's opposition to militarism and imperialism is not incompatible with his vigorous defence of laissez-faire. Hobhouse's attitude towards war and imperialism is an outgrowth of his harmony-principle, and reflects the value of a consistent theory.

97. Bogardus, *The Development of Social Thought*, pp. 288–90.

98. Peter Kropotkin, *Mutual Aid: a Factor in Evolution* (New York: Doubleday, Page & Co., 1902).

99. Bogardus, *The Development of Social Thought*, p. 386. Although Hobhouse wrote out of a background in which the problems of British colonial relations loomed large, it is contended that the principles expounded in his *Democracy and Reaction* (1904) have a wider application than the immediate temporal situation to which they referred. When read in the light of recent world history, the volume may be described as prophetic.

100. Case, *Social Process and Human Progress*, p. 116. A criticism of one-sided biological interpretations of society and progress is given by Ellwood in *The Psychology of Human Society*, pp. 278, 430–32. Similarly, the German writer, J. H. W. Stuckenberg, attacked the extreme biological theory that emanated from social Darwinism, according to which sociology is a socio-biological science that has no concern with ethical questions. Stuckenberg may be compared with Hobhouse, as Barnes has shown: ' . . . Stuckenberg takes the same general position as Hobhouse in holding that the growth of harmony and co-operative activities in social organization constitutes the soundest test of progress toward the ideal society. There must be efficient social organization, but this must not preclude the existence of all reasonable freedom for the individual' (Barnes, *An Introduction to the History of Sociology*, p. 808). Barnes also notes that Stuckenberg thought in terms of humanity, rather than the national state, and that 'he was, along with Stein and Hobhouse, one of the most ardent advocates among sociological writers of an adequate development of international political machinery . . .' (ibid., p. 815).

The biological school of sociology has been ably examined and criticized by Sorokin (*Contemporary Sociological Theories*, Chapter IV). He notes its main characteristics, criticizing them skilfully from the theoretical sociological point of view. Hobhouse, on the other hand, applied scientific arguments, but in relation to a practical situation in British social and political life. Sorokin gives a historical account and critical examination of the biological school as a whole, from the earliest representatives to modern times. But this criticism does not relate to 'progress' as interpreted by the biological school.

101. See Ellwood, *A History of Social Philosophy*, p. 564. See also Lester F. Ward, *Dynamic Sociology, or Applied Social Science, as Based Upon Statistical Sociology and the Less Complex Sciences* (New York: D. Appleton & Company, 1910), p. 57.

102. Barnes, *An Introduction to the History of Sociology*, p. 176.

103. See Albion W. Small, *General Sociology*, pp. 82–3.

104. According to Barnes, Hobhouse's insistence upon the need for harmonious social development as a goal of social evolution and upon the application of the best thought to this problem 'cannot be too highly commended' (*An Introduction to the History of Sociology*, p. 649). Both Ward and Hobhouse are outstanding for their emphasis upon human purpose as a social force. Barnes has said of Hobhouse that 'his social philosophy is the most effective English substantiation of Lester F. Ward's notion of *social telesis*' ('Some Typical Contributions of English Sociology to Political Theory, (II) Leonard T. Hobhouse and the Neo-Liberal Theory of the State', p. 442). It would appear, as Barnes notes (op. cit.,

p. 445) that Hobhouse has a greater command of the data of social and cultural evolution and so could speak with more exactness and authority. One of Hobhouse's distinctive contributions lies in his concept of social harmony and development as the essence of progress. Ward did not utilize this criterion. The need, expressed by Hobhouse, for an organic view of society and its advancement should also be mentioned.

105. Ellwood, *A History of Social Philosophy*, p. 528. An interesting similarity between Ward and Hobhouse is seen in their common use of the term 'achievement'. Ward says in regard to this: 'My thesis is that the subject-matter of sociology is human achievement. It is not what men are but what they do. It is not the structure but the function'—*Pure Sociology* (New York: Macmillan Company, 1903), p. 15. Ward equated achievement with invention, 'The artificial modification of natural phenomena', of which no animal is capable. *Pure Sociology* has a decidedly cultural emphasis. The cultural emphasis also runs through Hobhouse's works, and he defines culture as 'a fabric of human achievement' (*Social Evolution and Political Theory*, p. 102; see also *Social Development, Its Nature and Conditions*, pp. 170–72). For both men, the study of cultural products, or human achievement, constituted sociology.

It may be asked whether Hobhouse's definition of progress as the 'rational good' or harmonious development of society does not constitute a more adequate criterion than Ward's view of the increase of human happiness as progress. Similarly, Ward looked upon education as the mere imparting of knowledge, though Hobhouse also saw moral growth as a part of education, the development of emotions and feelings, as well as growth in knowledge. Both men, however, were similar in their synthetic outlook. They used knowledge from all sources that impinged on sociology, and did not restrict themselves to a narrow concept of their subject-matter. Since Hobhouse was later in time than Ward, he had the advantage of being able to utilize all that had been achieved in the realm of scholarship in the intervening years.

106. Robert Briffault, *The Making of Humanity* (London: Allen & Unwin, 1919). The great American opponent of these 'telic' views of progress is Spencer's disciple, William Graham Sumner, whose concern with folkways and mores led him to disbelieve in man's power to direct and guide his future. But Sumner apparently failed to give much consideration to the fact that the mores are transmitted by tradition, which is a cultural product arising from the mind of man. Sumner also appeared to place little emphasis upon the great culture-building factors of society, such as art, science and religion, whereby man remakes his world. In comparison, it should be noted that Hobhouse did actually engage in empirical research to show the role of intelligent purpose, and studied history from this viewpoint. Hobhouse was historical and empirical in his study of mind in evolution.

8 Summary and Conclusions

The present study has been an attempt to show some of the particular ways in which Leonard Trelawny Hobhouse made contributions to sociology. A partial summary of Hobhouse's work is seen in the breadth and scope of his publications.

His first book was *The Labour Movement* (1893, 1912), an analysis of the economic life of Britain, dealing with trade unions and the cooperative movement. He followed this with *The Theory of Knowledge* (1896), a study of the problems of logic and metaphysics from a realist point of view. *Mind in Evolution* (1901) traced the development of mind in terms of an increasing correlation, and summarized the comparative psychological research of Hobhouse in the realm of animal behaviour. *Democracy and Reaction* (1904) was a vigorous yet reasoned criticism of the imperialism and racial domination that was being 'justified' by the then current social Darwinism. The book is also a fine statement of the requirements of democratic rights. *Morals in Evolution* (1906) was his classic summary of the development of human customs, practices and ideas relating to conduct. *Social Evolution and Political Theory* (1911) set forth the three principles of kinship, authority and citizenship, in addition to indicating the fundamental distinction between evolution and progress. *Liberalism* (1911) was a brief but comprehensive statement of different types of liberty, and an exposition of the philosophical creed of the British Liberal Party at that time. It emphasized the importance of human rights, as did nearly all of his works. *Development and Purpose* (1913, 1927) was a statement of the philosophical implications of the theory of development and harmony. It considers the facts of history and sets forth a metaphysical system in which the power of mind is made the central force in all development.

Together with many other persons in both Britain and America, the present writer maintains that it is Hobhouse's greatest work.

The Material Culture and Social Institutions of the Simpler Peoples (1915) was a pioneer treatise in comparative anthropology. It was largely concerned with the relationship between economic organization and the other aspects of primitive culture.

The World in Conflict (1915) was an analysis of the forces that led to the First World War, and a statement of the requirements of a lasting peace. *Questions of War and Peace* (1916) consisted of a dialogue on the First World War, its causes and issues, and world affairs generally. A related work was *The Metaphysical Theory of the State, a Criticism* (1918), which was a vigorous refutation of the assumptions and implications of the German view of the omnipotent God-state, as interpreted by Hegel and Bosanquet.

The Rational Good (1922) set forth the concept of harmony as a norm of progress, considering it from a philosophical viewpoint, and *The Elements of Social Justice* (1921) shows how the principle of harmony may be applied to modern problems. It is an excellent study in applied social ethics.

Social Development, Its Nature and Conditions (1924) shows the conditions underlying human evolution, elaborates upon the meaning of the term, gives some non-ethical criteria by which societies may be judged, and reviews the growth of mind in human association.

In addition to the above list, Hobhouse was the author of several important articles. This vast body of writing covered many realms, in all of which Hobhouse made intellectual contributions of value.

In the realm of science, Hobhouse made an implied plea for the objective analysis of science and its ramifications by the social scientist. He insisted that it is not in the nature of science to assume the metaphysical theory of materialism at the outset of research, and that it is not the object of science to reduce all phenomena to matter. This is a consideration that is often overlooked in discussions of science and scientific purposes.

He gave a reasoned criticism of the mechanistic philosophy which was dominant in his day, and which still tends to persist in much social and natural science. He showed that mechanism rests upon false presuppositions and that it does not furnish an adequate explanation or interpretation of either the physical universe or the human organism. He pointed out the differences between the human body and the machine, and indicated that mechanism cannot account for the phenomena of purposeful activity.

He engaged in empirical research upon sub-human behaviour and showed thereby that the element of conation exists in animal life. He was one of the pioneers of comparative psychology and was enabled to formulate his philosophical theories upon an empirical study of the growth of mind on both the sub-human and the human levels.

He stressed the fact that assumptions are basic to logic and science, and that they underlie all scientific work. He showed the relation between assumptions and hypotheses, and pointed to the need for sound logic in the use of hypotheses. This involved the analysis of some of the dangers inherent in hypotheses.

He analysed the meaning of the empirical approach and noted the importance of not restricting the range of 'experience', though this restriction is often done in contemporary science and philosophy. He followed Comte in insisting that reason must be combined with observation. He also gave a more up-to-date statement of positivism or empiricism, stressing the importance of going to the facts of experience rather than building up a metaphysical system by *a priori* dogmas. A philosophical contribution lay in his helping to establish realism in British philosophy, despite the strong Hegelian current of thought that was dominant in the British and Scottish universities in the last quarter of the nineteenth century.

The inseparable connection between fact and theory was implicitly recognized by Hobhouse. He showed how an acquaintance with philosophy can be beneficial in the most rigidly empirical science. He also noted that science is not the sole gateway to valid knowledge; he has indicated that all areas of human experience have a claim in the kingdom of truth, and that the religious, aesthetic and philosophical approaches to knowledge rightfully demand autonomy of investigation.

He displayed the need for concepts to be based upon experience, and showed the dangers and limitations involved in deducing concepts from other concepts. He noted the tendency for concepts to form a world of their own into which all experience must fit or be considered unreal, and the tendency of concepts to solidify into hard moulds.

He wrote at length on the desirability of maintaining an attitude of mind that is tentative and experimental. He emphasized the fact that the present stage of knowledge is only a stage in human development and that there are therefore few unmodifiable truths.

He maintained that science should not be identified with mathematical measurement and he raised several thought-provoking questions regarding both the possibility and the desirability of interpreting the social reality in terms of mathematical-physics. In this connection, he noted that some of the most important factors in human experience are those very factors that are least amenable to mathematical treatment.

In a general prolegomena to sociology, he called attention to the imponderable and intangible factors in human association and pointed out that it is unscientific to assume that they do not exist merely because they cannot be reduced to mathematical terms. He was one of the few sociologists to emphasize human purpose as a social force that had to be considered in any realistic interpretation of societal interaction. He showed that the category of purpose was basic to the understanding of mental activity.

All through the writings of Hobhouse runs an emphasis, both implied and explicit, upon the need for sound theoretical foundations in sociology. He pointed out that theory underlies the research of those who would be quick to disavow any connection with philosophy, and he gave a good example in the work of Comte. Comte's whole system was based, as Hobhouse clearly indicated, upon a metaphysical theory.

Hobhouse has written at length on the desirability of maintaining a synthetic view of sociology. He expressed certain warnings regarding early trends in sociology, warnings which have been vindicated by future developments in the science. His warnings applied more particularly to the specialization that was taking place within the social sciences. The years since his time have seen the rise of specialities within sociology itself.

He also warned sociologists against the thraldom of intellectual fashions and fads in methods and approach. His own wide knowledge of history and philosophy suggests that greater perspective might be gained from an acquaintance with past developments in sociology, science and thought generally. He protested against monistic or one-sided views of social life and warned against the tendency to extend a method to all areas of experience simply because it had yielded good results in one particular field.

He portrayed a four-fold historical and philosophical heritage of modern sociology at the outset of his career, and insisted on the separation of the scientific and the philosophical approaches to sociology. For Hobhouse, the factual and the normative methods were equally legitimate in social study, but should be complementary to one another rather than fused.

He expressed a fundamental point in noting the importance of values as part of the subject-matter of sociology. Explicit references to this are not numerous in his works, but the importance of values in society and the view of individuals as *valuing* and *value-making* beings are inherent in his writings.

He has indirectly asserted the importance of sociological *understanding*, as distinct from the mere gathering of factual data. The importance of the latter function is not denied, but it may be contended that knowledge consists in the increase of the understanding of the facts, as well as in the attempt to gather additional facts. He emphasized the concept of reason as 'the method of growth in understanding', and expressed certain ideas pertinent to the formulation of sociological laws and generalizations.

In the realm of social evolution and progress, Hobhouse set forth some prolegomena to the sociological study of morality, and made an outstanding contribution in his own study of the evolution of moral ideas and practices. *Morals in Evolution* was one of the earliest works to provide an objective summary of the development of ethical consciousness in man, as portrayed in five main fields of human association.

The exposition of the three principles of kinship, authority and citizenship represent an illuminating theory for the understanding of social evolution, as well as furnishing a series of hypotheses for further research in this area.

He provided several pertinent preliminary considerations relating to social progress, and gave a norm of progress in the concept of 'harmony', the philosophical ramifications of which he discussed at length. The concept of harmonious growth became for Hobhouse the centre of a systematic treatment of society and its foundations. He applied the principle to the modern problems of economic life, industrial organization and international relations.

He gave a reasoned criticism of the individualistic philosophy of

Herbert Spencer and the social Darwinists, and pointed out that progress lies not in an unmitigated struggle for existence but in a rational humanitarianism. Similarly, he spoke out vigorously against militarism, exploitation and imperialism. By so doing, he showed that an evaluative approach to social problems, when synthesized with an impartial search for social facts, can enable the sociologist to transcend the ethos of the class, country and era of which he is a part.

He provided a criticism of the Hegelian view of the State, and showed the actual evolution of the state, insisting that it was only one of several institutions to which human beings owed allegiance. Allied with this contribution was a fine expression of the meaning of democratic humanitarianism.

He set forth arguments for the telic view of mind, based on an empirical study of mind and investigations into the human past. He provided a reasoned basis for the belief that human advancement is possible and that the concept of a self-directing humanity is valid.

He also did much for the rise of British sociology. The practical contributions of Hobhouse consisted in his years of work in connection with the improvement of labour conditions, the establishment of old-age pensions and the founding of the Department of Sociology at the London School of Economics and Political Science. With respect to the first two of these, it should be noted that Hobhouse founded several trade boards, and served on them, in an attempt to produce harmonious and just labour relations in Britain. Like his friend and colleague, Graham Wallas, he applied his social theories in the practical world of politics, and in turn supplemented his teaching and writing with insights drawn from this wider experience.

The development of academic sociology in Britain owes much to Hobhouse. The Department of Sociology at the London School of Economics and Political Science was for long the only centre of sociological instruction and research in the United Kingdom. It is interesting to note that several leading members of British governments have been connected with the above school, and so, in greater or lesser degree, came under the influence of Hobhouse. Among them may be mentioned the former Prime Minister Clement Atlee, who taught sociology at L.S.E., Harold Laski, Hugh Dalton, Hugh Gaitskell, and many civil servants. Although

Hobhouse was connected with the Liberal Party, his work brought him into contact with several Labour Party figures, and it is a reasonable inference that his teaching and outlook helped to mould their thinking.

Despite the early opposition to sociology as an academic discipline on account of entrenched university interests in England, Hobhouse did pioneer work in establishing the subject. A great deal of work had been done for long in fields broadly sociological—social philosophy, political science, history, anthropology, public adminstration, welfare and economics—fields that were, in England, often classified under the one heading of 'sociology'. But it is only since 1945 that sociology, as the field is now defined, has taken root in British universities. The social changes then accruing from the legislation of the Labour Party, the rise of a social consciousness on the part of more young people, the upheavals in social structure, the emergence of race problems upon the British scene and the academic influence of America as a new world leader have all probably played their part in this development.

By 1949, five new sociology departments were established—at the universities of Birmingham, Hull, Leicester, Manchester and Oxford. Since that date, the new science of society has enjoyed an unprecedented rise in terms of the number of new university departments established, the growth in students enrolled in sociology courses at both undergraduate and postgraduate level, and the number of books, articles and journals published. Some forty British universities now offer sociology as a degree subject, and it has become accepted as a subject in the new colleges of education. As an early founder, Hobhouse may well be regarded as an academic pioneer in the rise of sociology in Britain.

The present writer maintains that, for five reasons, Hobhouse may even be looked upon as 'the Albion W. Small of England'. Small was largely responsible for founding the Department of Sociology at the University of Chicago, regarded by many as the leading department in North America; he likewise played a great part in establishing the American Sociological Society and the *American Journal of Sociology;* in his work entitled *Between Eras, From Capitalism to Democracy*[1] he urged the establishment of industrial councils in which workers might be represented; and finally, in *The Meaning of Social Science,*[2] he indicated the dangers of overspecialization and departmentalism in the social sciences.

Similarly, Hobhouse was largely responsible for founding the London department, as has been seen. He took part in the founding of the Sociological Society in England, and served as the first Editor of the *Sociological Review*; he founded and served on industrial councils, and warned against specialization and departmentalism in sociology and social science.

In connection with his work at the University of London, it may be said that a further contribution lay in the influence he exerted upon Morris Ginsberg, who is to be regarded as a foremost contemporary sociologist of Great Britain. Hobhouse also exerted an undoubted influence upon the thinking of Charles A. Ellwood, his pupil of 1914 and 1915. In their emphasis upon the power of reason, in their humanitarianism, and in their concepts of a self-directing humanity, they show many similarities. How far Hobhouse was responsible for Ellwood's sociological outlook is a question that cannot be answered with precision, but it is well-known that Ellwood's cultural emphasis was partly derived from his year in England under Hobhouse, Marett and other social scientists there. Further similarities between Hobhouse and Ellwood can be seen in their view of the functions of science and rational-ethical religion. It should not be forgotten that Hobhouse gave a fine statement of the role of religion from the rationalist point of view.

Conclusions

Regarding the specific contributions that have been set forth, several conclusions may be stated.

1. It is at once apparent that Leonard Trelawny Hobhouse was one of the great minds in recent sociology, and one of the few modern systematizers. He possessed a vast knowledge which accrued from a combination of philosophical reflection and the power of sustained and detailed research. His scholarship was of a depth and breadth that are rare in modern social science. It enabled him to study society with a historical and philosophical perspective that freed him from any undue attachment to contemporary fashions in method or approach. He represented, on the contrary, a synoptic type of sociology in which knowledge is drawn from all reliable sources. However, despite his many remarkable achievements he is not widely known.

2. Hobhouse's strength lay, at least in part, in his philosophical approach to sociology. It is a truism that the term 'philosophical' has almost come to be one of disrepute in modern scientific sociology, largely on account of the attempt to follow the thought-patterns of the natural sciences. Carter's study of Hobhouse, for example, makes the statement[3] that Hobhouse was a great intellect and that he tried to bridge the gulf between philosophy and a science of society—a statement with which the present writer is in agreement. It is contended, however, that the disparagement of philosophy that runs through Carter's volume and through much modern sociology is unjustified. One aim of the present study has been to show that philosophy or theory can be of vital aid to the sociologist.

To say that Hobhouse was 'philosophical' does not thereby prove that he was unscientific. On the contrary, it is worthy of note that some of the greatest *scientists*, as distinguished from mere technicians, have been philosophers. Einstein is an excellent example, as are the fellow-countrymen of Hobhouse, A. N. Whitehead, Arthur Eddington and James Jeans. Einstein's great discovery was based upon a *philosophical* criticism of the basic *philosophical* presuppositions of Newtonian physics, and his contribution was a *theory* of relativity.

To condemn a sociologist on the ground that he is 'philosophical' is to condemn him for being reflective, analytical and possessed of ideas. It is granted that unfounded speculation should be minimized in sociology. Nevertheless, it may also be repeated that Hobhouse bears eloquent testimony to the distinction between unfounded speculation and rigid, comprehensive, logical analysis.[4]

3. The present writer rejects the charge that Hobhouse did little to forward the development of sociology as a *science*. He would maintain that this springs from a false and narrow concept of science, and that there is considerable question as to whether sociology should attempt to follow the methods and techniques of the natural sciences. To the extent that science is based upon impartial analysis and open-minded investigation, involving the ascertainment of facts, and the careful formulation of statements, Hobhouse was undoubtedly scientific. The writer contends that a mature science will be sanely philosophical and that philosophy will prosper when it is broadly scientific.

4. In connection with the present 'natural science trend' of

modern sociology, it is noteworthy that the natural sciences pre-suppose the existence of an ordered regularity in nature. In view of the great individuality and rich psychic heredity of human beings, is it possible to make the same assumption in the social sciences regarding an ordered regularity in the world of social relations? And does not the inventive and creative capacity of the human mind, with its great culture-building potentialities, invalidate this prime assumption?

5. The study of Hobhouse's works has led the writer to raise the question of whether the orthodox natural science technique (hypothesis, problem-formulation, empirical research, verifica-tion) actually gives many significant *insights* into human relations. The question is also raised as to whether this method has been the cause of many discoveries of data which were not actually known before the investigation in question. Is it not true that natural science techniques, when applied to sociology, often result in the mere restating, in scientific terminology, of what was previously known to any individual of insight and discernment?

6. Since some of the greatest advances in the natural sciences have been brought about through a study of the first principles of science (e.g. Einstein's theory of relativity), is it not reasonable to suppose that sociology might prosper through more philo-sophical analysis of its first principles and basic presuppositions? For example, sociologists *assume* the possibility of a social *science*. To what extent, and in what sense, is this possible?

7. A further conclusion is that scientific techniques cannot in themselves throw light on the problems of what sociology ought to involve and what its objectives should be. These, together with many of the basic questions and problems of sociology, are of the type that transcend science and its techniques. They are questions of theory, value and logic. They involve philosophical issues and value-judgements at every turn.

8. The wealth of ideas that Hobhouse manifested suggests the need for more philosophy, reflection and ideas in sociology. If, as the present writer maintains, ideas are vital social forces, then sociology should become a social force through its ideational content. If the charge should be made that no new sociological knowledge is to be gained or produced by studying the writings of a thinker such as Hobhouse, it may be repeated that such knowledge consists, not merely in the discovery of new factual

data, but in the deepening of *understanding* into human interaction, and that such understanding is to be gained from the study of a great mind in sociology.

9. The foregoing emphasis on knowledge and ideas leads to a further conclusion. Throughout the writings of Hobhouse runs a concern with thought in society, and in one connection it is explicitly stated[5] that sociology should analyse the relation between ideas, intellectual forces and culture. This would appear to be an indirect plea for 'the sociology of knowledge'. Hobhouse did, indeed, recognize that thought is socially conditioned, and his study of social development centred around the growth of *mind* in society. The implication would appear to be that the sociology of knowledge could play a valuable role in enabling sociologists to gain a perspective that would transcend the ethos and outlook of their class, country and time.[6] It could give an insight into the value-systems, thought-ways and dominating ideas of the cultural environment. By the sociology of knowledge there is implied a broad area of research into the historical and intellectual forces that have moulded contemporary culture.

10. The writer maintains that this particular branch of social science, the sociology of knowledge, has not received the attention it deserves. It is further contended that a greater 'objectivity' could be brought about towards the thought-ways of the natural and social sciences through greater interest in the sociological aspects of knowledge and thought. This might enable scientists to see, for example, whence their present outlooks and methodological viewpoints were derived. If scientists could so stand aside from their methods and look at *them* with the same objectivity that they apply to their subject-matter, some interesting revelations might result. If scientists, aided by the sociology of knowledge, were to look at the epistemological premises inherent in natural science, and note how they arose, their present outlooks and conclusions would appear in a fresh light. They would see, for example, that the modern view of science as the only gateway to truth, is, in actuality, a seventeenth-century idea, having grown up with the mathematical-physics of Newton and the epistemology of Locke. The writer therefore submits that more attention might profitably be paid to the roots of sociological and scientific knowledge, and in this task the sociology of knowledge could play a major role. Allied with this viewpoint is that fact that there are

important implications for sociology in Hobhouse's experimental and dynamic concept of knowledge. It suggests the constant need for more philosophical theory and logic, for the examination and revision of the first principles and basic assumptions of sociology and for the extension of the boundaries of research.

A final conclusion relates to the fact that for Hobhouse, as for Cooley, who was his American contemporary (1864–1929), sociology was both a science, a philosophy and an art. The present writer maintains that Leonard Trelawney Hobhouse was scientific in his concern for facts and empirical data, that he was philosophical in his interpretation and analysis of the relationships between facts, and that he was artistic in his recognition and portrayal of the dynamic, living content of sociology.

Notes and References

1. Albion W. Small, *Between Eras, From Capitalism to Democracy* (Kansas City: Intercollegiate Press, 1913).

2. Albion W. Small, *The Meaning of Social Science* (Chicago: University of Chicago Press, 1910).

3. Hugh Carter, *The Social Theories of L. T. Hobhouse* (Chapel Hill: University of North Carolina Press, 1927), p. 132.

4. A criticism may be made regarding the tendency of Hobhouse to follow McDougall's 'instinct psychology'. Had Hobhouse lived longer, it is more than reasonable to suppose that he would have revised his thinking here, as many contemporary sociologists and psychologists have been compelled to do. Nevertheless, this similarity to McDougall did not invalidate the remainder of his social thought. That Hobhouse recognized the difficulties inherent in the conception of 'instinct' is very apparent from a study of the Appendix to the 1926 edition of *Mind in Evolution*. For a competent examination of the concept of 'instinct', see Ronald Fletcher, *Instinct in Man, in the Light of Recent Work in Comparative Psychology* (New York: International Universities Press, 1957). To the charge that Hobhouse's writings during the First World War did not manifest scientific impartiality, it may be replied that in *The Metaphysical Theory of the State* he was concerned with attacking a philosophy that would restrict the rights and freedoms of all human beings, including scientists. In so doing he testified to his own recognition of the priority of human values over mere academic values.

5. L. T. Hobhouse, *The Rational Good* (New York: Henry Holt, 1921), pp. 17–19.

6. It would seem a valid contention that Hobhouse was, in many ways, singularly free from the domination of his class, country and time, so far as his sociological outlook was concerned. His rational humanitarianism, for example, was radically different from the conventional social philosophy of the class into which he was born. He similarly transcended any narrow nationalistic prejudices, in his insistence on humanity as the ultimate group. For these and other reasons, the writer agrees with J. A. Hobson that Hobhouse was 'one of the less known of the great men of our time'. See J. A. Hobson and Morris Ginsberg, *L. T. Hobhouse, His Life and Work* (London: Allen & Unwin, 1931), p. 72.

Bibliography of the Writings of Leonard Trelawney Hobhouse

A. Books

The Theory of Knowledge, a Contribution to some Problems of Logic and Metaphysics. London: Methuen and Co., 1896. xx, 627 pp.

Mind in Evolution. London: Macmillan and Co., 1901. xiv, 415 pp.

Democracy and Reaction. London: T. Fisher Unwin, 1904. vii, 244 pp.

Morals in Evolution, a Study in Comparative Ethics. London: Chapman & Hall, 1906. 2 volumes.

Government by the People. London: The People's Suffrage Federation, 1910. 26 pp.

Liberalism. London: Williams & Norgate, Home University Library, 1911. v, 254 pp.

Social Evolution and Political Theory. New York: Columbia University Press, 1911. ix, 218 pp.

The Labor Movement. New York: The Macmillan Company, 1912. 159 pp.

Mind in Evolution. London: Macmillan and Co., Limited, 1915. xix, 469 pp.

The World in Conflict. London: T. Fisher Unwin, 1915. 104 pp.

Questions of War and Peace. London: T. Fisher Unwin, 1916. 233 pp.

The Metaphysical Theory of the State, a Criticism. New York: Macmillan and Co., Limited, 1918. 156 pp.

Morals in Evolution, a Study in Comparative Ethics. New York: Henry Holt and Company, 1919. xvi, 648 pp.

The Rational Good. New York: Henry Holt and Company, 1921. xxii, 237 pp.

The Elements of Social Justice. New York: Henry Holt and Company, 1922. viii, 247 pp.

Social Evolution and Political Theory. New York: Columbia University Press, 1922. 218 pp.

Social Development, Its Nature and Conditions. New York: Henry Holt and Company, 1924. 348 pp.

Morals in Evolution, a Study in Comparative Ethics. New York: Henry Holt and Company, 1925. xvi, 648 pp.

Mind in Evolution. London: Macmillan and Co., Limited, 1926. 483 pp.

Development and Purpose, an Essay Towards a Philosophy of Evolution. London: Macmillan and Co., Limited, 1927. xxxix, 494 pp.

B. Articles

'The Principle of Induction', *Mind*, XVI: 80–91, January 1891.

'Induction and Deduction', *Mind*, XVI: 507–20, October 1891.

'The Ethical Basis of Collectivism', *International Journal of Ethics*, 8: 137–56, January 1898.

'The Laws of Hammurabi', *The Living Age*, XIX: 250–53, 25 April 1903.

'Faith and the Will to Believe', *Proceedings of the Aristotelian Society*, VI: 87–111, 1904.

'Editorial', *Sociological Review*, 1: 1–11, January 1908.

' The Law of the Three Stages', *Sociological Review*, 1: 262–279, July 1908.

Review of J. S. Mackenzie, *Lectures on Humanism, with Special Reference to its Bearings on Sociology* (London: Swan, Sonnenschein & Co., 1907) in *Sociological Review*, I: 305–306, July 1908.

'Ethical Evolution', review of E. A. Westermarck, *The Origin and Development* (London: Macmillan and Co., Limited, 1908) in *Sociological Review*, II: 402–5, October 1909.

'The Material Culture and Social Institutions of the Simpler Peoples, an Essay in Correlation', *Sociological Review*, VII: 203–31, July 1914. (Written in collaboration with G. C. Wheeler and Morris Ginsberg.)

'The Social Effects of the War', *Atlantic Monthly*, 115: 544–50, April 1915.

'The Soul of Civilization, a Dialogue', *Contemporary Review*, 108: 158–65, August 1915.

'Are Physical, Biological and Psychological Categories Irreducible?', *Life and Finite Individuality, Proceedings of the Aristotelian Society*, pp. 62–71, 1918.

'Democracy and Civilization', *Sociological Review*, XIII: 125–35, July 1921.

'Sociology', *Hasting's Dictionary of Religion and Ethics*, XI: 654–65, 1921.

'Competitive and Social Value', *Economics*, IV: 278–90, November 1924.

'The Place of Mind in Nature', *Methods of Analysis, Aristotelian Society*, Supplementary Volume V: 112–26, 1926.

'Aristocracy', *Encyclopedia of the Social Sciences*, II: 183–90, 1930.

'Christianity', *Encyclopedia of the Social Sciences*, III: 452–61, 1930.

'Comparative Ethics', *Encyclopaedia Britannica*, VI: 156–64, 14th edition, 1937.

'Comparative Psychology', *Encyclopaedia Britannica*, VI: 167–70, 14th edition, 1937

C. Books written in collaboration with others

Gore, Charles, *et al.*, *Property, Its Duties and Rights Historically, Philosophically and Religiously Regarded, Essays by Various Writers*. New York: The Macmillan Company, 1922. Pages 1–33, 'The Historical Evolution of Property, in Fact and in Idea'.

Hobhouse, L. T., and Hammond, J., *Lord Hobhouse, a Memoir*. London: Edward Arnold, 1905.

Hobhouse, L. T., Wheeler, G. C., and Ginsberg, Morris, *The Material Culture and Social Institutions of the Simpler Peoples, an Essay in Correlation*. London: Chapman & Hall, 1915.

Liveing, Susan, *A Nineteenth-Century Teacher, John Henry Bridges*. London: Kegan Paul, Trench, Trubner and Co., Ltd, 1926. Preface.

Marvin, F. S. (ed.), *The Unity of Western Civilization*. London: Oxford University Press, 1922. Pages 162–79, 'Science and Philosophy as Unifying Forces'.

Morgan, J. H. (ed.), *The New Irish Constitution, an Exposition and Some Arguments*. London: Hodder & Stoughton, 1912. Pages 361–72, 'Irish Nationalism and Liberal Principle'.

Muirhead, J. H. (ed.), *Contemporary British Philosophy*. London: George Allen & Unwin, Ltd, 1924. Volume 1, pages 149–88, 'The Philosophy of Development'.

Muller-Lyer, F., *The History of Social Development*, translated by E. C. Lake and H. A. Lake. London: George Allen & Unwin, Ltd, 1920. Introduction.

Steeves, H. R., and Ristine, F. H., *Representative Essays in Modern Thought*. New York: American Book Company, 1913. Pages 341–75, 'Law and Justice'.

Willis, Walter, *Trade Boards at Work, a Practical Guide to the Operation of the Trade Boards Acts*. London: Nisbet and Co., Ltd, 1920. Introduction.

Supplementary Bibliography

A. Books

Barnes, Harry Elmer, *Historical Sociology, Its Origin and Development, Theories of Social Evolution from Cave Life to Atomic Bombing.* New York: Philosophical Library, 1948.

Barnes, Harry Elmer, and Becker, Howard, *Social Thought from Lore to Science.* New York and Boston: D. C. Heath & Company, 1938.

Barnes, Harry Elmer, and Becker, Howard, *Contemporary Social Theory.* New York: D. Appleton-Century Company, 1940.

Bernard, L. L., *Social Control in its Sociological Aspects.* New York: The Macmillan Company, 1939.

Bogardus, Emory S., *The Development of Social Thought.* New York: Longmans, Green and Company, 1940.

Breasted, J. H., *The Dawn of Conscience.* New York: Charles Scribner's Sons, 1939.

Briffault, Robert, *The Making of Humanity.* London: George Allen and Unwin, Ltd, 1919.

Carter, Hugh, *The Social Theories of L. T. Hobhouse.* Chapel Hill: University of North Carolina Press, 1927.

Case, C. M., *Social Process and Human Progress.* New York: Harcourt, Brace and Company, 1931.

Case, C. M., *Essays in Social Values.* Los Angeles: University of Southern California Press, 1944.

Cooley, Charles Horton, *Life and the Student, Roadside Notes on Human Nature, Society, and Letters.* New York: Alfred A. Knopf, 1927.

Dewey, John, *The Quest for Certainty.* New York: Minton, Balch and Company, 1929.

Dewey, John, *Logic, the Theory of Inquiry.* New York: Henry Holt and Company, 1938.

Driver, G. R., and Miles, J. C. (eds.), *The Assyrian Laws.* Oxford: The Clarendon Press, 1935.

Eddington, Arthur S., *The Nature of the Physical World.* New York: The Macmillan Company, 1929.

Ellwood, Charles A., *Sociology in Its Psychological Aspects.* New York: D. Appleton and Company, 1914.

Ellwood, Charles A., *The Psychology of Human Society, an Introduction to Sociological Theory.* New York: D. Appleton-Century Company, 1925.

Ellwood, Charles A., *Cultural Evolution, a Study of Social Origins and Development*. New York: The Century Co., 1927.

Ellwood, Charles A., *Methods in Sociology, a Critical Study*. Durham: Duke University Press, 1933.

Ellwood, Charles A., *A History of Social Philosophy*. New York: Prentice-Hall, Inc., 1939.

Ginsberg, Morris, *Sociology*. London: Oxford University Press, 1947.

Ginsberg, Morris, *Reason and Unreason in Society, Essays in Sociology and Social Philosophy*. London: Longmans, Green and Co., 1947.

Green, T. H., *Prolegomena to Ethics*. Oxford: The Clarendon Press, 1890.

Gurvitch, Georges, and Moore, Wilbert E., *Twentieth Century Sociology*. New York: The Philosophical Library, 1946.

Haldane, J. S., *Mechanism, Life and Personality: an examination of the mechanistic theory of life and mind*. New York: E. P. Dutton, 1921.

Haldane, J. S., *The Philosophical Basis of Biology*, Garden City, N.Y.: Doran and Company, Inc., 1931.

Hobson, J. A., and Ginsberg, Morris, *L. T. Hobhouse, His Life and Work*. London: George Allen & Unwin, Ltd, 1931.

House, Floyd N., *The Range of Social Theory, a Survey of the Development, Literature, Tendencies and Fundamental Problems of the Social Sciences*. New York: Henry Holt and Company, 1929.

House, Floyd N., *The Development of Sociology*. New York: McGraw-Hill Book Company, Inc., 1936.

Joad, C. E. M., *Guide to Modern Thought*. New York: Frederick A. Stokes Company, 1933.

Kropotkin, Peter, *Mutual Aid: a Factor in Evolution*. New York: Doubleday, Page and Company, 1902.

Lecky, W. E. H., *History of European Morals from Augustus to Charlemagne*. London: Longmans, Green and Co., 1920.

Lundberg, George A., Bain, Read, and Anderson, Nels, (eds.), *Trends in American Sociology*. New York: Harper and Brothers, 1929.

MacIver, R. M., *Community, a Sociological Study*. London: Macmillan and Co., Limited, 1917.

MacIver, R. M., *Society, Its Structure and Changes*. New York: Ray Long & Richard R. Smith, Inc., 1931.

MacIver, R. M., *Society, a Textbook of Sociology*. New York: Farrar and Rinehart, Inc., 1937.

MacIver, R. M., *Social Causation*. Boston: Ginn and Company, 1942.

MacIver, R. M., *The Elements of Social Science*. London: Methuen & Co., Ltd., 7th edition, 1944.

Mill, John Stuart, *On Liberty*; *Representative Government*; *The Subjection of Women*. London: Oxford University Press, 1933.

Nash, Arnold S., *The University and the Modern World, An Essay in the Philosophy of University Education*. New York: The Macmillan Company, 1944.

Needham, Joseph (ed.), *Science, Religion and Reality*. New York: The Macmillan Company, 1925.

Nicholson, J. A., *Some Aspects of the Philosophy of L. T. Hobhouse: Logic and Social Theory*. Urbana: University of Illinois Studies in the Social Sciences, 1928.

Northrop, F. S. C., *Science and First Principles*. New York: The Macmillan Company, 1931.

Northrop, F. S. C., *The Logic of the Sciences and the Humanities*. New York: The Macmillan Company, 1947.

Park, Robert E., and Burgess, E. W., *Introduction to the Science of Sociology*. Chicago: University of Chicago Press, 1921.

Parsons, Talcott, *The Structure of Social Action, a Study in Social Theory with Special Reference to a Group of Recent European Writers*. New York: McGraw-Hill Book Company, Inc., 1937.

Ross, E. A., *Principles of Sociology*. New York: The Century Company, 1920.

Small, Albion W., *General Sociology: an Exposition of the Main Development in Sociological Theory from Spencer to Ratzenhofer*. Chicago: University of Chicago Press, 1905.

Small, Albion W., *The Meaning of Social Science*. Chicago: University of Chicago Press, 1910.

Small, Albion W., *Between Eras, from Capitalism to Democracy*. Kansas City: Intercollegiate Press, 1913.

Sorokin, Pitirim A., *Contemporary Sociological Theories*. New York: Harper and Brothers, 1928.

Sorokin, Pitirim A., *The Crisis of Our Age: the Social and Cultural Outlook*. New York: E. P. Dutton and Co., Inc., 1941.

Sorokin, Pitirim A., *Society, Culture, and Personality, their Structure and Dynamics, a System of General Sociology*. New York: Harper and Brothers, 1947.

Sorokin, Pitirim A., *The Reconstruction of Humanity*. Boston: The Beacon Press, 1948.

Spencer, Herbert, *Descriptive Sociology; or Groups of Sociological Facts Classified and Arranged*. New York: D. Appleton and Company, 1873–81.

Spencer, Herbert, *Principles of Sociology*, New York: D. Appleton-Century Company, 1914.

Spykman, Nicholas, *The Social Theory of Georg Simmel*. Chicago: University of Chicago Press, 1925.

Sumner, William Graham, *Folkways, A Study of the S:ciological Importance of Usages, Manners, Customs, Mores, and Morals*. Boston: Ginn and Company, 1906.

Sumner, William Graham, *What Social Classes Owe to Each Other*. New York: Harper and Brothers, 1920.

Thomas, W. I., and Znaniecki, Florian, *The Polish Peasant in Europe and America*. New York: A A. Knopf, 1927.

Ward, James, *Naturalism and Agnosticism*. London: Adam, 1903.

Ward, Lester F., *Pure Sociology*. New York: The Macmillan Company, 1903.

Ward, Lester F., *Dynamic Sociology, or Applied Social Science, as Based Upon Statical Sociology and the Less Complex Sciences*. New York: D. Appleton and Company, 1910.

Whitehead, A. N., *Science and the Modern World*. New York: The Macmillan Company, 1926.

B. Articles

Barker, Ernest, 'Leonard Trelawny Hobhouse, 1864–1929', *Proceedings of the British Academy*, XV: 1–21, 1931.

Barnes, Harry Elmer, 'Some Typical Contributions of English Sociology to Political Theory, (II) Leonard T. Hobhouse and the Neo-Liberal Theory of the State', *American Journal of Sociology*, 27: 442–85, January 1922.

Becker, Howard, 'Sociology', *Britannica Book of the Year*, 704–6, 1947.

Becker, Howard, 'Sociology', *10 Eventful Years, a Record of Events of the Years Preceding, Including and Following World War II, 1937 through 1946*, 4: 113–16, 1947.

Branford, Victor, 'The Sociological Work of Leonard Hobhouse', *Sociological Review*, XXI: 273–80, October 1929.

Bogardus, Emory S., 'Leonard T. Hobhouse, 1864–1929', *Sociology and Social Research*, XIV: 103, November–December 1929.

Bogardus, Emory S., 'Cooperative Research', *Research News* (University of Southern California, Graduate School), XI: 2, October 1946.

Bryson, Gladys, 'Early English Positivists and the Religion of Humanity', *American Sociological Review*, I: 343–62, June 1936.

Burgess, J. S., 'Certain Concepts, Methods and Contributions in the Social Science and Social Philosophy of L. T. Hobhouse', *Chinese Social and Political Science Review*, XIII: 119–43, April 1929.

Case, C. M., 'What is Social Progress?', *Journal of Applied Sociology*, X: 109–19, November–December 1925.

Cooley, Charles Horton, 'The Roots of Social Knowledge', *American Journal of Sociology*, 32: 59–79, July 1926.

Ellwood, Charles A., 'Scientific Method', *Science*, N. S., 37: 412–13, 14 March 1913.

Ellwood, Charles A., 'The Struggle over Method in the Social Sciences', *Social Science*, S:137–140, March–April 1930.

Ellwood, Charles A., 'Emasculated Sociologies', *Sociology and Social Research*, 17: 219–29, January 1933.

Ginsberg, Morris, 'Leonard Trelawny Hobhouse', *Journal of Philosophical Studies*, IV: 442–52, October 1929.

Ginsberg, Morris, 'The Contributions of Professor Hobhouse to Philosophy and Sociology', *Economica*, 27: 251–66, November 1929.

Ginsberg, Morris, 'Leonard Trelawny Hobhouse', *Encyclopedia of the Social Sciences*, VII: 396–7, 1932.

Harper, Ernest B., 'Sociology in England', *Social Forces*, XI: 335–42, March 1933.

Lindeman, Eduard C., 'Sociology Synthesized', review of Howard W. Odum, *Understanding Society: The Principles of Dynamic Sociology* (New York: The Macmillan Company, 1947), *Saturday Review of Literature*, XXX: 12–13, 27 December 1947.

Nordskog, John Eric, 'Leonard T. Hobhouse: Internationalist', *Sociology and Social Research*, XIV: 373–82, March–April 1930.

Owen, John E., 'The Sociological Thought of L. T. Hobhouse', *Transactions of the Westermarck Society*, II: 26–46, 1953.

Palmer, Vivien M., 'Impressions of Sociology in Great Britain', *American Journal of Sociology*, 32: 756–61, March 1927.

Sinnott, Edward W., 'Science', *Time*, I: 95, October 1947.

Sorokin, Pitirim A., 'Improvement of Scholarship in the Social Sciences', *Journal of Social Philosophy*, II: 237–45, April 1937.

Wilde, Norman, review of *Morals in Evolution*, *Journal of Philosophy, Psychology, and Scientific Methods*, 4: 183, 28 March 1907.

Wallas, Graham, 'Address by Professor Graham Wallas at the Hobhouse Memorial Service, St Clement Dane's Church, 27 June, 1929', *Economica*, IX: 247–50, November 1929.

Index